Models and Reality in Economics

ADVANCES IN ECONOMIC METHODOLOGY

General Editor: Warren J. Samuels, *Professor of Economics, Michigan State University, USA*

This major series presents original and innovative work in economic methodology, including all aspects of the philosophy, sociology and rhetoric of economics as well as the relationship of economics to other disciplines.

The series reflects interest in all aspects of economic methodology, as well as the deepening sense of conceptual and technical crises plaguing the economics profession, which involve deep methodological considerations. The series also contributes to the better understanding and solution of the economic problems of both mature and developing countries and is open to all points of view and approaches.

Titles in the series include:

Models and Reality in Economics

Steven Rappaport

ADVANCES IN ECONOMIC METHODOLOGY

Edward Elgar
Cheltenham, UK • Northampton, MA, USA

Published by
Edward Elgar Publishing Limited
8 Lansdown Place
Cheltenham
Glos GL50 2HU
UK

Edward Elgar Publishing, Inc.
6 Market Street
Northampton
Massachusetts 01060
USA

HB
141
, R36
1998

A catalogue record for this book
is available from the British Library

Library of Congress Cataloguing in Publication Data

Rappaport, Steven, 1945–
        Models and reality in economics / Steven Rappaport.
            (Advances in economic methodology)
        Includes bibliographical references and index.
        1. Econometric models. 2. Economics—Methodology. I. Title.
    II. Series.
    HB141.R36 1998
    330'.01'5195—dc21   97–43551
                                                                            CIP

ISBN 1 85898 575 7

Printed and bound in Great Britain by Biddles Ltd, Guildford and King's Lynn

Contents

Acknowledgments

I wish to thank several journals for granting their permission to use previously published material. Chapter 3 is a revised version of 'Is economics empirical knowledge?', *Economics and Philosophy*, Vol. 11 (1995) No 1, 137–58, and is reprinted by permission of Cambridge University Press. Most of Chapter 5 appeared as 'Abstraction and unrealistic assumptions in economics', *The Journal of Economic Methodology*, Vol. 3 (1996) No. 2, 215–36, and is reprinted by permission of Routledge. Portions of Chapter 8 appeared in 'Economic models and historical explanation', *Philosophy of the Social Sciences,* Vol. 25 (1995) No. 4, 421–41, copyright (c) 1995 by Sage Publications, Inc. This material is reprinted by permission of Sage Publications, Inc.

I am grateful to my wife Sandy without whose encouragement this book would never have seen the light of day. I am indebted to Edward Elgar and the people at his publishing house who handled my book. Their support and editorial assistance are much appreciated. I also wish to thank Laine Gates for her word processing effort.

1. Introduction

This book is an essay in economic methodology. Economists themselves sometimes express dissatisfaction with methodology, finding it too removed from what they actually do. In a recent review of a book on methodology David Colander says this:

> Just as economics has become remote from the real-world economy, so too has economic methodology become remote from what economists do. Methodology has become an end in itself, quite separate from a description of what is done in economics, or a prescription for what should be done. (Colander, 1997, p. 141)

Yet economic methodology can be relevant to economic inquiry in a number of ways, several of which are suggested by Colander's remarks. One way economic methodology might be relevant to economics as it actually exists is to provide a *description*, albeit at a rather general level, of what in fact economists do. This book purports to provide such a description. My focus here is to present an image of economics that does justice to various central facets of the discipline as it is actually pursued. The discussion is intended as a contribution to the effort by philosophers and philosophically minded economists to understand what economics is all about as it actually exists.

Secondly, economic methodology can be relevant to economics in that methodologists can offer advice to economists about how to do a better job of acquiring economic knowledge. And some methodologists do offer such advice (see Hausman, 1992a, Chapter 14). However, my book offers relatively little in the way of prescriptions to economists as to how to pursue their discipline. A third way that economic methodology can be relevant to economics is as an aid to resolving some disagreements among economists on substantive issues. Disagreements among practitioners of a discipline over substantive issues sometimes reflect differing methodological commitments. And economics is no different than physics, geology or medicine on this score. Economic methodology

1

might be germane to the practising economist in helping to resolve disagreements on economic issues that are at least partly caused by different methodological commitments. But this book does not discuss contentious issues within economics reflecting methodological disagreement. Accordingly, the book should not be viewed either as a set of prescriptions for economic inquiry or as an aid to resolving any disputes within economics, but rather as a description of the conduct of inquiry in economics.

Other thinkers have tried to understand economics as it is. A recent and radical effort to understand both economics and its metatheory has been made by Donald McCloskey. McCloskey argues that the traditional metatheory of economics – as practised by J.S. Mill and J.E. Cairnes in the nineteenth century through to Blaug, Friedman, Hausman and Rosenberg in the twentieth century – should be replaced with the rhetoric of economics. And correlatively, economics itself is simply an exercise in rhetoric. Chapter 2 of this book serves a dual purpose. It is a sustained argument for the inadequacy of McCloskey's rhetorical conception of economic metatheory, as well as a critique of views about economics implied by the rhetorical conception of metatheory. Chapter 2 also sets out and defends the traditional conception of economic metatheory, a rather modest version of which is pursued in the remainder of the book.

More traditional efforts to understand economics have often approached the task by asking of economics 'Is it an empirical science?' The 'Is it science?' approach comes in several distinct varieties. One variety first lays down some methodological rule or standard that a science must meet; anything that fails to meet the standard is non-science. Then an attempt is made to determine whether or not economics meets the proposed methodological standard. As Laudan (1996, pp. 213–5) notes, the view that science is marked off from non-science by the methodology of the former arose in the nineteenth century along with the fallibilist idea that all scientific theories are corrigible. In the 1930s Karl Popper proposed a demarcation criterion requiring that to be scientific, a theory must be falsifiable. One of the more influential forms of the methodological rule version of the 'Is it science?' approach to economics, applies the litmus test of Popper's demarcation criterion to economics. This form is found in the work of Mark Blaug, T.W. Hutchinson, and others. But Popper's demarcation criterion has been shown to be unacceptable.[1] As a result, the Popperian form of the methodological rule version of the 'Is it science?' approach to economics has somewhat fallen out of favour. However, the methodological rule version refuses to die. An important recent form of it is Alexander Rosenberg's position.

Rosenberg requires that a science exhibit predictive improvement over time. And he argues that economics, as it has in fact developed, does not meet this standard for empirical science. Chapter 3 of this book shows that Rosenberg's position fails to present an adequate picture of economics.

Despite the efforts of many talented people – Blaug, Rosenberg, *et al.* – the methodological rule version of the 'Is it science?' approach to economics has failed to shed any real light on the discipline. But there is a second generic version of the 'Is it science?' approach that may seem to hold more promise. This makes a discipline being a science conditional upon its having a certain kind of content. What particular content is required yields different forms of the special content version of the 'Is it science?' approach to economics. One important tradition in the philosophy of science views science as a search for laws which can be used to construct explanations and predictions of phenomena in the real world. And a science itself includes a corpus of scientific laws some of which are theoretical or fundamental laws – this is the special content required of a science. This conception of empirical science is associated with the positivist tradition from Comte and J.S. Mill in the nineteenth century through Hempel and Carnap in the twentieth. One form, then, of the special content version of the 'Is it science?' approach to economics requires that to be a science, a discipline must include a body of laws some of which are fundamental or theoretical laws.

One important economic methodologist has claimed that economics does meet this standard for science. Daniel Hausman says that neoclassical microeconomics includes a ten-membered set of fundamental laws – he calls these laws taken together 'equilibrium theory'. Borrowing J.S. Mill's distinction between exact and inexact sciences, Hausman views the generalizations of equilibrium theory as inexact laws. They are qualified by vague *ceteris paribus* clauses and, so qualified, they can reasonably be regarded as genuine scientific laws. Chapter 4 sets out Hausman's position in detail. But it is argued that Hausman does not succeed in showing that the generalizations of equilibrium theory are laws; and moreover, it is unjustifiable to regard all of these generalizations as laws. However, there is a very weak resemblance between economics and a discipline which meets the standard for science associated with nineteenth and twentieth century positivism. The concluding remarks of Chapter 4 describe this weak resemblance.

Another form of the special content version of the 'Is it science?' approach to economics derives from the conception of the content of science associated with Galileo and his study of terrestrial motion in the first half of the seventeenth century. On this conception, a scientist assumes away one or more factors always operating in a real world situation or system of some kind, and then formulates a hypothesis or theory interrelating other key factors or variables always operating in systems of the kind in question. Such hypotheses and theories may be called 'ideal' in that they are about cases that do not exist in reality but only in idea. Ideal hypotheses are fairly common in physics. The law for the period of a simple pendulum and Galileo's law that bodies fall to Earth with a constant acceleration, are just two examples. On the Galilean conception of the content of a science, a science is largely a body of ideal hypotheses or theories. And if we know that the ideal hypotheses or theories truly or correctly interrelate the variables with which they are concerned, then the science is a valid Galilean science affording genuine scientific knowledge of the world.

Critics of economics have long noted that the subject, and especially neoclassical microeconomic theory, relies heavily on unrealistic assumptions. And these critics have seen this circumstance as defeating any claim economics might have to afford knowledge of real world economic phenomena. In their textbooks and elsewhere, some economists and economic methodologists have attempted to justify reliance of economics on unrealistic assumptions by saying that its unrealistic assumptions are the result of abstraction, and abstraction is necessary to understand complex, real world economic phenomena. The idea behind this defence of unrealistic assumptions is that economists assume away various complexities of the real world, eliminating unimportant detail, and then formulate hypotheses interrelating a small number of key variables. This view of economic theorizing appears to reflect the Galilean conception of the content of science. Chapter 5 first shows that the appeal to abstraction to defend unrealistic assumptions in economics is a failure. It then indicates that the reason for this failure also justifies saying that, as economics has so far developed, it cannot be said to be a genuine Galilean science.

The three varieties of the 'Is it science?' approach to economics discussed in Chapters 3, 4 and 5 lead to no positive characterization of economics that illuminates the discipline for us. The 'Is it science?' approach to economics appears to be a dead end. Chapter 6 begins a different approach to understanding economics. In a paper published several years ago, Gibbard and Varian (1978, p. 676) note that 'Much economic theorizing consists not of an overt search for economic laws, not of forming explicit hypotheses about situations and testing them, but of investigating models'. This book takes seriously Gibbard and Varian's remark in that one of its central themes is that economic thinking is in a large measure the investigation of models.

Chapter 6 begins the discussion of economic models by making a distinction between global theories and mini-theories. A mini-theory is a single, well-defined set of statements which are systematically interrelated. Global theories are harder to characterize. Thomas Kuhn's classic *The Structure of Scientific Revolutions* (1970) first brought global theories in science into prominence. Kuhn's views about paradigms – or, as he also calls them, 'disciplinary matrices' – offer a distinctive and highly controversial account of the role of global theories in science. Imre Lakatos and Larry Laudan are two other important thinkers who have emphasized the importance of global theories in science. Chapter 6 presents a brief account of the mini-theory/global theory distinction, and then locates economic models in relation to the distinction. Chapter 6 also treats the utilization of models in two cognitive activities of central importance in economics – Chapter 8 discusses a third key cognitive activity and the role models play in it. The pair of cognitive activities discussed in Chapter 6 are the resolution of normative problems and the resolution of conceptual problems. The discussion of Chapter 6 warrants adopting a partial instrumentalism about economics. It is argued that this partial instrumentalism is entirely compatible with the claim made in Chapter 2 that economics is in pursuit of truth. Finally, Leontief, McCloskey and others have criticized contemporary economics for its excessive formalism. Chapter 6 argues that the central role of models in economic thinking is not responsible for any excessive formalism exhibited by economics.

Chapter 7 continues the effort begun in Chapter 6 to characterize the nature of economic models. The literature on economic methodology contains a number of philosophical theories about the nature of economic models. The three most prominent ones are the lawlike generalization theory, the structuralist theory and the modal theory. Chapter 7 compares the relative merits of the three theories, and makes a case for the modal theory as the best account of the character of economic models.

Chapter 8 treats a key use of economic models. Economics is to a significant degree an explanatory enterprise; it aims to provide explanations of real world economic phenomena. And models play a crucial role in economic explanation. A causal theory of explanation of why something happened is introduced in Chapter 8 and used to illuminate explanation in economics. The heuristic and other functions which models serve in economists' causal explanations are brought out. William Dray's notion of explanation-what in history is also explicated in Chapter 8; and it is argued that economics resembles history in providing explanations-what of real world phenomena, with models playing an essential role in explanations-what in economics. A theme of Chapter 8 is the close similarity between economics and history in the two disciplines providing both causal explanations of phenomena as well as explanations-what.

Chapters 2 to 5 are largely critical, demonstrating the inadequacy of a number of approaches to understanding the character of economics as it actually exists. These chapters do make a contribution to the construction of the positive image of economics this book seeks to convey. For instance, Chapter 2 defends the idea that economics is in pursuit of truth in a sense in which truth is distinct from being persuasive to the community of economists, or what Donald McCloskey calls 'the citizenry of the intellect'. Chapter 4 brings out a resemblance, albeit it a very weak one, between economics and a science built around a body of scientific laws. But it is Chapters 6 to 8 that largely present the important facets of the image of economics that I wish to convey. The picture of economics that emerges in Chapters 6 to 8 places models centre stage in economics. These chapters develop in detail the view that much economic thinking is the construction of models and/or their utilization in cognitive activities such as resolving conceptual problems and explaining real world economic phenomena.

NOTES

1. Hausman (1992a, Ch. 10) and Laudan (1996, pp. 218-22) give good accounts of the difficulties that fatally bedevil Popper's demarcation criterion.

2. Economic Methodology

2.1 THE TRADITIONAL CONCEPTION OF METHODOLOGY

A standard view of the method of a discipline is described by Richard Rudner as follows:

> For the methodology of a scientific discipline is not a matter of its transient techniques but of its *logic of justification*. The method of a science *is*, indeed, the rationale on which it bases its acceptance or rejection of hypotheses or theories. (Rudner, 1966, p. 5, italics in original)

The method of a discipline consists of the types of reasoning or arguments which are used in that discipline to justify acceptance or rejection of hypotheses and theories. The methodology of a discipline can be viewed as the *study of* the types of reasoning, or procedures of justification, used by that discipline. The methodology of economics is, then, the study of the types of arguments used by economists to justify acceptance or rejection of hypotheses and theories. This view of economic methodology may be called 'the epistemological conception'. For epistemology is the study of the grounds on the basis of which statements are, or should be, accepted or rejected. The epistemological conception of economic methodology can also be described by saying that it views the task of economic methodology as setting out the *criteria* used by economists in appraising the cognitive or epistemic worth of theories and hypotheses. This is equivalent to the characterization of the epistemological conception as having the job of setting out the types of reasoning used to justify acceptance or rejection of economic theories. For a style of reasoning usable to justify acceptance or rejection of an economic theory will invoke, explicitly or implicitly, a criterion for appraising the epistemic merit of a theory. And a criterion for appraisal in effect constitutes an instruction for devising an argument to justify acceptance or rejection of a theory.

The epistemological conception of methodology can be adopted in a *naturalistic* form. Two questions can be distinguished:

(1) What kinds of arguments or justification procedures *do* economists use to justify acceptance or rejection of theories?
(2) What kinds of arguments *ought* economists to use to justify acceptance or rejection of theories?

A naturalistic version of the epistemological conception would say that question (1) must be answered in order to answer question (2); the answer to question (1) *is* relevant to answering question (2).[1] A *radical* naturalism would say that question (2) may be replaced with question (1). But one could adopt the naturalistic form of the epistemological conception of methodology, and yet reject this radical version. That the epistemological conception of methodology can be held in a naturalistic form has been overlooked recently by Donald McCloskey. He says this:

> Rappaport claims that epistemology can provide 'standards' for warranted belief in economics. There's that word again, and again with no rational backing. I believe his claim is unwarranted, illogical, and non-cognitive. He offers no empirical evidence for it .... (McCloskey, 1994, p. 214)

McCloskey's sharply negative assessment of the claim that epistemology can provide standards for warranted belief in economics rests on a misconception of epistemology. He appears to think that epistemology, as applied to economics, is only concerned with supplying an answer to question (2) above, *and* it regards answering question (1) as totally irrelevant to answering question (2). That McCloskey adheres to this extreme anti-naturalistic conception of epistemology is confirmed by his (1989, p. 5) saying 'Epistemology has not yet solved its self imposed problem - its only problem - of getting outside human conversations to decide what to believe on grounds other than what is persuasive to humans'. But once again, epistemology, as applied to economics, can be conceived along naturalistic lines. And McCloskey cannot legitimately reject epistemology in a naturalistic form on the basis of a claim that the extreme anti-naturalistic conception of epistemology is unacceptable.

The epistemological conception of economic methodology, whether in a naturalistic or anti-naturalistic form, does not by any means describe *all* of what has been done under the rubric 'economic methodology'. In the following passage Daniel Hausman characterizes some of the issues, in addition to that of the criteria for theory appraisal in economics, which have occupied economic methodologists:

Although theory appraisal is a central issue, about which I shall have a great deal to say, there are other philosophically interesting questions to ask about economic theory. One should also inquire about the *structure* of microeconomics and general equilibrium theory, about the *strategy* and *heuristics* that guide contemporary economics, about the *goals* of economic theorizing, and about the relations between economic theory and policy questions. (Hausman, 1992a, pp. 4–5, italics in original)

Some of the issues cited here – especially that of the goals of economic theorizing – are related to the issue of theory appraisal in economics. But the issues Hausman identifies in the above passage at least to some degree can be pursued independently of the issue as to what types of arguments are, or ought to be, used by economists. Let us use the term 'the traditional conception of methodology' to refer to the view that economic methodology consists of two parts. The first part has as its task setting out the kinds of arguments economists do or should use to justify acceptance or rejection of theories. In short, the first part of the traditional conception is identical with the *entire* task of methodology on the epistemological conception of methodology described above. The second part of the traditional conception sees its job as resolving issues other than that of the criteria for theory appraisal in economics; important examples of these issues are identified by Hausman in the passage quoted above. Work in the metatheory or second-order study of economics from J.S. Mill and J.E. Cairnes in the nineteenth century to Alexander Rosenberg, Mark Blaug, Daniel Hausman and many others in the twentieth, falls squarely under the traditional conception of economic methodology.

2.2 THE RHETORICAL CONCEPTION OF ECONOMIC METATHEORY

Recently a *competing* view of the nature of economic metatheory has arisen, a view most elaborately developed by Donald McCloskey. On this conception, the metatheory of economics is a branch of rhetoric, and the proper pursuit of the metatheory of economics consists in something that resembles a literary analysis of economic texts. This rhetorical conception of metatheory is associated with views about the nature of economics which, I believe, are seriously mistaken. Moreover, were the rhetorical conception to replace the traditional conception of economic methodology, the discussion in this monograph would have to be quite different than it is going to be. Accordingly, it is worthwhile saying why the rhetorical conception of metatheory should be abandoned. This will clear the way for the adoption of the traditional conception of methodology in the remainder of this monograph.

The central tendency of McCloskey's concept of rhetoric is one tracing its origins to Aristotle. McCloskey says:

> The word 'rhetoric' here does not mean a verbal shell game, as in 'empty rhetoric' or 'mere rhetoric' (although form is not trivial either, and even empty rhetoric is full). Rhetoric is the art of speaking. More broadly, it is the study of how people persuade. (McCloskey, 1985a, p. 29)

In his recent, book-length defence of his rhetorical approach, McCloskey (1994, p. 40) endorses the same concept of rhetoric expressed in the quoted passage. Thus, rhetoric is the study of the means or devices people use to persuade others. Aristotle (1954, p. 24) defines rhetoric as '...the faculty of observing in any given case the available means of persuasion'. McCloskey's conception of rhetoric is, then, the classical or Aristotelian one.

However, there are two very different kinds of rhetorical devices. An *evidential* rhetorical device is one having this feature: in using the device, the speaker affirms a set of statements P which he adduces in support of another statement C. Thus an evidential rhetorical device is an *argument* in the sense in which philosophers use this term. An argument in the philosopher's sense consists of one or more premises together with a conclusion purportedly supported by those premises. The second kind of rhetorical device is the *non-evidential* device. This is simply a rhetorical device that is *not*, either explicitly or on analysis, an argument in the philosopher's sense. Irony and sarcasm are examples of non-evidential rhetorical devices. Sarcasm threatens the opponent with scorn, irony threatens ridicule. Neither consists of a set of premises together with an intended conclusion allegedly supported by those premises. It is important to note how broad a category is encompassed by evidential rhetorical devices. Such devices include demonstrative or deductively valid arguments. But much more besides is included. *Inductive arguments* – arguments by analogy, inferences to the best explanation, statistical syllogisms, statistical generalizations, and so on – *are* all evidential rhetorical devices. In 1988 *Economics and Philosophy* published a symposium on McCloskey's work. I contributed a paper to the symposium. In his reply to me in the symposium and again in his recent book, McCloskey (1988, p. 155; 1994, p. 210) says inductive reasoning is *excluded* from the category of evidential rhetorical devices. But in my rejoinder to McCloskey in the 1988 symposium, I (Rappaport, 1988, p.

170) plainly said that inductive inferences are *included* in the class of arguments, and therefore are counted as evidential rhetorical devices. McCloskey seems to think that evidential rhetorical devices, being arguments in the philosopher's sense, are restricted to syllogisms, or a few forms of argument of interest in formal logic. But once again, this is simply not true.

McCloskey is sceptical of my evidential/non-evidential distinction. He says:

> So *any* proposition can be reformed into a syllogism if sufficient pragmatic context is allowed. Any speech act can be reduced to syllogism. For instance: sneering at people undermines their authority; people with less authority are less persuasive; and so on to the conclusion that the argument sneered at is overturned. Therefore Rappaport's distinction between 'evidential' and 'non-evidential' does not hold. (McCloskey, 1994, p. 207)

So McCloskey thinks that any putative *non*-evidential rhetorical device, by incorporating enough material from the context of its use, is analysable as an argument in the philosopher's sense, that is, a set of premises and a conclusion it purportedly supports. For example, suppose a person *A* makes a remark that constitutes sneering at a person *B*, sneering being an expression of derision or contempt. I take sneering to be a non-evidential rhetorical device. But McCloskey seems to think that an *act* of sneering in a particular context is constituted by presenting or running the following argument:

(1) Sneering at people undermines their authority.
(2) People with less authority are less persuasive. Therefore,
(3) the argument or remark (of the person sneered at) is overturned.

But *A* sneering at *B* is *not* the same as *A* presenting or using this two premise argument. (Presenting or using an argument is affirming the premises and the conclusion, as well as adducing the premises in support of the conclusion.) *A* might present the above argument and yet *not* perform an act of sneering at all. Indeed, let the reader try to sneer *just by presenting* the argument '(1) and (2); therefore, (3)'. Also, *A* might sneer at *B* (who has just made some claim) by saying, with just the right tone of voice, 'That is a stupid thing to say'. But obviously *A*'s act of sneering does *not* consist in presenting the argument '(1) and (2); therefore, (3)'. McCloskey is mistaken, then, to suggest that non-evidential devices like the sneer are analysable into arguments in the philosopher's sense of 'argument'. Even if an argument can be constructed drawing on the context in which a non-evidential rhetorical device is used, it is not true that presenting that argument is constitutive of using the non-evidential rhetorical device in question. The evidential/non-evidential rhetorical device distinction does hold.[2]

McCloskey's resistance to recognizing this distinction is abetted by an unfortunate use of the term 'argument' and its cognates like 'arguing'. For example, in commenting on my contribution to the 1988 symposium, McCloskey (1988, p. 154) says 'Banning such a common mode of *argument* as metaphor signals a radically conservative move' (emphasis added). This suggests strongly that for McCloskey *any* rhetorical device is an argument. But metaphors, for instance, are *not* generally arguments in the philosopher's sense of the term. Heraclitus' metaphor 'War is father and king of all' is not a *group* of statements one of which is the conclusion purportedly supported by the rest of the statements in the group. Of course, in a context in which the metaphor is expressed, the speaker might provide another statement *P* that is intended as a supporting reason for 'War is father and king of all'. In this case *P* plus the metaphor *together* would be an argument in the philosopher's sense. But *by itself* 'War is father and king of all' is simply not an argument, explicitly or on analysis. Anyone who uses the term 'argument' to refer to *all* rhetorical devices, as does McCloskey, *blurs* the useful distinction I have drawn between evidential and non-evidential rhetorical devices, inasmuch as I have explained the distinction by saying the former are arguments whereas the latter are not.

To sum up, on the Aristotelian or classical concept of rhetoric, rhetoric studies *both* evidential and non-evidential rhetorical devices. And so, on McCloskey's rhetorical conception of economic metatheory, the second-order study of economics should identify, analyse, and evaluate the rhetorical devices, evidential as well as non-evidential, which are found in the discourse of economists. The implication is that economic discourse itself is simply an exercise in persuasion. McCloskey (1985a, p. 57) notes that his view of economic metatheory makes it resemble a literary analysis of economic discourse, in the sense that the economic metatheorist will say many of the same sorts of things about economic texts that people say about poetry, novels, and drama. McCloskey himself can be found practising the rhetorical conception of metatheory in Chapters 4 to 9 of his 1985 book *The Rhetoric of Economics*.

2.3 ECONOMICS AND THE PURSUIT OF TRUTH

I now turn to indicating why the rhetorical conception of economic metatheory should be abandoned. Three distinct considerations will be offered to support this prescription. The first has to do with truth. Economics, like any science or organized body of putative knowledge, pursues truth.[3] Even McCloskey now nominally acknowledges this. He (1994, p. 204) says 'I myself, for example, believe that economics is a report on the real, that reason will reveal its *truths,* and that empirical work is essential for economic science' (emphasis added). However, McCloskey's rhetorical conception of metatheory does *not* enable us to see truth as a key goal of economics in the *ordinary* sense of 'truth' employed in remarks like 'Engel's law is a truth' (said by an economist). Thus, the rhetorical conception is unable to present an adequate account of the goals of economic inquiry.

To say that economics pursues truth is not to say that the *only* goal of economic inquiry is truth. No doubt economists pursue a variety of goals like the resolution of puzzlement, income, the good opinion of fellow economists, and so on. In saying economics is in pursuit of truth, I mean that one goal of economics, and an especially important one, is to come to adopt true hypotheses and theories. It should be noted that in identifying truth as a goal of economics, I am not begging the question in favour of a *realist* as opposed to an *instrumentalist* view of economic theorizing. It will be sufficient for present purposes to say that realists hold that economists put forward their (first-order) theories and hypotheses as true, or close to true, descriptions of the real world; while instrumentalists say that economists do not generally accept their hypotheses and theories as even approximate truths about the real world, but instead see them as convenient devices for such tasks as generating predictions or providing a vocabulary for describing real world economic phenomena.[4] But even on an instrumentalist view of economics, economics *is* in pursuit of truth. It is just that on instrumentalism, economists do not accept as true *first-order* theories like the theory of perfect competition or the neoclassical model of demand for labour by firms. Instead they accept *as true* hypotheses *about* first-order theories, such as 'The neoclassical model of the demand for labour is useful for generating predictions about the effects of minimum wage legislation.' On instrumentalism, economists seek truths of the form 'T is useful' or 'T is useful for such-and-such', with T representing first-order theories.

In my initial contribution to the 1988 symposium in *Economics and Philosophy*, I cited, and developed in detail, the objection to McCloskey's rhetorical view of economic metatheory that it *unhooks* economics and the pursuit of truth, an objection Martin Hollis briefly urged against McCloskey in 1985. In his reply to me in the 1988 symposium McCloskey tries to meet this objection, and what he says is repeated with some changes in the 1994 book *Knowledge and Persuasion in Economics*. McCloskey's effort to meet this objection consists in accusing me of stipulatively defining a useless notion of truth which he expresses using phrases like 'Big-T Truth' and 'Truth'. McCloskey (1994, p. 210) admits that using this notion of truth, '... there will be no difficulty in showing that rhetoric does not pursue truth'. But, McCloskey claims, there is an *ordinary* concept of truth which he expresses with such phrases as 'true (small t)' and 'small-t true'. And rhetoric is not hostile to or unconnected with small-t truth. In short, McCloskey's reply to the objection that his rhetorical conception disconnects economics and the pursuit of truth is that if we but understand truth correctly, we will see that the objection fails.

What is McCloskey's distinction between Big-T Truth and small-t truth? McCloskey (1985a, pp. 46–7) says 'The very idea of Truth – with a capital T, something beyond what is merely persuasive to all concerned – is a fifth wheel, inoperative except that it occasionally comes loose and hits a bystander'. Thus Big-T Truth has the following feature: a statement *S* can be persuasive to all concerned (all are persuaded of *S*) at a given time and *S* is *not* Big-T True at that time. I take it that this feature of being persuasiveness-independent is what is meant by McCloskey's talk of Big-T Truth being 'something beyond what is merely persuasive'. McCloskey says other things about Big-T Truth. For instance, he (1994, p. 319) says that we humans could not know whether a statement is Big-T True, only God could. But the persuasiveness-independence feature seems the *central* aspect of Big-T Truth. One suspects, then, that the key feature of small-t truth is that it is *not* persuasiveness-independent. And indeed, McCloskey confirms this suspicion:

> The 'relation between persuasiveness and truth' is not 'incidental', as Rappaport says. The relation is close, *as close as we poor humans are going to get*. What is persuasive to a citizenry of the intellect is what is true, for now. That's if you want to keep the word 'truth' in sight, recognizing that Big-T 'Truth' is unattainable anyway. (McCloskey, 1994, p. 211, italics in original)

This passage, together with the context from which it is drawn, suggests strongly that McCloskey's small-t truth is definable in the following fashion:

(Df1) A statement *S* is small-t true at time *t* iff *S* is persuasive to a citizenry of the intellect at time *t*.

I am not quite sure what McCloskey means by 'a citizenry of the intellect'.[5] But whatever lack of clarity attaches to this phrase will turn out to be of little moment.

Now if small-t truth as defined by (Df1) is identical with the *ordinary* or vernacular sense of 'true' used in remarks like 'It is true that there is a dark side to the moon' (said by an astronomer), then McCloskey's rhetorical view of economic metatheory would enable us to see truth in the vernacular sense as a goal of economic inquiry. The rhetorical view represents economists' discourse as consisting in employing rhetorical devices with a view to persuading each other of some hypothesis or theory. But if a theory being persuasive to economists at a given time just is for the theory to be true at that time as (Df1) implies, then the rhetorical conception in effect represents economists as using rhetorical devices to reveal truth. However, in point of fact, (Df1) does *not* capture the *ordinary* concept of truth. Small-t truth and the sense of 'true' used in 'The weak form of the efficient-market hypothesis is pretty nearly true' (said by an economist), are not at all the same notion.

A hypothesis or theory in economics, or any science, could be persuasive to whatever group of humans you like at time *t* – a citizenry of the intellect, good people, etc. – and *not* be true at time *t* in the ordinary sense of 'true'. This is a consequence of the *inductive underdetermination* of scientific theories and hypotheses.[6] The evidence or arguments which persuade scientists of a theory at a time *t* are ultimately of a broadly *inductive* nature. But inductive arguments or inferences are *nondemonstrative*. Wesley Salmon deftly characterizes this concept as follows:

> A *nondemonstrative* inference is simply one that fails to be demonstrative. Its conclusion is not necessitated by its premises; the conclusion could be false even if the premises are true. (Salmon, 1967, p. 8, italics in original)

Thus, the premises of the arguments ultimately persuading scientists of a theory *T* at a time *t* could be true, the evidence for *T* could be just as it is, and yet *T* is *not true at time t*. And this point holds in the vernacular sense of 'true'; no sense of 'true' invented or stipulatively defined by philosophers is being used here. The fact is that the *ordinary* concept of truth has the persuasiveness-independence feature McCloskey attributes to Big-T Truth. It follows that (Df1) above is *not* a correct account or analysis of the ordinary sense of 'true', for (Df1) does not allow for the possibility that a hypothesis or theory is persuasive to scientists at time *t* yet is not true at time *t*.[7]

McCloskey might acknowledge that the ordinary notion of truth is persuasiveness-independent, and then say that this fact simply makes truth in the ordinary sense unattainable by us humans. After all, he says only God could attain Big-T Truth on the basis of the persuasiveness-independence of Big-T Truth. And McCloskey might then withdraw his claim that (Df1) *describes* the ordinary concept of truth, and instead recommend that we *replace* the ordinary concept with the notion of truth (Df1) defines. But this line of thought contains a bad mistake. Let us assume that a statement *S* is true in the ordinary sense, and therefore *S*'s truth is persuasiveness-independent. It hardly follows that we humans cannot know or have good reason to believe that *S* is true. Imagine that we have very good *inductive evidence* for *S* on the basis of which we believe that *S*. The truth of *S* *is* epistemically attained by us. It is just that our evidence for believing that *S*, being inductive, is logically compatible with *S* not being true. Anyone who, like McCloskey, thinks that we humans *cannot* know or justifiably believe that a statement is true in a persuasiveness-independent sense of 'true', is *ignoring* the fact that we can, and sometimes do, justifiably accept statements on the basis of inductive evidence which does not logically guarantee the truth of the statements accepted. Inductive evidence makes persuasiveness-independent truth attainable by us. Thus, McCloskey will not be able to justify *replacing* the ordinary, persuasiveness-independent concept of truth with small-t truth as defined by (Df1).

The foregoing discussion warrants viewing as a failure McCloskey's effort to render his rhetorical conception of economic metatheory consistent with the fact that economics pursues truth in the *ordinary* sense of the term. The rhetorical conception represents the conversation among economists as an exercise in rhetoric whose goal is persuasion. But achieving this goal is *not* necessarily to attain truth in the ordinary sense of 'truth'. This follows from the fact that McCloskey's (Df1) above does not accurately define the ordinary concept of truth. Thus, McCloskey's rhetorical conception of metatheory does not enable us to see economics in pursuit of truth in the vernacular sense of 'truth'. But, as economics *does* pursue truth in this sense, McCloskey's rhetorical view of metatheory is unable adequately to characterize the goals of economics. This is a strong reason to abandon the rhetorical conception.

2.4 ECONOMIC METATHEORY AND JUSTIFICATION

The second reason to jettison McCloskey's rhetorical conception of economic metatheory has to do with justification. Economists nowadays, as well as in the past, in some sense *accept* various economic theories and hypotheses. In his textbook presentation of microeconomic theory (price theory), McCloskey (1985b, p. 4) goes so far as to say 'Confident skill in price theory defines an economist ...'. Presumably confident skill in microeconomic theory presupposes acceptance, in some sense, of that theory. And McCloskey makes clear that he believes that there is widespread acceptance of microeconomic principles among economists today. This belief of McCloskey's is surely correct – see the evidence that McCloskey (1985b, pp. 1-3) marshals in its support. There is also wide agreement among economists nowadays on *some* macroeconomic hypotheses – an example might be 'Persistent growth in the money supply considerably beyond the growth of real GDP is a cause of inflation.' Given economists' acceptance of various theories and hypotheses, the following pair of questions are appropriate:[8]

(3) Are economists *justified* in accepting the theories and hypotheses they do?
(4) *How* do economic theories and hypotheses come to be justified?

McCloskey himself admits the importance of justification. He says:

> Justified true belief is an admirable ideal. If people are not made to justify their assertions and do not believe them, the conversation will, of course, be a poor one.... (McCloskey, 1989, p. 5)

We might add that if people, including economists, are *unable* to justify their assertions, then they will have succeeded in achieving their main cognitive goal of believing what is *true* at best by accident.[9]

Recall that the traditional conception of economic methodology discussed in section 2.1 holds that methodology in part studies the types of reasoning used by economists to justify acceptance or rejection of hypotheses and theories. McCloskey's rhetorical view of economic metatheory can offer *nothing* in answer to question (4) over and above what the traditional conception can give us in answer to (4). Nor can the rhetorical view of metatheory provide any assistance in answering (3) which the traditional conception is unable to provide. The rhetorical conception of economic metatheory is otiose as far as answering (3) and (4) is concerned. And this is a second ground on which to set aside the rhetorical conception.

The reason that McCloskey's rhetorical conception is useless in dealing with (3) and (4) has to do with the distinction between evidential and non-evidential rhetorical devices treated in section 2.2. Beginning with (4), if we want to know how economic theories come to be justified, it is of no use examining *non*-evidential rhetorical devices economists employ. Whatever credibility attaches to an economic theory or hypothesis must derive from its relation to *other statements*; and the hypothesis together with these other statements regarded as supporting reasons is an argument (in the philosopher's sense), that is, an *evidential* rhetorical device. A non-evidential device an economist employs – metaphor, a sneer, irony, and so on – cannot *qua* non-evidential device confer any warrant on a hypothesis or theory.[10] Though of course the economist's use of the non-evidential device may play a role in persuading others of the theory or hypothesis. On the traditional conception of economic methodology, methodology can answer question (4). For the traditional conception views methodology as in part the study of the arguments usable in economics to justify the acceptance or rejection of claims. But the portion of economic metatheory that, on the rhetorical conception of metatheory, studies *non*-evidential rhetorical devices, is *useless* in answering question (4). And whatever information might be provided in answer to (4) by the part of rhetorical metatheory that studies *evidential* rhetorical devices is *already* supplied by methodology as pursued according to the traditional conception. In sum, economic metatheory as viewed by McCloskey's rhetorical conception is otiose as far as answering question (4) goes.

There are a number of different approaches which might be taken to question (3). These are applications of general positions nicely described by Roderick Chisholm in the following passage:

We can formulate some of the philosophical issues that are involved here by distinguishing two pairs of questions. These are: A) '*What* do we know? What is the *extent* of our knowledge?' B) 'How are we to decide *whether* we know? What are the *criteria* of knowledge?' ... There are people – philosophers – who think that they do have an answer to B and that, given their answer to B, they can figure out their answer to A. And there are other people – philosophers – who have it the other way around: they think that they have an answer to A and that, given their answer to A, they can figure out the answer to B. ... I suggest, for the moment, we use the expressions 'methodist' and 'particularists'. By 'methodists', I mean, not the followers of John Wesley's version of christianity, but those who think they have an answer to B, and who then, in terms of it, work out their answer to A. By 'particularists' I mean those who have it the other way around. (Chisholm, 1982, pp. 65–6)

Narrowing Chisholm's questions A) and B) to apply to just economics and replacing knowledge in A) and B) with the notion of justified acceptance, the result is our questions (3) and (4). Borrowing Chisholm's terminology, let us say that *economic particularists* assume that hypotheses and theories accepted by (nearly) all economists (at time *t*) are justified (at time *t*), and then they try to find out *how* these hypotheses and theories acquire credibility. So, economic particularists start out by assuming that 'Yes' is the answer to question (3). But *economic methodists* first assume an answer to question (4), and then, using that answer, try to find out what economists really are justified in believing.[11]

McCloskey's rhetorical conception of economic metatheory is of no use to an economic particularist – nor, for that matter is the traditional conception of methodology of aid to the particularist. For the economic particularist does *not* reach his assumption that economists are justified in believing the things they do by applying a principle or criterion for identifying instances of justified belief or theory acceptance. And, whatever one's conception of economic metatheory, *such* a principle or criterion is all that could be expected from metatheory that might be of use in deciding whether economists are justified in believing the things they do.

Suppose that instead of being economic particularists, we adopt economic methodism. In this case we will need some principle or criterion for identifying instances of justified theory acceptance in economics. And such a criterion or principle will come from economic metatheory. But metatheory, on McCloskey's rhetorical conception, cannot provide any assistance in finding the criterion in question in addition to that provided by methodology on the traditional conception. For, according to the rhetorical conception, a portion of economic metatheory studies *non*-evidential rhetorical devices economists use. But *this* part of metatheory as viewed by the rhetorical conception is useless in finding a criterion for justified belief in economics. Again, non-evidential rhetorical devices cannot confer justification on a hypothesis or theory. And whatever assistance might be supplied by the part of metatheory that studies *evidential* rhetorical devices, is *already* provided by methodology as viewed by the traditional conception. Thus, economic metatheory on the rhetorical conception is useless for an economic methodist. Whatever rhetorical metatheory might do for the methodist is done by methodology on the traditional conception.

The issue of justification in economic metatheory divides into questions (3) and (4) above. It has been argued that economic metatheory, on McCloskey's rhetorical conception, is unable to provide any assistance in resolving the issue of justification that is not provided already by methodology on the traditional conception.

2.5   THE RHETORICAL CONCEPTION AND SOCIAL CONSTRUCTIVISM

This section is more conjectural than previous ones in this chapter. Its central conjecture is that a specific form of social constructivism about scientific knowledge is a major motive behind McClosky's adoption of the rhetorical conception of economic metatheory. As noted at the end of section 2.2, McCloskey's rhetorical view has it that economic metatheory is a sort of literary analysis of economic discourse. And McCloskey's own practice of economic metatheory gives emphasis to this aspect of his rhetorical view of metatheory. This is readily confirmed by reading Chapters 4 to 9 of *The Rhetoric of Economics*. But viewing economic metatheory as something like literary analysis of economic texts implies that economic discourse itself is rather like literature, that is, poetry, novels, and drama. This implication suggests the idea that some sort of social constructivist view is behind the rhetorical approach to economic metatheory. The generic social constructivist position can be expressed by the slogan 'Science is the social construction of reality'.[12] But this slogan admits of different interpretations. I will suggest that there is an interpretation of it on which McCloskey accepts the slogan. However, the form of social constructivism implicit in McCloskey's work is unacceptable, inasmuch as it represents an unpalatable form of anti-realism. And once the form of social constructivism in question is brought out into the open and seen to be the mistake that it is, a substantial part of the motivation to adopt the rhetorical conception of economic metatheory disappears. The rhetorical conception is plausibly seen as largely the solution to the problem of what in the world economic metatheory could do *once* social constructivism about knowledge is adopted. But rejecting social constructivism of the variety to be described below, removes the need to bring in the rhetorical conception to give economic metatheory something to do that is consistent with social constructivism.

In a recent essay George Levine suggests that the view that science is literature is motivated by a number of assumptions common nowadays among literary theorists and critics. The assumptions are identified by Levine in the following passage:

> I construct this hypothetical *Times* report to locate myself and, I expect, my
> readers inside a discourse that is so comfortably shared by literary critics and

theorists that they do not question – perhaps at times do not even recognize – the prima facie peculiarity of their assumptions. The assumptions I am thinking about are three: 1) All we have is representation (and representation always contains within it a politics that is disguised and 'naturalized'). 2) Thus all knowledge is culturally constructed; 'facts' are ideologically loaded representations, not ontologically real phenomena. 3) All knowledge is thus a play for power not for truth, although often in the name of truth. I do not want to deny these assumptions but to emphasize their peculiarity.... (Levine, 1994, p. 65)

Levine's 1) to 3) constitute a particular interpretation of the slogan 'Science is the social construction of reality', an interpretation Richard Boyd (1992, p. 132) has called 'debunking constructivism'. Debunking constructivism can be succinctly expressed like this: the content of scientific theories is largely determined by power relations among scientists and the non-scientific community. Levine does not argue that debunking constructivism is behind the view that science is literature. But Levine's view that debunking constructivism is one route to the conclusion that science is literature, certainly appears plausible.

It is partly the plausibility of this view of Levine's which suggests to me at any rate that McCloskey's belief that economics is like literature, and indeed, his entire rhetorical conception of economic metatheory, is motivated by some sort of social constructivism. But it is doubtful that McCloskey adopts debunking constructivism. It smacks too much of the left-wing politics that McCloskey rejects – he is a libertarian. But I think McCloskey adopts a position which bears a family resemblance to debunking constructivism, and is an interpretation of the slogan 'Science is the social construction of reality'. It is expressed by something like the following pair of claims:

(5) There is nothing outside of our representations (thoughts and utterances), in economics and elsewhere, which those representations could be seen as accurately representing.
(6) As a result, there is no theory-independent reality for knowledge in economics or any other scientific discipline to be about. To be sure, there are rocks, trees, planets, bacteria, consumers like you and me, and firms like General Motors. But these objects are just social constructs, not inhabitants of a theory-independent reality or world; there is no such world.

Given the social constructivism expressed by (5) and (6), economics, physics, chemistry, historiography, and so on are naturally seen as a kind of *writing*. And I am talking about writing in the sense that Derrida takes philosophy to be a kind of writing, at least on Richard Rorty's (1982, pp. 91–95) interpretation of Derrida. But then the efforts of traditional methodologists from J.S. Mill to Alexander Rosenberg and Daniel Hausman would seem to be seriously misguided. For traditional methodology in the sense of section 2.1 does not view economics as a kind of writing in the manner of Derrida. Nor, I submit, do traditional methodologists accept (5) and (6). Typically traditional methodologists believe that there is a theory-independent world for economists to investigate, and they try to find out – and perhaps assess – how economists go about acquiring knowledge of this world.

However, the rhetorical conception of economic metatheory is entirely compatible with claims (5) and (6). On the rhetorical conception, economics is an exercise in rhetoric. Rhetoric has as its object persuasion, not acquiring knowledge about a theory-independent reality. Persuasion certainly can, indeed often does, take place without any *such* knowledge being acquired. Moreover, for rhetoric to operate, there does not have even to be a theory-independent reality outside of the representations of economists, or other scientists. Economics can be viewed as a kind of writing whose aim is to persuade, and writing with the aim of persuasion does not require that there be a theory-independent world. The view that economics is an exercise in rhetoric, and its metatheoretical correlate the rhetorical conception of economic metatheory, are comfortably compatible with the social constructivism expressed by claims (5) and (6). Indeed, were one to adopt (5) and (6), the rhetorical view of economic metatheory would be a very natural position to embrace. Embracing it would certainly solve the problem of how to see economic metatheory in light of claims (5) and (6). Thus, if I can marshal evidence that McCloskey accepts (5) and (6), it will not seem so implausible to say that his acceptance of social constructivism motivates his adoption of the rhetorical conception of metatheory.

Evidence that McCloskey adopts (5) and (6) is contained in the following passage:

> As Niels Bohr said, 'It is wrong to think that the task of physics is to find out how nature is. Physics concerns what we can say about nature ... We are suspended in language ... The word "reality" is also a word, a word we must learn to use correctly'.... (McCloskey, 1994, p. 41)

Bohr's view quoted in this passage – and McCloskey quotes it approvingly – certainly looks like claim (5) to me. Claim (6) follows from claim (5). But independent confirmation exists that McCloskey accepts

(6). In an interesting, critical treatment of social constructivism, J.E. McGuire (1992, pp. 167–8) expresses (6) by saying '... scientific theories and facts are constituted solely by social constructs. On this view, there are no factual referents "out there" independent of social constructs to which these constructs refer'. McCloskey seems to accept the position expressed in this passage. For example, he (1994, p. 41) says 'Studies of science over the past few decades have repeatedly shown that facts are *constructed* by words' (emphasis added). To be sure, as indicated in section 2.3 above, McCloskey acknowledges that economists seek truth. But this is small-t truth which is merely what a citizenry of the intellect, a batch of human intellectuals, is persuaded of. Small-t truth is *not* necessarily truth about a theory-independent world, and small-t truths can exist in abundance even if there were no theory-independent reality. McCloskey's view that economics pursues small-t truth is perfectly consistent with the social constructivism expressed by claims (5) and (6). McCloskey (1994, p. 204) also says 'I myself, for example, believe that economics is report on the real ...'. But this assertion is just an adventitious addition to McCloskey's position to deflect criticism; he does nothing to *show* that this assertion literally interpreted can be made consistent with and integrated into his rhetorical conception of economic metatheory. McCloskey appears, then, to accept claims (5) and (6). Given how natural it would be to move from (5) and (6) to the rhetorical conception, I suggest that McCloskey's adoption of (5) and (6) in part at least motivates his acceptance of the rhetorical conception of metatheory.

Social constructivist views of one sort or another have enjoyed considerable popularity in recent decades. And the intellectual sources of constructivist views about knowledge are diverse and complicated. They include: left-wing social theorists from Marx to current feminists; continental European intellectuals like Foucault and Derrida; American philosophers and literary theorists like Richard Rorty and Stanley Fish; and sociologically oriented studies of science such as Latour and Wolgar's *Laboratory Life: The Construction of Scientific Facts*. I will make no effort here to discuss this rather vast literature. But I will mention one difficulty with the social constructivist position expressed by claims (5) and (6) above. Bernard Williams in effect identifies this difficulty in a discussion of Rorty's views. Williams says this:

> These ideas contribute, *from within scientific reflection itself*, to an image of the objects of science which Rorty says we should not have; they contribute, that is, to a conception of the world as it is, independently of our enquiries.... In a revealing passage he says that 'pragmatism denies the possibility of getting beyond the ... notion of "seeing how things hang together" – which, for the

bookish intellectual of recent times, means seeing how all the various vocabularies of all the various epochs and cultures hang together.' That may be a programme for the successor to philosophy, or for the literary studies from which he does not want that successor to be distinct, but it is certainly no programme for science. The sense that one is not locked in a world of books, that one is confronting 'the world', that the work is made hard or easy by what is actually there – these are part of the driving force, the essential consciousness of science.... (Williams, 1990, p. 31)

Williams notes that scientists generally think of themselves as investigating a world that is already there, a theory-independent reality.[13] And Williams rightly thinks this self-conception of scientists is central to their activities as scientists; Williams describes it as part of 'the essential consciousness of science'. It is not at all clear how science could continue in the way it has were scientists to cease thinking of themselves as investigating a world already there, and instead view themselves as merely producing texts, or, as Williams puts it, 'making comparisons within a web of texts'.

But the point Williams makes about scientists generally applies to economists. In large parts of economics – industrial organization, economic forecasting, and economic history to name just a few – economists think of themselves as investigating a theory-independent world. To be sure, a good deal of economic theorizing consists in investigating models in abstraction from their being applied to the real world. Yet, as the discussion in Chapters 7 and 8 will indicate, economists also apply models to the real world. And they typically believe that the world to which they are applying their models exists *antecedent to* economic inquiry. D. Wade Hands expresses the point being made here. He says:

The main problem is that most economists are epistemologically quite traditional. For most economists there is simply a world 'out there' and good science represents that world accurately. (1994, p. 97)

This is as good a statement as you could wish for of Williams's point applied to economists.

However, the social constructivist view expressed by claims (5) and (6) does *not* allow economists to *correctly* see themselves as investigating a theory-independent world. The two claims deny that there is such a world. It might be objected that (5) and (6) acknowledge the existence of consumers, business firms and products like bales of cotton and pairs of running shoes. The social constructivist who adopts (5) and (6) may say that economists investigate a world consisting of such objects as these.

And why is this not sufficient for economists rightly viewing themselves as inquiring into a theory-independent reality? To meet this objection, it will be helpful to remove an ambiguity in the notion of a theory-independent reality. Roberto Salinas describes the two interpretations of this notion as follows:

> Davidson's antirealism results from the rejection of any coherent concept of independent 'theory neutral' reality. Yet the notion of 'theory-independent reality' is itself ambiguous between the loose notion of an intrinsically interpretation-free world of inaccessible noumena and the much more robust notion of the world as a structured realm of independent items like rocks and trees. (Salinas, 1989, p. 111)

Let us use the term 'Kantian theory-independent reality' to refer to an intrinsically interpretation-free world, uncontaminated by theory. And let us use the term 'commonsense theory-independent reality' to refer to a structured domain of entities like stars and trees independent of human knowledge and awareness.

I take Williams's point that scientists view themselves as investigating a theory-independent reality, to affirm that scientists, including economists, take themselves to be inquiring into a *commonsense* theory-independent reality. But the social constructivism expressed by claims (5) and (6) is *not* consistent with economists *rightly* viewing themselves as investigating a commonsense theory-independent world. Claims (5) and (6) deny that there is anything – Kantian theory-independent reality, commonsense theory-independent reality, or whatever – which economists' representations could represent accurately. (6) does acknowledge that consumers, firms and products like bales of cotton exist. But according to (6), such objects are simply social constructs. So conceived, consumers, firms, and bales of cotton cannot be part of a commonsense *theory-independent* world. On the social constructivism expressed by (5) and (6), economists' representations may be about firms, consumers, etc. But this does not mean that economics concerns a commonsense theory-independent reality. Emily Brontë's text *Wuthering Heights* is about Heathcliff and Catherine Earnshaw. But of course, this does not mean that Heathcliff and Catherine are part of a reality independent of Emily Brontë's text; they are just constructs of the text.

It has been argued that the social constructivism expressed by (5) and (6) does not allow economists to correctly view themselves – as they in fact mostly do – as investigating a commonsense theory-independent reality. And this is a serious drawback of (5) and (6). Now the social constructivist may simply reply that economists are under an illusion in viewing themselves this way. But this reply is not cogent. The social constructivism expressed by (5) and (6) is a form of anti-realism.[14] Realism says that there is some sort of reality existing independently of knowledge or representations of it. And commonsense realism says that the familiar world of rocks, trees, planets, stars and animals exists independently of knowledge or representations of it. Claims (5) and (6) conflict with commonsense realism, and therefore constitute a form of anti-realism. It is not the task of this book to defend commonsense realism. Adequate defences of it are readily available, such as Michael Devitt's.[15] But given the acceptability of commonsense realism, and its incompatibility with claims (5) and (6), these two claims should be rejected. Thus, economists and other scientists can *correctly* see themselves as investigating a (commonsense) theory-independent world. Claims (5) and (6), being unacceptable, afford no legitimate basis for saying that economists or other scientists are under an illusion in seeing themselves this way.

I have shown that the social constructivism expressed by claims (5) and (6) is unable to preserve the natural view of economists and other scientists that they are investigating a theory-independent world. And this is reason to reject the social constructivism (5) and (6) represent. But I suggest that it is precisely this social constructivism that in a good measure motivates McCloskey's adoption of the rhetorical conception of economic metatheory. Casting aside the social constructivism which (5) and (6) express undercuts the motivation to adopt the rhetorical conception, and should provide another ground to simply abandon it.

2.6 CONCLUDING REMARKS

Recall that the epistemological conception of economic methodology sets methodology the task of characterizing the kinds of arguments or justification procedures to be used by economists to justify acceptance or rejection of theories. And the epistemological conception may be held in a naturalistic form which requires the methodologist to regard as relevant to this task the answer to 'What kinds of arguments *do* economists employ?' The much broader *traditional* conception of economic methodology incorporates the epistemological conception, and adds to the methodologist's tasks the resolution of those problems, other than the theory appraisal issue, which methodologists have historically treated. The rhetorical conception of economic metatheory, for ·which Donald McCloskey is largely responsible, has arisen in the last decade or so as a serious rival to the traditional conception of methodology. It has been argued here that the rhetorical conception should be abandoned. Accordingly, the traditional conception of methodology still deserves to be seen as the reasonable view of economic metatheory.

The remainder of this book will deal with various issues that have occupied those who have pursued economic methodology on the traditional conception. Criteria for theory appraisal in economics will be discussed. For instance, Chapter 3 evaluates what I dub 'predictive empiricism' as a standard economic theories allegedly must meet in order to afford scientific knowledge. And in Chapter 8 I discuss an important style of argument economists in fact use to establish causal hypotheses. But a good deal of the discussion in this book is directed at issues in economic methodology other than the theory appraisal issue, issues of the sort identified toward the end of section 2.1 above. Overall, the discussion in this book – especially in Chapters 6, 7 and 8 – purports to present an image of economics that does justice to various central facets of the discipline. This chapter has already put in place two pieces of the image of economics this monograph aims to convey. One of them is that economics is in pursuit of truth in a sense of the term in which truth is persuasiveness-independent. The other is that (most) economists see themselves to some extent as trying to acquire knowledge about a theory-independent world. And commonsense realism ensures that there is such a world for them to find out about.

NOTES

1. Here I borrow from Hilary Kornblith's (1985, pp. 1–13) account of naturalized epistemology. It should not be automatically assumed that there is a single, timelessly valid answer to questions (1) and (2). The styles of reasoning economists use, or ought to use, to justify theory acceptance or rejection may change over time. And questions (1) and (2) allow for this possibility.
2. McCloskey criticizes the evidential/non-evidential distinction in another way than the one so far discussed. He (1994, p. 209) correctly notes that ordinary statements like 'It is raining' occur in the absence of arguments. He asks whether this makes them *non*-evidential. Instead of trying to answer this question – if the statements in question are rhetorical devices, the answer is of course 'Yes' – he simply concludes that 'something has gone wrong with the criterion dividing evidential from non-evidential devices'. But, as far as I can see, this conclusion is a total non-sequitur.
3. Roy Weintraub apparently would dissent from what I have said. He (1988, p. 158) affirms that (A) science is not a truth seeking enterprise. His reason for (A) is (B) there is no attribute of truth shared by all true propositions about which anything philosophically interesting can be said. But Weintraub's reasoning from (B) to (A) is a glaring non-sequitur. Suppose that we accept the deflationary or disquotational account of truth according to which to say that, e.g., 'Snow is white' is true, is just to affirm that Snow is white. On this account, truth is not a property of true propositions.

But still we can say, consistently with the deflationary theory, that science pursues truth. This simply means that science seeks true hypotheses. And *this* use of 'true' is easily understood along the lines of the deflationary theory. To say hypothesis *H* is true, is just to affirm *H* itself. So, accepting (B), as an advocate of the deflationary theory does, hardly commits one to Weintraub's (A).

4. This account of scientific realism versus instrumentalism is deployed in Michael Gardner, 1983.

5. In his reply in the 1988 symposium, McCloskey uses the term 'good people' in place of 'a citizenry of the intellect'. He (1988, p. 155) says 'What is persuasive to good people is what is true, for now'. In a recent, valiant effort to make sense of McCloskey's views about truth, Uskali Mäki (1995, p. 1309) ascribes to McCloskey a position resembling (Df1), though Mäki expresses his interpretation of McCloskey in the language of a coherence theory of truth. Mäki rightly emphasizes McCloskey's commitment to being able to identify a suitable, privileged group of people such that what is persuasive to them is the touchstone of truth.

6. The *inductive* underdetermination of scientific theories by the evidence for them is not the same as the *empirical* underdetermination of theories (Ellis, 1985, p. 62). The former simply says that the falsity of a theory is compatible with the supporting evidence for the theory available at a given time. The empirical underdetermination of theories says that for a given theory, there is an incompatible theory which is empirically equivalent in that no observational evidence *could* distinguish between the two theories.

7. McCloskey's view that the notion of truth defined by (Df1) *is* the ordinary concept of truth, is in effect a crude version of a consensus theory of truth. Consensus theories of truth link the concept of truth with the notion of consensus by some social group. For example, Peirce analyses truth as what scientists will in the long run reach consensus on. But even Peirce's relatively sophisticated consensus theory has not fared well at the hands of critics. See Rescher, 1978, *passim*. It is worth noting that consensus theories of truth can seem to gain a specious credibility on the basis of the fact that the distinction between what a group of people are persuaded of at time *t* and what is true cannot be *applied* by people in the group at time *t*. But this fact does not warrant collapsing the distinction between being persuasive to all and being true. For people in the group may find out *after* time *t* that what they believed at *t* was false at *t*.

8. McCloskey (1994, pp. 215-7) distinguishes between practitioners of a discipline like economics and outsiders or non-practitioners. He suggests that outsiders cannot legitimately appraise or assess the cognitive status of a discipline from their armchairs. This seems to imply that *philosophers* are in no position to provide answers to questions (3) and (4). I certainly think that philosophers who hope to say anything useful about economics ought to study the subject seriously and learn some economics. But any blanket dismissal of what philosophers might say in answer to (3) and (4) is unwarranted. How can McCloskey, or anyone, know the value of a particular philosopher's remarks in answer to (3) and (4) in advance of examining that philosopher's remarks?

9. On the connection between justification and believing what is true, see the illuminating discussion in Bonjour, 1985, pp. 7-8.

10. In an insightful paper Christina Bicchieri (1988) argues that metaphors are not merely ornamental but convey knowledge. But this conclusion does not contradict my claim that non-evidential rhetorical devices, like metaphor, cannot confer warrant on economists' claims. Bicchieri's conclusion just means that an economist's use of a metaphor may constitute a *claim* to knowledge, and so the question of the justification

of that claim can arise. But a single claim to knowledge, whether conveyed by a metaphor or not, generally confers no warrant on anything taken by itself. Of course, if a claim to knowledge C1 conveyed by a metaphor is adduced in support of another claim C2, then the metaphor may confer warrant on C2. But 'C1; therefore, C2' is an argument rather than a non-evidential rhetorical device.

11. Alexander Rosenberg is a prominent economic methodist. See Rosenberg, 1992, Chapters 1 and 2.

12. This is Richard Boyd's formulation. See Boyd, 1992, p. 132.

13. This is not to say that scientists are realists as opposed to instrumentalists. Instrumentalist scientists would think of themselves as investigating a theory-independent world, and would view their first-order theories as devices for such purposes as generating predictions about such a world.

14. McCloskey appears to view himself as a realist. He (1994, p. 203) says '"Realism" ... seems to mean that the world exists independent of our perceptions of it ... But if "*our* perceptions" are taken to mean "the perceptions about which we speak to each other, testing by conversation their mutual reasonableness and freedom from illusion," then I am a realist, and so is every working scientist.' However, it is not clear that his definition of 'our perceptions' in the realist's claim really preserves what realists intend. Moreover, if McCloskey really does adopt realism, he is accepting a position inconsistent with the social constructivism he certainly appears to embrace.

15. See Devitt, 1991. But I would not want to endorse everything Devitt says in defence of commonsense realism. For one, I do not think Devitt appreciates the fact that a metaphysical relativist like Nelson Goodman can be a commonsense realist. For an effort to show that this indeed the case, see Rappaport, 1993, pp. 77–8. Also, an interesting discussion of some of the confusions that engender social constructivism is found in J.E. McGuire, 1992.

3. Economics and Predictive Empiricism

3.1 ROSENBERG'S SCEPTICISM ABOUT ECONOMICS

As indicated in the Introduction (Chapter 1), a major traditional effort to understand economics is by asking 'Is it an empirical science?' One version of the 'Is it science?' approach first lays down a methodological rule or standard an empirical science must meet. An attempt is then made to determine whether or not economics meets the methodological standard. Alexander Rosenberg's position is the most important recent example of the methodological rule version of the 'Is it science?' approach to economics. The outcome of Rosenberg's application of this approach is his endorsement of the sceptical view that economics does not constitute scientific empirical knowledge. He says:

> However, anyone with much knowledge of the history of economic theory will agree that the discipline does not seek to respond to empirical data in the way characteristic of an empirical science – even a theoretically impoverished one. If social contract theory is too Procrustean a bed for economic theory, and empirical science is too demanding a status, is there not some other interpretation of the aims and methods of economic theory that will do full justice to its scope and insulation from data. (Rosenberg, 1992, p. 228)

How does Rosenberg manage to arrive at the conclusion that 'empirical science is too demanding a status' for economics? Rosenberg has provided an answer to this question in several works. But the most extended argument for Rosenberg's scepticism about economics is found in his book *Economics - Mathematical Politics or Science of Diminishing Returns?* Accordingly, I will concentrate my attention here on the line of thought in this book.

Rosenberg's argument for his scepticism appeals to a pair of premises. The first is that knowledge or warranted belief in empirical science is dependent on predictive attainment, while the second premise is a denial that economics exhibits the required predictive attainment. My formulation of the first premise is a vague statement of the methodological rule or standard which Rosenberg thinks an empirical science must meet. The second premise denies that economics measures up to the standard. It will be argued here that Rosenberg's argument fails to support its sceptical conclusion. And the failure of Rosenberg's argument spells the failure of the most important, recent example of the methodological rule version of the 'Is it science?' approach to economics.

We need a more precise statement of Rosenberg's argument for his scepticism about economics. It is a common belief that at least part of what qualifies the findings of the natural sciences as knowledge or warranted belief is their predictive accomplishments. Let us use the term 'predictive empiricism' to refer to the doctrine that predictive success or improvement is at least a necessary condition for knowledge or justified belief in empirical science. Predictive empiricism received clear endorsement in the writings of some logical positivists (Ayer, 1946, p. 99). But the doctrine has also been popular among economic methodologists. For example, in his classic article on methodology Milton Friedman (1953, p. 9) affirms '... a theory is to be judged by its predictive power ...' And in the preface to the second edition of his well-known book on economic methodology Mark Blaug (1992, p. xiii) states '... the only way to know that a theory is true or rather not false is to commit ourselves to a prediction about acts/states/events that follow from the theory ...' Rosenberg plainly commits himself to predictive empiricism when he says this:

> It seems evident that if forced to, most neoclassical economists would endorse an empiricist account of knowledge which makes the proximate goal of science the successful testing of its claims by experience, and more specifically, by prediction ... I share the economists' commitment to predictive success as at least a necessary condition of knowledge. (Rosenberg, 1992, p. 17)

This passage clearly makes predictive success a necessary condition for scientific knowledge. (Following Rosenberg, I will use 'science' and its cognates as short for 'empirical science'.)

But what is predictive success? Though Rosenberg acknowledges some difficulty in defining the notion, he does specify conditions for predictive success in the following passage:

> There are even more fundamental problems facing any simple claim that predictive success is a necessary condition for knowledge or an end to be sought above others in science. One of them is the problem of stating exactly and unobjectionably what counts as a confirmation of a prediction. But this is a philosopher's problem, not an economist's. Like other social scientists, the economist knows a confirmed prediction when he or she sees one, and of

course what is crucial in science is not the sheer number of confirmed predictions a theory makes, but the proportion of right predictions to wrong ones and the precision of the predictions it makes, along with the amount of surprise generated by its predictions. (Rosenberg, 1992, p. 18)

The quoted passage implies that a theory T exhibits predictive success to the degree that (A) the ratio of correct to incorrect predictions is high, (B) T's predictions are precise, and (C) T generates surprising or novel predictions.[1]

However, Rosenberg often emphasizes predictive *improvement*, rather than predictive *success*, as a necessary condition for scientific knowledge. For example, he says:

In Chapter 1 I held that long-term improvement in predictive success is a necessary accomplishment of any discipline that claims to provide knowledge, and especially to provide guidance for policy. (Rosenberg, 1992, p. 56)

This passage implies that for a discipline D to afford scientific warranted belief or knowledge, D must exhibit predictive improvement over time. In other words, to be scientific knowledge, D must show an *increasing degree* of predictive success, which implies that D must exhibit an increasing ratio of correct to incorrect predictions, more precise predictions, and more novel or surprising predictions.[2]

Which is it that Rosenberg takes to be necessary for scientific knowledge? Is it predictive success, or is it predictive improvement? The two properties are not entirely identical, as Rosenberg himself rightly suggests in the following remarks:

Friedman's argument for the predictive success of economics turns out to be much less vigorous than it appears, but perhaps the demand that economic theory reflect substantial predictive success is too strong. After all, a discipline must walk before it can run. Perhaps the most we should expect of neoclassical economic theory is improvement in predictive success. (Rosenberg, 1992, p. 62)

So a discipline or theory can show predictive improvement over a period of time *without* exhibiting *substantial* predictive success by the end of that period. In other words, a *low* degree of predictive success at time t can coexist with predictive improvement over the period up to time t. Though continued predictive improvement of a theory or discipline must *eventually* bring a high degree of predictive success. Moreover, predictive improvement over a period of time spells *some* degree of predictive success by the end of the period, as predictive improvement just is an increase in predictive success. In light of these points, we can say that Rosenberg takes predictive *improvement* over time to be at least necessary for scientific justified belief. But this implies that some degree of predictive success is necessary for science, inasmuch as predictive improvement over a period of time entails some degree of predictive success by the end of the period. So, the answer to the question as to whether Rosenberg takes predictive improvement *or* predictive success to be essential to science, is that he takes both to be essential, though the emphasis is on predictive improvement. I will, therefore, take Rosenberg's predictive empiricism to affirm that for a theory or discipline to be scientific justified belief or knowledge, the theory or discipline must exhibit predictive improvement over time.

However, Rosenberg takes condition (C) for predictive success to be less important for economics than conditions (A) and (B). He (1992, p. 18) says 'The two predictive criteria of proportion of hits to misses and precision are especially important for economics'. And this leads Rosenberg to relax his requirements for predictive improvement. He says:

> For the purposes of this book, I stipulate the following implication of the economists' commitment to an empiricist epistemology: a scientific discipline should be expected to show a long-term pattern of improvements in the proportion of correct predictions and their precision. (Rosenberg, 1992, p. 18)

So, in the context of his discussion of economics, Rosenberg is apparently willing *not* to demand that a discipline which furnishes scientific knowledge must come up with a larger number of novel or surprising predictions. Instead, for a discipline to be scientific knowledge, it is only required that the discipline exhibit an increasing ratio of correct to incorrect predictions, and to generate more precise predictions. Again, Rosenberg's predictive empiricism affirms that for a theory or discipline to be scientific knowledge, the theory or discipline must show predictive improvement over time. And in light of what has just been said, we should interpret predictive improvement as requiring that a theory or discipline exhibit an increasing ratio of correct to incorrect predictions, as well as generate more precise predictions.

3.2   TROUBLES WITH PREDICTIVE EMPIRICISM

Before proceeding, we need to use the discussion in section 3.1 to give a precise statement of Rosenberg's argument for his sceptical view about economics. Here, then, is Rosenberg's argument:

(P1) A necessary condition for a theory or discipline counting as scientific knowledge is that it exhibit predictive improvement over time. (P2) At least since the marginalist revolution of the 1870s, economic theory has failed to show predictive improvement.
So, (C) economics does not constitute scientific knowledge or justified belief.

It was argued above that (P1) is Rosenberg's version of predictive empiricism. That Rosenberg adopts (P2) is clear from the following remarks:

> In this chapter I take up the burden, and try to share it with economists who are on record as defending the predictive success of their discipline! I try to show that their methodological position would be pointless except against a background of failure to improve the predictive power of economic theory. (Rosenberg, 1992, p. 57)

> It is not that economic theory has no predictive power; rather the problem is that it does not have enough. And it never seems to acquire any more than it had at the hands of, say, Marshall in the late nineteenth century. (Rosenberg, 1992, p. 67)

The conclusion (C) of Rosenberg's argument expresses his sceptical or negative thesis about economics. It is this negative thesis which has led Rosenberg to search for a cognitive status for economics other than science. Rosenberg's rather notorious positive thesis that neoclassical microeconomics is a branch of applied mathematics is a large part of the outcome of that search.

The two premises of Rosenberg's sceptical argument clearly entail the conclusion (C). In the remainder of this section I will argue that premise (P1), which expresses Rosenberg's methodological standard for science, is false. But I want the case against Rosenberg's methodological rule version of the 'Is it science?' approach to economics to rest on several pillars. Accordingly, in subsequent sections of this chapter I will show that Rosenberg fails to substantiate premise (P2) of his sceptical argument. In other words, Rosenberg does not succeed in determining whether or not economics meets his methodological standard.

As noted above, Rosenberg's predictive empiricism *entails* that for a theory *T* to count as scientific justified belief, *T* must exhibit some degree of *predictive success*. But this entailment is *not* true. As a matter of fact, in science empirical data that are already known can incrementally confirm or raise the credibility of a theory.[3] Glymour supplies some familiar examples in the following passage:

Scientists commonly argue for their theories from evidence known long before the theories were introduced. Copernicus argued for his theory using observations made over the course of millennia, and not on the basis of any startling new predictions derived from the theory, and presumably it was on the basis of such arguments that he won the adherence of his early disciples. Newton argued for universal gravitation using Kepler's second and third laws, established before *Principia* was published. The argument that Einstein gave in 1915 for his gravitational field equations was that they explained the anomalous advance of the perihelion of Mercury, established more than a half century earlier. Other physicists found the argument enormously forceful, and it was a fair conjecture that without it the British would not have mounted the famous eclipse expedition of 1919. Old evidence can in fact confirm new theory .... (Glymour, 1980, pp. 85–6)

In the cases Glymour cites, the epistemic worth of a theory increases due to the theory being able to account for or explain already known data. But if the ability to explain old data can raise the credibility of a theory, then presumably the ability of a theory to account for more and more already known data should raise the theory's credibility more and more. And at some point, through this process the theory will be absolutely confirmed, that is, its credibility will be high enough to justify acceptance. But in this event, the theory in question is acceptable *without* exhibiting any degree of predictive success, and so predictive empiricism is false. The predictive empiricist may reply that, though explaining old data can raise the credibility of a theory, it can never raise it enough to absolutely confirm the theory. But this is implausible. If accounting for more and more old evidence can continue to increase a theory's epistemic worth and so bring the theory closer and closer to being worthy of acceptance *simpliciter*, what could prevent the theory from finally gaining enough credibility to constitute rational acceptance or knowledge? Nothing, as long as some finite amount of evidence for the theory is enough for rational acceptability. So, a theory or discipline *can* constitute scientific knowledge *without* exhibiting any degree of predictive success. (I assume that should the individual theories within an entire discipline become knowledge just through substantially increased ability to explain old data, the discipline itself would become scientific knowledge, even in the absence of any predictive improvement on the discipline's part.) Since Rosenberg's predictive empiricism entails that a theory or discipline must have some degree of predictive success to be knowledge, it follows that his predictive empiricism is false.

A second argument for rejecting Rosenberg's predictive empiricism is worth presenting here. I will develop the argument for an individual theory, but insofar as entire disciplines contain theories, the argument is easily modified to apply to disciplines. As others have pointed out, the distinction between a theory accounting for old data and the theory predicting new data is merely one of chronology, and thus of no epistemic significance. John Maynard Keynes made this point some time ago when he said this:[4]

> The peculiar virtue of prediction or predesignation is altogether imaginary. The number of instances examined and the analogy between them are the essential points, and the question as to whether a particular hypothesis happens to be propounded before or after their examination is quite irrelevant. (Keynes, 1948, p. 305)

Bearing this in mind, let us tell two stories about an imaginary scientific theory T. In story one T is justifiably accepted by a community of scientists. At least one determinant of the rational acceptance of T is that T exhibits predictive improvement over a long period of time, that is, the ratio of T's correct to incorrect predictions has increased, etc. Thus, in story one the predictive empiricist condition for warranted scientific belief is met. In story two everything is the same except that the *same* empirical data making T's predictions true in story one were known or available *prior to* T's construction; and T is able to explain or account for all the data in question. (Though T was not constructed specifically to account for these data.) In story two T has generated *no* correct predictions, and so has not exhibited predictive improvement over time. Thus in story two the scientists' acceptance of theory T fails to meet the predictive empiricist requirement for scientific knowledge. Does this mean that in story two the scientists are not justified in accepting theory T? Surely not. The *same* data predicted by theory T in story one are all accounted for or explained by T in story two. And in light of the fact that there is no epistemic significance to the relation between the time a theory is generated and the time supporting data or evidence come to be known, the data explained in story two lend the *same evidential support* to theory T as do those data predicted in story one.[5] But if this is so, then theory T must *also* be justified in story two. For T has the same amount of evidential support in story two as it does in story one, and T is justified in story one. It follows that Rosenberg's predictive empiricism is false. A scientific theory may be justified or known – as is theory T in story two – even though it has not exhibited predictive improvement.

The argument of the previous paragraph may be subject to the following objection. It might be said that the major intuition behind predictive empiricism is the following principle:

(I) If data D are known before theory T is developed and T merely implies D, then D cannot confirm or support T nearly as strongly as they would had T correctly anticipated or predicted D.

But, the objection continues, the argument of the previous paragraph ignores or overlooks (I). Specifically, (I) conflicts with the claim made by the argument that theory T has the *same* evidential support in story two as it does in story one. Since by (I), T has *less* evidential support in story two than it does in story one. In response to this objection, (I) may seem plausible. Suppose that a scientist knows of data D and then devises a theory T specifically to imply D, and T has no stronger probative relation to T than being implied by T. In this case it would appear that D do not support T as strongly as they would had T correctly predicted D. However, the argument of the preceding paragraph does not really conflict with (I). The argument relied upon the following principle:

(K) If data D are known before theory T is developed, then D *can* provide the *same* degree of confirmation or evidential support as they would had T correctly predicted D.

(K) is the conclusion I took to be implied by the fact that the distinction between a theory accounting for known data and the theory predicting those data, is of no epistemic import. And (K) and (I) are entirely compatible, for the antecedents of the two conditionals represent different states of affairs. The antecedent of (I) represents known data D merely being implied by a theory T, a theory that has perhaps been invented specifically to account for D. But the antecedent of (K) does not envisage that known data D have played a role in the very construction of theory T. Evidence or data D *can* be known prior to the development of a theory T, and yet T is not devised, even in part, to account for D. Indeed, evidence available prior to the development of a theory may even be thought hostile to the theory, and only subsequently are advocates of the theory able to figure out a way for their theory to accommodate the initially nonconfirming evidence. Nor does the antecedent of (K) rule out that there is a stronger evidential relation between D and T than D being implied by T. Moreover, in story two of the previous paragraph, it was not assumed that theory T has no stronger probative relation to the known data D than implying those data. Nor was it assumed in story two that T was invented specifically to account for D. Since the antecedent of (I) is not fulfilled in story two, (I) cannot be used to conclude that theory T has less evidential support in story two than it does in story one. I conclude, then, that the objection under consideration fails.

I have argued that predictive empiricism is a false epistemological doctrine. And the doctrine's falsity causes the breakdown of Rosenberg's argument for the conclusion that economics is not scientific justified belief or knowledge. In other words, premise (P1) of Rosenberg's argument as stated at the start of this section is false, and so the argument fails to justify its sceptical conclusion. But I want to emphasize that nothing that has been said here implies that prediction is not important in science. Scientists often seek to *test* theories, and in one sense testing a theory involves getting it to yield a prediction and ascertaining the accuracy of the prediction. Indeed, it seems common for a theory that is accepted in a scientific discipline to rest on a combination of the theory's ability to account for data known prior to its development, *and* to generate predictions which turn out to be correct. However, none of this entails the view that predictive improvement is a *necessary* condition for justified belief in science or any organized empirical discipline. In addition, Rosenberg (1992, p. 56) affirms that any discipline like economics which purports to be relevant to policy must show predictive improvement over time. There is some truth to this claim.[6] Specific policy proposals typically must in part be based on predictions; and to *justify* a policy proposal, the prediction it is based on must be correct. So, if a discipline is to increase its warranted policy proposals over time, then it must generate an increasing number of correct predictions, which at least may spell an increase in the discipline's ratio of correct to incorrect predictions. (Recall that predictive improvement as Rosenberg construes it requires an increasing ratio of correct to incorrect predictions.) It is an important goal of science to enable us to make beneficial changes in the natural and social orders. And generating an increasing number of correct predictions is a condition for implementing this goal. But neither this goal nor any condition for its implementation should be confused with a necessary condition for warranted belief about the natural or social orders. Warranted belief is not necessarily useful belief.

3.3   IS ECONOMICS PREDICTIVELY IMPOVERISHED?

Premise (P2) of Rosenberg's argument for economics not being science affirms that economics has not exhibited predictive improvement over time. This premise expresses Rosenberg's view on the question of whether or not economics meets the methodological standard set by predictive empiricism. In this section and the next it will be argued that Rosenberg fails to justify premise (P2). This will complete my negative evaluation of Rosenberg's example of the methodological rule version of the 'Is it science?' approach to economics.

One way Rosenberg attempts to justify premise (P2) of his sceptical argument is via a demonstration that a number of prominent economists are committed, expressly or implicitly, to economics' lack of predictive improvement. But the evidence Rosenberg marshals in this regard is so weak that one could acknowledge Rosenberg's evidence and still rationally refuse to accept premise (P2).

Given the account of predictive improvement we finally settled on in section 3.1, premise (P2) of Rosenberg's sceptical argument affirms the disjunction of the following pair of claims:

(C1) The ratio of correct to incorrect predictions in economics has not increased over time.

(C2) There has been negligible improvement in the precision of economic predictions.

Rosenberg thinks that Milton Friedman is one prominent economist whose methodological views presuppose the failure to improve the predictive record of economics. He interprets Friedman as admitting that the record of neoclassical economics in predicting *individual* economic choice, as opposed to marketwide phenomena, is very poor. But on Rosenberg's interpretation, Friedman then denies that the falsity of neoclassical theory's predictions about individual choice is relevant to the appraisal of the theory. Rosenberg challenges this denial of Friedman's, and further claims that neoclassical micro theory, even when restricted to marketwide phenomena, is predictively very weak. To support this claim, Rosenberg (1992, p. 60) says that at least half of the predictions of the theory of perfect competition have turned out to be false. However, Rosenberg's discussion of Friedman does little to support claims (C1) or (C2). No evidence is provided that at least half of the predictions of the theory of perfect competition have been falsified. Moreover, elsewhere I have indicated that Friedman is an advocate of the 'as-if' view of economic motivational hypotheses like 'Business firm managers seek to maximize profits'. And on the as-if view, many of the allegedly false predictions of neoclassical microeconomics about individual agents are *not* really implied by neoclassical theory at all.[7] As a result, I am disinclined to accept Rosenberg's claim that Friedman *admits* that neoclassical micro theory has a miserable record in predicting individual choice. And if no such admission is really forthcoming from

Friedman, Rosenberg can derive little support for (C1) or (C2) from what Friedman says.

Another prominent economist Rosenberg appeals to is Wassily Leontief. Rosenberg (1992, p. 63) says 'Leontief does not argue that economic theory has made little progress in predictive power. He simply assumes it'. He adds that Leontief has a *reason* for the belief in economics' lack of predictive power. The reason is that an area in which predictive improvement might especially have been expected, to wit, econometrics, has not managed to improve the predictive record of economics.[8] But Leontief's view that econometrics has not improved the predictive record of economics is apparently controversial among economists.[9] For example, Lawrence Klein is a major figure in the area of constructing macroeconometric models and using them to make macroeconomic forecasts or predictions. And Klein believes that, despite some failures in forecasting with macroeconometric models, there have been many good forecasts. Klein (1984, pp. 8–9) cites a number of successful forecasts he himself made using macroeconometric models. I am not suggesting that what Klein says provides anything like clear-cut evidence that econometrics has improved the predictive record of economics – Klein does not even unequivocally provide evidence that he managed to increase the *percentage* of correct macroeconomic predictions. But the existence of dissenters like Klein from Leontief's negative assessment of econometrics' predictive record, should at least make us hesitate to accept (C1) or (C2).

There is another reason for scepticism regarding Rosenberg's appeal to Leontief's claim about econometrics in support of his premise (P2). Estimated econometric models are not the only basis for economic prediction or forecasting. Another approach to economic prediction, ignored in Rosenberg's discussion, bases predictions at least partly on generalizations affirming correlations among economic phenomena. For example, a few years ago the economist Richard Hoey made the following prediction about inflation in the US economy:

> I believe that we are about at the cyclical lows for inflation for this cycle but that the initial rise in inflation should be gradual. My expectation is for a saucer-shaped low in inflation followed by a gradual upward trend. I just don't see evidence for a dramatic upsurge in inflation. (Hoey, 1993, p. 3)

What is Hoey's basis for predicting that inflation will trend upward only gradually after the low in inflation the US economy experienced around mid-1993? In part it is the following generalization:

(G1) The lowest rate of inflation tends to occur early in the expansionary phase of the business cycle, with inflation gradually drifting up thereafter.

(G1) just affirms a rough correlation between different rates of inflation and earlier and later states in an economic expansion. (Hoey's overall argument for his prediction about inflation also appeals to generalizations of a causal character like 'Rapid money supply growth tends to produce inflation'.)

Another example of the use of correlational generalizations like (G1) to make economic prediction is the index of leading economic indicators. This index, currently compiled by the Conference Board, is a composite of eleven variables (as of mid-1996) such as changes in business inventories, average work week in manufacturing, and new residential housing permits. The use of the index to make predictions about overall economic activity is based partly on the following generalization:

(G2) Ups and downs of the index of leading indicators tend to foreshadow ups and downs of the economy (real GDP).

(G2) affirms a rough correlation between the behaviour of the index and the behaviour of the overall economy. Of course, sometimes the index has fallen and no recession has followed. But the general tendency of the index of leading indicators over a period of several months, especially together with other information like the behaviour of the lagging indicators, is still a useful tool for predicting aggregate economic activity. And its use has afforded a large number of *correct* forecasts of overall economic activity.[10]

As this example illustrates, especially since the 1930s economists have increased the number of correct economic predictions through increased knowledge of how one set of data is correlated in time with another set. It might be said that this increase has little connection with economic *theories* such as neoclassical micro theory, Keynesian macro theory and new classical macro theory. And so the larger number of correct predictions afforded by the sort of knowledge represented by the index of leading indicators can do nothing to show that economics as a discipline exhibits any predictive improvement however modest. In response to this, economics certainly is characterized in a large measure by what in Chapter 5 of this book will be called 'global theories', neoclassical micro theory being a prime example of a global theory. But as anyone who teaches economics knows, there is more to economics then these global theories and the specific models (the model of perfect competition, the model of the rational consumer, and so on) partly constituting the global theories. For instance, economics includes knowledge of the workings of real world economic institutions – for example, knowledge of how the Federal Reserve System affects the growth of the money supply through open market operations and other tools. In addition, economics incorporates a number of true generalizations which are separate or separable from the specific models in any of economics' global theories. (G2) above is only one example. Others are 'A convertible bond rarely sells below its conversion value', Engel's law, the law of demand and Gresham's law. Additions to the stock of such generalizations over the last century or two have enabled economics to increase the number of its correct predictions. (Gresham's law 'Bad money drives out good' was stated in a proclamation issued in 1560 by the government of Elizabeth I of England, and so Gresham's law goes back more than just a couple of centuries.) To be sure, an increase in the number of correct predictions a discipline generates does not by itself constitute predictive improvement, though an increasing number of correct predictions spells an increasing *percentage* of correct predictions as long as the number of incorrect predictions does not rise proportionally. But the fact that economics has made more correct predictions due to the augmentation of its stock of warranted generalizations like (G2) negatively affects Rosenberg's appeal to Leontief in support of premise (P2). Suppose Leontief is right in claiming that *econometrics* has done little or nothing to improve the predictive record of economics. Still, placing this consideration alongside the fact that in areas of economics *other* than econometrics the number of correct predictions *has* increased, our *total* evidence fails to justify the claim that economics has exhibited no predictive improvement over the last century or two.

The third prominent economist to whom Rosenberg appeals to support premise (P2) of his sceptical argument is Paul Samuelson. Rosenberg (1992, p. 71) claims that economics has been able so far to provide *only* qualitative as opposed to quantitative predictions, a claim pretty much admitted by Samuelson. Other economists have made this same claim. Mark Blaug expresses it in the following passage:

> We must begin by disenchanting ourselves of the idea that economic predictions must be quantitative in character to qualify as scientific predictions. Clearly, the predictions of most economic models are qualitative rather than quantitative in nature: they specify the directions of the change of the endogenous variables in consequence of a change in the value of one or more exogenous variables, without pretending to predict the numerical magnitude

of the change. In other words, all neoclassical economics is about the *signs* of first- and second-order partial derivatives and that is virtually all it is about. (Blaug, 1985, p. 701, italics in original)

Now how is the claim that economics has not moved beyond qualitative or generic predictions supposed to bear on claims (C1) or (C2)? Rosenberg (1992, p. 70) does say that improvement in predictive power requires supplanting qualitative with quantitative predictions. (C2) ties predictive improvement to making predictions that are more precise, and perhaps Rosenberg thinks that replacing qualitative with quantitative predictions is supplanting imprecise predictions with more precise predictions. But qualitative predictions are not necessarily imprecise. To see this let us look at an example of the sort of thing Rosenberg expressly counts as a qualitative prediction. Consider a single good market model whose demand and supply functions are given by the following equations:

$$Q = a - bP \qquad a, b > 0 \qquad (3.1)$$
$$Q = -c + dP \qquad c, d > 0 \qquad (3.2)$$

The reduced form solution for the endogenous variable P is given by the following:

$$\bar{P} = (a + c) / (b + d) \qquad (3.3)$$

Equation (3.3) expresses the equilibrium value of P as a function of the parameters a, b, c and d. Using a little calculus it is easy to show that

$$\frac{\partial \bar{P}}{\partial c} = 1 / (b + d) \qquad (3.4)$$

And given the restrictions on the signs of the parameters b and d specified in (3.1) and (3.2), we can infer that

$$\frac{\partial \bar{P}}{\partial c} > 0 \qquad (3.5)$$

Now equation (3.5) seems to be a case of a qualitative or generic prediction for Rosenberg. He says 'The qualitative predictions that we can test against data are roughly the signs, positive or negative, of the partial differentials of the changes in the values of economic variables we set out to measure' (Rosenberg, 1992, p. 68). But is the qualitative prediction (3.5) imprecise? Speaking intuitively, (3.5) seems quite precise. But if qualitative predictions like (3.5) can be precise, the claim that economics gives us only qualitative predictions fails to provide any evidence for (C2).

It appears that Rosenberg's appeal to Friedman, Leontief and Samuelson provides little in the way of support for his contention that economics has shown no predictive improvement over the last century or two. I want to emphasize that no effort has been made in this section to provide evidence for saying economics *has* exhibited predictive improvement in Rosenberg's sense of the term. All I have done is show that Rosenberg's appeal to prominent economists does not succeed in supporting premise (P2) of his argument for the sceptical conclusion that economics is not science.

3.4　PREDICTIVE POVERTY AND SCIENTIFIC LAWS

Rosenberg's appeal to Friedman, Leontief and Samuelson is not his only basis for his claim that economics has not exhibited predictive improvement. Another seemingly more profound basis for the predictive poverty of economics can be found in Rosenberg's writings. Rosenberg offers a philosophical explanation for economics' lack of predictive improvement. Though I have argued in section 3.3 that Rosenberg has not established the existence of the explanandum phenomenon, the explanans itself may well seem to warrant saying that not only has economics so far failed to show predictive improvement, but that the discipline as we know it will never improve predictively. However, the explanans of Rosenberg's philosophical explanation for the alleged predictive poverty of economics is subject to a number of difficulties that undercut its persuasiveness.

Rosenberg (1980, pp. 90–91) has long believed that any theory which attempts to explain human behaviour in terms of *intentional* concepts like belief and desire, is doomed to predictive sterility. This view is used to explain the predictive failure of economics. Rosenberg says:

> As we have seen, the real source of trouble for the attempt to find *improvable* laws of economic behaviour is something that has only become clear in the philosophy of psychology's attempts to understand the intentional variables of common sense and cognitive psychology. What we saw in Chapter 5 is that 'beliefs' and 'desires' – the terms in which ordinary thought and the social sciences describe the causes and effects of human action – do not describe 'natural kinds'. They do not divide nature at the joints. They do not label types

of discrete states that share some manageably small set of causes and effects and so cannot be brought together in causal generalizations that improve on our ordinary level of prediction and control of human action, let alone attain the sort of continuing improvement characteristic of science. We cannot expect to improve our intentional explanations of action beyond their present level of predictive power. But the level of predictive power of our intentional theory is no higher than Plato's. (Rosenberg, 1992, p. 235, italics in original)

I will set out Rosenberg's explanation for economics' lack of predictive improvement as a series of numbered propositions. Doing so will facilitate understanding and assessment of the explanation. Here, then, is the explanans of Rosenberg's explanation:[11]

(R1) Economics views individual actions and aggregates of them as resulting from *intentional states*, specifically preferences and expectations; intentional states are the explanatory variables of economic theory.

(R2) To exhibit improvement in predictive power, a discipline must uncover *laws* or generalizations which can be improved in the direction of laws.

(R3) There are neither any laws nor any improvable generalizations formulated using intentional concepts like preference and expectation.

I will treat (R1), (R2) and (R3) as the premises of a philosophical argument for premise (P2) of Rosenberg's case for economics not being science. It does look as if these three premises together imply that economics has not predictively improved, and there is no hope for improvement in its predictive power as long as it appeals to intentional states to explain economic behaviour.

Some clarification of (R2) and (R3) is required, and Rosenberg's reason for (R3) needs to be brought out. (R2) is a variant of the view, sometimes associated with logical empiricist accounts of scientific explanation, that predictions must be justified by appeal to other statements which include scientific laws. And on this view, predictive improvement results from *adding* to the stock of laws available to warrant predictions. However, (R2) allows that generalizations which are not strictly laws can ground predictions, but to do so, such generalizations must be capable of a certain kind of improvement or refinement. Rosenberg thinks that genuine scientific laws are exceptionless generalizations that are not qualified, explicitly or implicitly, by *ceteris paribus* clauses.[12] I will call this view of laws 'the logical empiricist conception'. On this conception, a generalization that is not, strictly speaking, a law may be refinable or improvable in the direction of a genuine law. Rosenberg (1985, p. 402) accepts Donald Davidson's distinction between homonomic and heteronomic generalizations. A generalization is homonomic if it is improvable within the vocabulary used in its original formulation; and a generalization is heteronomic if the process of refining it requires switching to a different vocabulary. Note that both homonomic and heteronomic generalizations are refinable in the direction of laws. At the terminus of the process of refining or improving a generalization is the genuine or finished law. But what sort of improvement is required of a generalization that eventually turns it into a real law? The following passage conveys Rosenberg's answer:

> In the natural sciences, predictive and explanatory power of generalizations are improved at least very often by sharpening up the specification of the values of causal variables instanced in a particular sequence that the law subsumes. Thus we can improve the precision of our prediction of the pressure of a gas consequent on a change in its temperature if we can improve our measurement of the temperature. If an alcohol thermometer is correct to one degree Celsius, and a mercury thermometer to one-tenth of a degree Celsius, the latter will enable us to predict the effects of a change in temperature on changes in pressure to an order of magnitude's greater precision. (Rosenberg, 1985, pp. 402–03)

So, improving or refining a generalization in the direction of a law is a matter of getting better and better methods of *measuring* the variables in the generalization. And Rosenberg (1985, p. 403) would add that these methods of measurement must not presuppose the truth of the generalization; the methods must be applicable independently of the generalization itself. In light of these remarks, we can see that (R2) affirms that a discipline exhibits predictive improvement to the extent that it discovers laws, or generalizations improvable in the way just described, which can then be used to warrant predictions.

Now (R3) says that there are no laws, or generalizations improvable in the direction of laws, connecting intentional states to one another or to human actions. Why does Rosenberg adopt (R3)? The answer is largely contained in the following passage:

> If anomalous monism is correct, there are no prospects for similar improvements in a law like L. [L is the psychological or intentional generalization '(x)(if x is in belief state B and has desires D, then x does action A'.] For in order to improve our specification of initial conditions, we need a means independent of L for identifying those conditions, we need a measuring instrument that will enable us to identify propositional attitudes of agents

independent of each other and their subsequent effects in action. Holism is the thesis that this cannot be done. But anomalous monism is the argument for this thesis. For anomalous monism holds that any type of propositional attitude may be realized by any of a vast and heterogeneous disjunction of brain states. It in effect rules out the existence of a neurophysiological 'measuring instrument' for intentional states. (Rosenberg, 1985, p. 403)

The initial part of this passage affirms that (A) intentional generalizations such as L are not improvable in the direction of laws. And on the assumption that we must first have improvable generalizations to eventually get laws, (A) implies that (B) there are no laws couched in intentional terms.[13] The conjunction of (A) and (B) is of course (R3) above. The *reason* for (R3) which the quoted passage suggests is *holism of the mental.* Holism says that it is impossible to identify an intentional state of a person apart from *other* intentional states of the person and actions in which these intentional states eventuate. But the improvability of intentional or psychological generalizations demands that we improve the methods of 'measuring' or determining intentional states expressed by terms like 'desire' in intentional generalizations. And holism of the mental precludes this, as it implies that there is no way to 'measure' intentional states by getting outside of the circle of intentional states and actions.[14]

I turn now to evaluating Rosenberg's philosophical argument for premise (P2) of his argument for economics not being science. Let us start with (R3). Again, (R3) affirms the conjunction of (A) there are no generalizations couched in intentional terminology that are improvable in the direction of laws, and (B) there are no laws couched in intentional terms. Claim (A) has been plausibly challenged (Henderson, 1991). But it is claim (B) that I want to focus on here. Given Rosenberg's logical empiricist conception of scientific laws, it may be true that there are no laws couched in intentional terminology like 'desire' and 'belief'. Indeed, it may be that there are no laws at all, even in physics, on the logical empiricist conception (Giere, 1988). But we do not have to adopt the logical empiricist conception. There is a different conception of laws which some philosophers have proposed as especially applicable to disciplines that employ intentional concepts. On this conception of laws – call it 'the hedged law conception' – laws are generalizations; moreover, they are lawlike generalizations by the familiar criterion of supporting counterfactual conditionals. Laws are, however, qualified by *ceteris paribus* clauses. Laws are subject to exceptions, and therefore false when their *ceteris paribus* clauses are detached, but they are true when qualified by their *ceteris paribus* clauses.[15] Even if laws so conceived turn out *not* to be improvable in the manner Rosenberg requires, this does not compromise their status as laws. For according to the hedged law conception, laws without their *ceteris paribus* clauses (explicitly or implicitly) attached have exceptions which do not have to be removed by improvement à la Rosenberg in order to be laws.

As a matter of fact, there are some hedged laws couched in intentional terminology. An important example from economics is the following:

(LD) *Ceteris paribus*, the quantity of a good demanded and the good's own price are negatively or inversely related.

The explicit *ceteris paribus* clause in (LD), which is the law of demand, subsumes factors such as consumers' preferences and consumers' expectations. Changes in these factors are among the disturbances or influencing factors that are excluded by the *ceteris paribus* clause in (LD). But as the notions of preference and expectation are intentional concepts, (LD)'s formulation uses intentional terms. (LD) is true. Alleged exceptions to (LD) such as Giffen goods remain theoretical possibilities whose existence in the real world has yet to be confirmed (Nicholson, 1978, pp. 102–4). The evidence for (LD)'s truth is various and extensive. One sort of evidence is the numerous *negative* estimates of price elasticities of market demand for different goods which economists have obtained by using multiple regression analysis with real world market data (Nicholson, 1978, pp. 139–40). Also, casual observation of peoples' purchasing behavior when business firms put goods on sale – people buy more at the lower sale prices – is further evidence in support of (LD). And note that given the relatively short duration of typical sales, the factors subsumed under the *ceteris paribus* clause in (LD) change little if at all during the sale. *Ceteris* is pretty much *paribus* for the duration of your typical sale. In addition, (LD) is a law-like generalization, as it supports counterfactual conditionals. For instance, (LD) implies the counterfactual 'If the prices of personal computers had been reduced yesterday at stores across the Silicon Valley, then, *ceteris paribus*, the quantity of personal computers sold yesterday in the Silicon Valley would have been greater'. In sum, (LD) is a hedged intentional law.[16]

Once again, Rosenberg's (R3) affirms both that (A) there are no generalizations using intentional concepts that are improvable in the way required for laws, and (B) there are no laws formulated in terms of intentional concepts. But (B) is false unless the term 'law' is arbitrarily restricted to refer only to laws as understood by the logical empiricist conception described above. For, as we have just seen, there are hedged scientific laws formulated in intentional terms. And hedged laws have as much right to be considered genuine scientific laws as do laws viewed by the logical empiricist conception. Again, (R3) is a premise of Rosenberg's philosophical argument for step (P2) of his case for economics not being science. But, as (R3) is erroneous, Rosenberg's philosophical argument for (P2) fails to justify its conclusion.

(R3) is not the only weak link in Rosenberg's philosophical argument for (P2). (R2), another premise of the argument, is false. It is not true that either laws in the logical empiricist sense, or generalizations improvable in the direction of such laws, are required to ground predictions. And it is not true that for a discipline to exhibit predictive improvement, it has to discover more laws or improvable generalizations, or actually improve the generalizations it already has in the direction of laws. As Michael Scriven (1959a, p. 480) long ago pointed out, a prediction can be justified by appeal to a statement of a correlation, and the statement of a correlation need not be a law or a generalization improvable in the direction of a law. The use of the index of leading indicators to predict overall economic activity is an example of this. Consider again the following generalization:

(G2) Ups and downs of the index of leading indicators tend to foreshadow ups and downs of the economy (real GDP).

(G2) affirms a rough correlation between the behaviour of the index and the behaviour of the economy. Surely (G2) is no law on a reasonable conception of what a law is. One test of whether or not a generalization expresses a law is the ability of the generalization to support counterfactual conditionals. Laws support or entail such conditionals. But what counterfactual conditionals does (G2) entail? Not something like

(CF) If the index of leading indicators had turned down during the first quarter of 1987, then real GDP would have turned down within a few months.

For (G2) is true, but (CF) is false. In early 1987 the real economy in the United States was healthy enough to continue growing even if the index of leading indicators had turned down, due, say, to a sharp decline in stock prices and the real M2 money supply (two variables in the index). Is (G2) improvable or refinable in the direction of a law in the way Rosenberg requires? Well, the index of leading indicators is capable of modification and improvement – new variables more tightly correlated with future real GDP changes might be added to the index, or a better measure of stock prices might be used. But this does not mean that (G2) itself is improvable in the direction of a law according to Rosenberg's standard of improvability. Should better methods of measuring the variables in the index be found this would not move (G2) any closer to being a law; though it could make predictions grounded by (G2) more precise. For it would still be hard to see what counterfactual conditionals (G2) entailed. After all, the variables in the index of leading indicators are just rough and ready indicators, however well measured. In sum, Rosenberg's (R2) is mistaken. A discipline could increase its proportion of correct to incorrect predictions by finding non-nomological correlations which improve the discipline's ratio of correct to incorrect predictions. Better methods of measuring the variables involved in the statement of these non-nomological correlations could also increase the precision of the discipline's predictions. Should these two things happen, this would entail that the discipline exhibits predictive improvement in Rosenberg's sense, despite a failure to uncover any laws or generalizations improvable in the direction of laws.

There is another reason for rejecting (R2) that is connected with my evaluation above of (R3). A discipline can improve its predictive power by uncovering more laws as described by the hedged law conception of scientific laws. Hedged laws can and do ground predictions. For instance, consider again the law of demand formulated above as (LD). A business firm might want to move more quickly some merchandise, say, mens' dress shirts. The firm knows that over a period of a few days or even a few weeks the variables covered by the *ceteris paribus* clause in the law of demand – buyers' income, the number of buyers, prices of substitutes and complements, and so on – are unlikely to change appreciably. In other words, *ceteris* is likely to be *paribus*. So, on the basis of the law of demand the firm *predicts* that they will sell more of the mens' shirts if they lower the price per shirt. This prediction is justified in part by the law of demand, which is a hedged law. Hedged laws are not laws in the logical empiricist sense, nor are they typically improvable in the direction of such laws. So, a discipline may uncover more hedged laws, and, by using these hedged laws to generate predictions, the discipline increases its ratio of correct to incorrect predictions. In addition, there is no *a priori* reason to rule out the ability of hedged laws to increase the precision of some of a discipline's predictions. Therefore, Rosenberg's (R2) is mistaken in saying that a discipline showing an improvement in predictive power requires either discovering laws in the logical empiricist sense, or finding generalizations refinable in the direction of such laws. That a discipline manages to find more hedged laws can also result in it exhibiting predictive improvement.

As indicated at the start of this section, Rosenberg offers a philosophical explanation for what he takes to be the fact that economics has failed to exhibit predictive improvement. The explanans consists of (R1), (R2) and (R3). Section 3.3 argued that Rosenberg fails to establish the existence of the explanandum phenomenon, to wit, economics' lack of predictive improvement in the last century or two. In this section I reinterpreted his explanation as an argument designed to *establish* the conclusion that economics has failed to show predictive improvement. But it has been argued in this section that Rosenberg's argument fails to establish this conclusion, as (R2) and (R3), two key premises of the argument, should not be accepted. Again I emphasize that I have not tried to show that economics has exhibited predictive improvement in Rosenberg's sense. I have only tried to show that Rosenberg fails to justify the claim – which is premise (P2) of his sceptical argument about economics – that economics has not exhibited predictive improvement in the last century or two. Frankly, I do not know whether or not economics has predictively improved by Rosenberg's standard. I am agnostic on the issue. But Rosenberg affirms that economics has not shown predictive improvement. And I have argued that he has not justified this affirmation.

3.5 CONCLUDING REMARKS

The methodological rule version of the 'Is it science?' approach to economics first lays down a methodological rule or standard an empirical science must meet. An attempt is then made to determine whether or not economics meets the standard. Alexander Rosenberg is the most recent proponent of this approach to economics. Predictive empiricism is the methodological standard which he applies to economics, and he thinks the discipline fails to measure up to the standard. It has been argued here that Rosenberg fails to justify his claim that economics does not meet the predictive empiricist standard, and in any case, predictive empiricism itself is false. Rosenberg's methodological rule version of the 'Is it science?' approach fails to shed any real light on economics. This failure should fuel an appropriate general scepticism about the viability of the methodological rule version of the 'Is it science?' approach to economics. So far no one, including Rosenberg, has managed to illuminate economics by pursuing this approach to the discipline.

NOTES

1. Giere (1991, p. 31) notes that sometimes one speaks of predicting data which are already known. But as 'prediction' is being used here, the term does not cover statements recording the occurrence of known data, but only statements putatively recording the occurrence of new data. And this seems to be Rosenberg's own use of 'prediction'. For example, (Rosenberg, 1992, p. 18) *contrasts* prediction with '... retrospective application of new theory to old data...' In sum, I take 'prediction' in Rosenberg's sense to refer to *ex ante* predictions of unknown data.

2. Uskali Mäki (1996, pp. 5–6) says that for Rosenberg predictive improvement only requires an increasing ratio of correct to incorrect predictions, and more precise predictions. A rising number of novel predictions is not required for predictive improvement. But this view ignores the connection Rosenberg initially makes between predictive improvement and predictive success. Predictive improvement is just an increase in predictive success, and Rosenberg (1992, p. 18) explicitly says that 'the amount of surprise' of predictions generated is a condition for predictive success. Yet Mäki's view is a correct account of how Rosenberg qualifies his initial conception of predictive improvement for the purposes of discussing economics. As we will shortly see, Rosenberg drops the condition requiring increasing novelty of predictions in the context of his treatment of economics.

3. Earman (1992, p. 114) remarks that in some cases scientists even regard old data as more strongly confirming a theory than data predicted by the theory.

4. For a recent development of Keynes' point, see Schlesinger, 1991, pp. 125–36. Oddly, Rosenberg almost acknowledges the point in question. He (1992, p. 18) says 'I accept that the difference between prediction and other sorts of empirical testing, like retrospective application of new theory to old data, may not be epistemic'. I say 'oddly' because once the point in question is conceded, it seems but a fairly short step to the conclusion that predictive empiricism is false.

5. For a theory T to be confirmed or supported by data D, it is not really sufficient that T account for D, nor that T correctly predict D. For D to be accounted for or predicted by T it is only necessary that we be able to reason from T to the occurrence of D. And that we can reason from a theory to data we already know to exist, or data we later find out exist, does not by itself raise the credibility of, and so does not confirm, the theory. This is one lesson of the failure of a simple hypothetico-deductive account of confirmation. (For a discussion of this failure in connection with economic methodology, see Rappaport, 1986a, pp. 35–6, 49–53). My own view is that for already known or predicted data D to confirm theory T, T must afford the *best explanation* of D. But this view is not assumed by my critique of predictive empiricism, and I make no assumption here about what the specific conditions are that are required for D to confirm T additional to being able to reason from T to the occurrence of D. But I do assume that these additional conditions for confirmation, whatever they are, are met in stories one and two.

6. Rosenberg (1992, p. 70) thinks that to be relevant to policy, economics must provide quantitative, not just qualitative, predictions. But this is not correct. Economic policy proposals are not always of such a nature that their assessment or implementation requires quantitative predictions. For example, an economist may propose that a certain city privatize garbage collection in the city. The economist may base this proposal on the prediction that a privately owned and operated garbage collector will collect garbage at a lower cost than a city owned garbage collection agency. (The economist may want to add that this prediction has a greater chance of being true if

the private garbage collection firms sign contracts directly with residents and businesses rather than signing a contract with the city government.) Note that the prediction here, though only qualitative, provides support for the policy proposal.

7. See Rappaport, 1992, especially pp. 95–8.

8. Following Leontief, Rosenberg (1992, p. 65) allows that agricultural economics has exhibited substantial predictive improvement. But Rosenberg discounts this on the ground that the confirmed predictions in agricultural economics are largely technological rather than strictly economic.

9. To some extent econometrics implies limitations on its own predictive power. Suppose a regression model of the form $Y = a + bX + U$, with U the error term. Using observed data on X and Y, the parameters a and b are estimated using ordinary least squares. But now we want to use the estimated regression model to *predict* a value of Y corresponding to X_1, a certain value of X. Econometric theory tells us that the predicted value of Y will be less accurate the further X_1 is from the mean of the X values. For the standard deviation of the estimate or prediction of Y is larger as the X value is further from the mean of the X values. See Kennedy, 1992, pp. 269–70.

10. A good discussion of the theoretical basis of the leading indicators and the history of their performance, is found in Klein and Moore, 1983, pp. 119–35.

11. I have drawn on a number of sources in putting together (R1) to (R3). (R1) is affirmed by Rosenberg, 1992, pp. 118–19, 149. (R2) is strongly suggested by the long passage quoted above. (R2) is clearly presented by Rosenberg, 1995, p. 8. To be sure, in that context he is simply setting out two opposing positions in the philosophy of social science. But anyone familiar with his philosophical views can see that the position including (R2) is Rosenberg's own. Finally, (R3) is developed in Rosenberg, 1992, Chapter 5. It is also illuminatingly developed in Rosenberg 1980 and 1985.

12. Rosenberg (1995, p. 9) says 'Our search ultimately leads to laws of chemical reactions that never have exceptions but ultimately underwrite the rough generalizations that experience leads us to frame'. The context from which this passage is drawn makes clear that Rosenberg thinks that it is not only the laws of chemistry that are generalizations true without exception. In his first book on the philosophy of economics *Microeconomic Laws*, Rosenberg ruefully seemed to allow that a generalization might be a law and still be qualified by a *ceteris paribus* clause (Rosenberg, 1976, p. 137). But in his more recent work Rosenberg thinks that *ceteris paribus* clauses get filled in or removed as we refine generalizations in the direction of genuine laws (Rosenberg, 1995, p. 41).

13. In the passage just quoted above Rosenberg calls the intentional generalization L a law. But he must be speaking loosely. Rosenberg believes that there are no laws couched in intentional terms. He affirms (1985, p. 402) 'It's not just, as Davidson notes, that intentional generalizations are heteronomic and cannot be independently refined. The trouble is that they cannot be refined at all. They are neither heteronomic nor homonomic; they are non-nomic.'

14. Rosenberg's twin bases for holism of the mental are what he calls 'anomalous monism', which in effect rules out any neurophysiological method of measuring intentional states, and the failure of behaviourism to provide a behavioural measuring instrument for intentional states. See Rosenberg, 1985, pp. 403–4.

15. The hedged law conception is applied to the social sciences by Jerry Fodor, 1983 and 1990, Chapter 5, and by Terence Horgan and John Tienson, 1990. But Horgan and Tienson (1990, p. 258, pp. 266–67) distance themselves from Fodor by viewing laws of intentional psychology as having exceptions stated in the language of intentional psychology itself. The *ceteris paribus* clauses that, explicitly or implicitly, qualify hedged

laws will be discussed in detail in Chapter 4.

16. A more extensive discussion of scientific laws will be supplied in Chapter 4 below. As noted there, this monograph adopts the standard philosophical conception of a law. According to this conception, the central feature of a law is that it is a true, lawlike generalization. There are two other more peripheral features of laws on the standard conception. One is that laws are not definitions or logical consequences of definitions, and the other is that laws are descriptive or positive statements rather than normative claims. Clearly (LD) is not a normative claim. Nor is it a definition or a deduction from one or more definitions.

4. Economics and Scientific Laws

4.1 SCIENCE AS THE SEARCH FOR LAWS

Positivism is a philosophical movement of the nineteenth and twentieth centuries. August Comte and J.S. Mill are well-known nineteenth century figures in the movement. And the logical positivism of Schlick, Reichenbach, Hempel and Carnap is the most important twentieth century manifestation of positivism. Von Wright provides the following general account of positivism:

> One of the tenets of positivism is *methodological monism*, or the idea of the unity of scientific method amidst the diversity of subject matter of scientific investigation. A second tenet is the view that the exact natural sciences, in particular mathematical physics, set a methodological ideal or standard which measures the degree of development and perfection of all the other sciences, including the humanities. A third tenet, finally, is a characteristic view of scientific explanation. Such explanation is, in a broad sense, 'causal.' It consists, more specifically, in the subsumption of individual cases under hypothetically assumed general laws of nature, including 'human nature.' (Von Wright, 1971, p. 4, italics in original)

I want to emphasize an aspect of positivism suggested by Von Wright's account. According to positivism, science as a process is primarily the search for scientific laws, and science as a product includes a corpus of laws. J.S. Mill (1970, p. 552) conveys this view in saying, 'Any facts are fitted, in themselves, to be a subject of science, which follow one another according to constant laws; although these laws may not have been discovered, nor even be discoverable by our own existing resources'. Mill is saying that the subject matter of a science, as opposed to a non-science, is governed by laws. This implies that a science itself must include the laws to which the phenomena it studies are subject.[1] May Brodbeck is a twentieth century positivist. She (1968, p. 9) says '... the scientist looks for laws or connections among facts in order to explain and predict phenomena'. This passage plainly conveys the positivist

55

conception of scientific inquiry as the quest for laws, with the product or outcome of that quest being a corpus of laws.

As we have just seen, the positivist movement is associated with the position – let us call it 'the positivist condition' – that it is necessary and sufficient for a discipline being a science that it include the laws to which the phenomena it studies are subject. So stated the positivist condition is not as illuminating as it might be about what a science is supposed to be like. The following remarks by J.S. Mill suggest a more useful expression of the positivist condition:

> But in order to give a genuinely scientific character to the study [of Human Nature], it is indispensable that these approximate generalisations, which in themselves would amount only to the lowest kind of empirical laws, should be connected deductively with the laws of nature from which they result – should be resolved into the properties of the causes on which the phenomena depend. In other words, the science of Human Nature may be said to exist in proportion as the approximate truths which compose a practical knowledge of mankind can be exhibited as corollaries from the universal laws of human nature on which they rest.... (Mill, 1970, pp. 554–5)

Though Mill is explicitly only talking about the science of man or human nature here, his remarks reflect a general conception of science. According to this conception, scientists observe or discover uniformities or regularities in a group of phenomena of interest. These uniformities are stated or expressed by generalizations which Mill refers to as 'empirical laws' and 'approximate generalisations'. Scientists seek to *explain* these empirical laws or approximate generalizations by appeal to more basic or fundamental laws. (Mill actually says in the quoted passage that science requires that empirical laws be *deductively connected* with other laws; but for Mill explaining one law by another law is the same thing as showing how the first law may be deduced from the second.) This conception of science is familiar to philosophers of science. Nancy Cartwright (1983, p. 100) says 'A long tradition distinguishes fundamental from phenomenological laws....' The distinction between what Cartwright calls 'fundamental laws' and 'phenomenological laws' is sometimes marked with the terms 'theoretical laws' and 'empirical laws', especially by logical positivist philosophers of science. Carl Hempel says:

> Theories are usually introduced when previous study of a class of phenomena has revealed a system of uniformities that can be expressed in the form of empirical laws. Theories then seek to explain those regularities, and, generally, to afford a deeper and more accurate understanding of the phenomena in question. To this end, a theory construes those phenomena as manifestations

of entities and processes that lie behind or beneath them, as it were. These are assumed to be governed by characteristic theoretical laws, or theoretical principles, by means of which the theory then explains the empirical uniformities ... (Hempel, 1966, p. 70)

As this passage suggests, those who advocate the conception of science we are examining often talk about *theories* explaining phenomenological or empirical laws. But a theory is a systematically related set of fundamental laws. And so to view theories as explaining phenomenological laws is in effect to see fundamental laws as doing the explaining.

I submit that we can use the conception of science just adumbrated to give a more useful or illuminating statement of the positivist condition for being a science. It is this:

(PC) It is necessary and sufficient for a discipline D being a science that it fits the following description. The accepted general statements of D include a collection of empirical laws, or at least generalizations that are approximately true. These express uniformities that have been observed or discovered in the class of phenomena which D studies. The accepted general statements of D also include a body of fundamental laws (perhaps organized into one or more theories) which explain the empirical laws or approximate generalizations.

It is clear that thinkers in the positivist tradition from Comte and J.S. Mill to Carnap and Hempel believe that without scientific laws there is no science. But of course, according to (PC) a discipline without any fundamental laws that explain uniformities would not be a science. Do positivist thinkers really believe that without fundamental laws there is no science? Would not positivists allow that a discipline which included a corpus of phenomenological laws yet no fundamental laws is still a science? Perhaps some positivists would allow this. But there is a marked tendency for positivists to regard phenomenological or empirical laws so-called as not genuine laws or as having an inferior epistemic status. J.S. Mill says the following:

An Empirical Law (it will be remembered) is an uniformity, whether of succession or of co-existence, which holds true in all instances within our limits of observation, but it is not of a nature to afford any assurance that it would hold beyond these limits ... The empirical law derives whatever truth it has from the causal laws of which it is a consequence. If we know those laws, we know what are the limits to the derivative law; while, if we have not yet accounted for the empirical law – if it rests only on observation – there is no safety in applying it far beyond the limits of time, place, and circumstance in which the observations were made. The really scientific truths, then, are not these empirical laws, but the causal laws which explain them. (Mill, 1970, pp. 562–3)

Mill does not regard empirical laws as being 'really scientific truths'. Carl Hempel makes similar remarks. Speaking of empirical generalizations like 'Iron rusts in damp air' and Kepler's laws of planetary motion, he says the following:

> Many general statements in terms of observables have indeed been formulated; they constitute the empirical generalizations mentioned in the preceding section. But, vexingly, many if not all of them suffer from definite shortcomings: they usually have a rather limited range of application; and even within that range, they have exceptions, so that actually they are not true general statements. (Hempel, 1965, pp. 179–80)

Hempel regards at least many empirical laws so-called as false, and so strictly speaking they are not scientific laws at all. For on the standard philosophical conception of laws – which will be discussed below – laws are *truths*. It is common, then, for positivists to express a deprecatory attitude toward empirical laws. And for such positivists, without fundamental laws there is indeed no science. Accordingly, I think that the positivist condition for science formulated above as (PC) correctly captures a central tendency within the positivist tradition by making it a necessary condition for a discipline being a science that it include fundamental laws, that is, laws explaining a range of uniformities discovered in the phenomena the discipline studies. And from now on when I speak of the positivist condition for being a science, I refer to (PC) as stated above.

In the Introduction (Chapter 1) I noted that a generic version of the 'Is it science?' approach to economics makes a discipline being a science conditional on its having a certain kind of content. As we have just seen, the positivist movement is associated with the positivist condition for science formulated as (PC). One form of the special content version of the 'Is it science?' approach assumes (PC) and asks 'Does economics fit the description which (PC) claims is necessary and sufficient for being a science?' I will use the term 'naturalism about economics' to denote a 'Yes' answer to this question, and use 'anti-naturalist about economics' to denote a 'No' answer to the question. Note that whether or not one is a naturalist or an anti-naturalist about economics is not dependent on acceptance of the positivist condition for science. One could accept the positivist condition (PC) and be a naturalist or an anti-naturalist, depending on the answer one gives to the question 'Does economics fit the description which (PC) claims is necessary and sufficient for being a science?' But an interest in this question is certainly motivated by acceptance of the positivist condition for science.

It will prove useful to make some remarks about scientific laws, the central concept of the positivist condition for science. On a view about laws standardly adopted by philosophers, laws are general statements that are true, or more briefly, generalizations that are true. As Hausman (1992b, p. 94) says 'In the usage of most philosophers, to call a statement a law is of course to imply that it is true'.[2] The term 'generalization' is construed broadly here. Sometimes laws are said to be generalized conditionals of the form 'For any x, if x is F then x is G', or more briefly, 'All F are G'. But this is too narrow a construal of laws. And the class of generalizations as understood here includes but is broader than the class of generalized conditionals. For instance, the term 'generalization' as used here also denotes statistical generalizations such as 'Convertible bonds rarely sell below their conversion values' and 'The probability of tossing an ace with a regular die is 0.167'. In addition, in section 3.4 I represented the logical empiricist conception of laws as holding that laws are generalizations that are true without exception and which are not qualified by *ceteris paribus* clauses. But though laws as viewed by this conception fall under the standard philosophical notion of laws adopted here, laws on the standard philosophical conception are a broader category than exceptionless generalizations unqualified by *ceteris paribus* clauses. Recall the hedged law conception also discussed in section 3.4 according to which laws without their *ceteris paribus* clauses attached (explicitly or implicitly) have exceptions and so are false. But with their *ceteris paribus* clauses attached, hedged laws are true generalizations, and so would fit the standard philosophical conception of laws. Yet hedged laws are not of course exceptionless generalizations unqualified by *ceteris paribus* clauses. It follows that laws viewed as true generalizations are a broader class than laws on the logical empiricist conception.

It is generally agreed among philosophers that being a true generalization is not sufficient for being a scientific law. There is a distinction between lawlike and accidental generalizations. And a true generalization that is accidental is not a law. Philosophers have suggested a number of ways to draw the lawlike/accidental generalization distinction. One way which seems reasonable is to say that lawlike generalizations entail counterfactual conditionals, whereas accidental generalizations do not. For instance, the lawlike generalization 'Copper expands when heated' entails the counterfactual 'If a certain piece of copper destroyed two days ago had been heated yesterday, then it would have expanded'. But the accidental generalization 'All the coins in my left pocket today are dimes' does not entail the counterfactual 'If a certain quarter had been in my left pocket today, then it would have been a dime'. But many philosophers would not regard the entailing counterfactual conditionals criterion as a stopping place in the process of analysing the lawlike/accidental generalization distinction. For they would say that the concept of a counterfactual conditional is as much in need of analysis as the lawlike/accidental generalization distinction. However, it is outside the purview of this discussion to pursue further the philosophical issue of the nature of scientific laws. It is sufficient for our purposes in the rest of this chapter to say that being a true, lawlike generalization is the central feature of a law. And thinking of laws as true, lawlike generalizations is the standard philosophical conception of scientific laws. I am of course aware that this description of laws provides little philosophical illumination, leaving unanswered the more profound questions about laws to which philosophers have sought answers.

Two more peripheral features of scientific laws are worth brief mention here. Some general statements are definitions or mere logical consequences of definitions. An example from economics is the equation of exchange '$MV=PY$', with M being the money supply, V being velocity, P being the price level, and Y being real GDP. The equation of exchange is deducible from the definition of velocity '$V=GDP/M$', and the definition of real GDP rewritten as '$PY=GDP$'. (Note 'GDP' denotes nominal GDP.) But neither definitions nor logical consequences of definitions are scientific laws on the standard philosophical conception of laws. In addition, some general statements are normative claims. An example from economics is the Pareto principle 'A change is desirable if it makes at least one person better off and no one else worse off'. But on the standard philosophical conception of scientific laws, laws are descriptive statements, not normative claims.

4.2   HAUSMAN'S NATURALISM

The aim of this chapter is to see if the special content version of the 'Is it science?' approach to economics that assumes the positivist condition (PC), sheds any real light on economics. Some prominent methodologists have adopted the positivist condition, and have inquired as to whether economics fulfils this condition. For instance, in *Microeconomic Laws*, his first book on the philosophy of economics, Alexander Rosenberg seems to adopt the positivist condition on being a science. He says this:

No one will deny that it is the mark of a developed discipline that it issues in general statements which can be used to account for the phenomena with which the discipline deals. It is equally clear that the paucity of such propositions is among the most notorious features of the social sciences ... Of course, within the social sciences there are occasional general statements of the statistical or summary sort, such as 'Legislators vote as their party directs 50 percent of the time' ... But these, so to speak, summarize research. They are not explanatory general propositions of the same systematic connection and explanatory power as, for example, the higher-order propositions of the kinetic theory of gases. They are not what we would call 'laws,' or alternatively, they are what Stephen Toulmin has called 'phenomenological laws': They are neither couched in a special theoretical language nor part of a theoretical framework which will account for them and the phenomena with which they deal. (Rosenberg, 1976, p. 7)

If we read the term 'developed discipline' in the first sentence of this passage as meaning 'science', then the passage rather strongly suggests an endorsement of the positivist condition (PC) for being a science. And in his first book on the philosophy of economics Rosenberg goes part way toward defending naturalism about economics. (Recall that this doctrine says that economics does fit the description of a science that (PC) claims is necessary and sufficient for science.) In *Microeconomic Laws* Rosenberg argues that the accepted general statements of neoclassical microeconomics are *lawlike*. He (1976, p. 183) says that in the book he '... conducts an extended argument to show that microeconomic general statements are *lawlike* statements'.

Of course, even if Rosenberg's argument were successful, he still would not have done enough to establish naturalism about economics. A crucial additional task would be to show that the lawlike generalizations of neoclassical microeconomics are *true*. For the laws, and especially the fundamental laws, which naturalism about economics requires the existence of are truths. But in *Microeconomic Laws* Rosenberg shies away from the issue of truth. He (1976, p. 183) says 'Whether they [the lawlike generalizations of microeconomics] are laws, that is, whether they are true, is largely a question for economists and not philosophers'. Rosenberg's more recent work in economic methodology casts economics in a far less complimentary light than his first book on the subject. Chapter 3 above dealt with the negative or sceptical thesis about economics Rosenberg has defended in his more recent work. Any concern to defend naturalism about economics seems to have disappeared altogether from Rosenberg's later work. But another prominent methodologist appears to have stepped into the breach. In a number of books and a series of articles Daniel Hausman has undertaken a searching effort to understand economics. And in his important book *The Inexact and Separate Science of Economics,* Hausman defends a 'Yes' answer to the question 'Does economics fit the description which (PC) claims is necessary and sufficient for a discipline being a science?' Much of the remainder of this chapter will be devoted to determining whether Hausman is successful in defending naturalism about economics. His case is the most sophisticated and well-argued defence of naturalism about economics extant.

Below I will justify my claim that Hausman does defend naturalism about economics in his early 1990s work. But I am unable to provide adequate evidence that he accepts the positivist condition (PC), though I am rather inclined to think he does accept it. (Recall that acceptance of naturalism about economics is not dependent on acceptance of (PC).) Hausman certainly seems to adopt the positivist idea that to be a science a discipline must include scientific laws. He (1994a, p. 10) says 'Most philosophers have recognized that science proceeds by the discovery of theories and laws'. The context from which this passage is drawn does not indicate that Hausman *exempts himself* from this generalization about philosophers. Thus, the passage quoted provides evidence that Hausman himself thinks that science 'proceeds by the discovery of theories and laws'. Theories as Hausman views them are collections of lawlike generalizations that are related in a systematic way (Hausman, 1992a, p. 75). So the quoted passage suggests that for Hausman a science must include a body of laws. For the outcome or result of scientists discovering (true) theories and laws is of course a body of laws. But passages of the sort I have just quoted do not afford clear-cut evidence for thinking that Hausman accepts (PC). As we will see below, Hausman does accept the distinction between fundamental and phenomenological laws – he prefers the term 'derivative laws' to 'phenomenological laws' – upon which (PC) relies. Furthermore, he takes economics to be a *science*, albeit an inexact one. And the reason he takes economics – more precisely, neoclassical microeconomics – to be an inexact science, as opposed to an exact one, is that he regards its fundamental laws as inexact laws. All this does suggest acceptance by Hausman of the positivist condition (PC). But the evidence cited here does not seem strong enough to definitively ascribe (PC) to Hausman. However, whether or not Hausman accepts (PC) does not in the end matter much for the argument of this chapter. For, the primary aim of the chapter is to answer this question: does the special content version of the 'Is it science?' approach to economics that assumes (PC) shed real light on the discipline? And examining Hausman's defence of naturalism about economics would still be highly relevant to the primary question of this chapter, regardless of Hausman's own attitude toward (PC).

Hausman's work in economic methodology focuses almost entirely on neoclassical microeconomics. He pretty much ignores macroeconomics, the other branch of mainstream economic theorizing. This would seem reasonable if Hausman accepts the positivist condition for science, and simply wants to determine whether or not economics meets that condition.[3] For the positivist condition (PC) requires that the *accepted* generalizations of a scientific discipline include a body of laws, and especially fundamental laws. But there do not appear to be many widely accepted generalizations in macroeconomics nowadays that might qualify as scientific laws. Probably most macroeconomists would accept generalizations such as 'There is a strong positive association between large increases in the money supply and large increases in the price level' (Colander, 1993, p. 335; Barro, 1984, pp. 152–8), and Gresham's law 'Cheap money drives out good money, assuming a fixed exchange rate between cheap and dear money' (Friedman and Schwartz, 1971 p. 27 note 16.) But it seems macroeconomics nowadays is characterized by extensive *disagreement* about theory, two of the main competing 'paradigms' or global theories being Keynesian macro theory and new classical macro theory. Dissensus rather than consensus seems the order of the day at the level of theory in macroeconomics – and partly as a result, there is also substantial disagreement among macroeconomists about government policies for stabilizing free enterprise economies. For this reason it does not appear that there are many broadly accepted generalizations in macroeconomics that could count as fundamental laws, or indeed laws of any kind. But in microeconomics it is different. At least among mainstream economists, there is a single 'paradigm' or global theory accepted (in some sense) by nearly all, and of course it is neoclassical microeconomic theory. One indication of this fact is that textbook presentations of microeconomics at the principles as well as the intermediate level almost always present only neoclassical micro theory. (On the other hand, macroeconomics texts, especially at the principles level, frequently present the chief competing 'paradigms' or global theories, though the authors themselves often favour one of the global theories over the others.) So, if the positivist condition for science is adopted without complaint, then there may seem little point in looking beyond neoclassical microeconomic theory in order to find out whether economics meets the positivist condition (PC). But this highlights a drawback of the positivist condition itself. Should there be dissensus within a large part of a discipline at the level of theory – as there is in macroeconomics – then the positivist condition is of limited use in helping us understand that part of the discipline, even if that condition does correctly specify a condition for being a science. Later in this chapter we will return to this point. But for now let us focus on the prospects for naturalism about economics. And to see what these prospects are we need to set out Hausman's position in some detail. Again, it is the best case extant for naturalism about economics.

What Hausman regards as the *conceptual structure* of neoclassical micro theory is partly built on the distinction between phenomenological and fundamental laws. Hausman himself seems to prefer the pair of terms 'derivative laws' and 'fundamental laws' to mark the distinction (1992a, p. 134). He initially introduces the distinction with the following remarks:

> So those economists interested in theory – and not all economists are or should be theoretically inclined – have gone deeper in another direction. Their research agenda has been to uncover 'deeper' laws concerning human behavior to explain, systematize, and unify causal generalizations concerning market behavior. Just as Newton's theory of motion and gravitation accounts for (and corrects) Galileo's law of freely falling bodies or Kepler's laws of planetary motion, so a deeper theory of the economic behavior of individuals *might* account for and possibly correct generalizations concerning market behavior. (Hausman, 1992a, p. 30, italics in original)

The generalizations concerning market behaviour to which Hausman alludes in this passage are phenomenological or derivative laws of neoclassical microeonomics, as Galileo's law and Kepler's laws of planetary motion are derivative laws of physics. These generalizations concerning market behaviour include the law of demand. Hausman (1992a, p. 28) expresses this by saying 'One of the central generalizations of economics is the law of demand, which can be oversimplified as: at higher prices, less of any commodity or service will be wanted'. Generalizations about market supply are also included among the derivative laws of neoclassical micro, such as 'A higher price for a product brings forth a larger quantity supplied, and a lower price reduces quantity supplied' (Hausman, 1992a, p. 42).

Hausman thinks that neoclassical microeconomics includes just seven fundamental laws, or just ten fundamental laws depending on how one counts them. He says this:

> ...this chapter and the last have set forth basically all there is to fundamental microeconomic theory. It consists in my view of seven laws: those of the theory of consumer choice, those of the theory of the firm, and the assertion that markets 'clear' or come quickly to equilibrium. (Hausman, 1992a, p. 51)

The seven laws to which Hausman alludes here constitute according to him the fundamental theory of microeconomics. He (1992a, p. 53) also refers to these seven, or ten, laws taken together as 'equilibrium theory'. Here is pretty much Hausman's formulation of the fundamental laws of micro theory counting them as ten in number:[4]

(PL1) Individuals have complete preferences.

(PL2) Individuals have transitive preferences.

(PL3) Individuals have continuous preferences.

(PL4) Individuals maximize utility, i.e., individuals prefer no option (of those attainable) to the one they choose.

(PL5) Individuals' preferences are defined over bundles of commodities, there are no interdependencies between the preferences of different individuals, and, up to some point of satiation, individuals prefer larger commodity bundles to smaller bundles.

(PL6) Individuals' marginal rates of substitution diminish, that is, an individual is willing to give up less of a commodity Y for a unit of a commodity X as the amount of Y the individual has relative to the amount of X he has decreases.

(PL7) If a firm uses more and more of a variable input while the other inputs are held constant or fixed, then, over the normal range of input use, the marginal product of the variable input declines.

(PL8) A firm's production function exhibits constant returns to scale, that is, if all the inputs the firm uses are multiplied by some constant, then output of the firm is multiplied by that same constant.

(PL9) Firms seek to maximize profits.

(PL10) Markets clear or come quickly to equilibrium.

So, for Hausman, neoclassical microeconomics has just a *single* theory consisting of the fundamental laws (PL1) to (PL10). As Hausman (1992a, p. 95) says in speaking of microeconomics 'For an orthodox [economic] theorist, it is in effect a one-theory science'. Hausman does recognize the existence of the theory of consumer choice and the theory of the firm. But these are simply proper subsets of the fundamental laws (PL1) to (PL10); they are not theories distinct from the single theory of neoclassical microeconomics. This single theory serves to explain the generalizations concerning market behaviour which I briefly treated above. For instance, Hausman (1992a, p. 30) says 'The theory of consumer choice [which consists of (PL1) to (PL6) above] is supposed to explain the causal generalizations discussed above concerning market demand'. Hausman supplies a detailed account of how the theory of consumer choice explains such generalizations as the law of demand, an account that is much the same as is found in standard microeconomics textbooks (see Hausman, 1992a, pp. 33–9).

Below I will argue that in his early 1990s work Hausman does regard (PL1) to (PL10), suitably qualified with *ceteris paribus* clauses, as genuine scientific laws. Given this view of Hausman's, he does indeed take neoclassical microeconomics to fulfil the description which the positivist condition (PC) claims is necessary and sufficient for being a science. As we have just seen, Hausman thinks that the accepted generalizations of neoclassical microeconomics include a collection of derivative laws or approximate generalizations such as the law of demand. And crucially, Hausman takes neoclassical microeconomics also to include a body of fundamental laws which serve to explain the derivative laws. Assuming I am correct in thinking that Hausman takes (PL1) to (PL10) to be scientific laws, he is then committed to saying that neoclassical microeconomics meets the positivist condition (PC) for a discipline being a science. That is, Hausman does adopt naturalism about economics in his early 1990s work.

On Hausman's analysis of its conceptual structure, there is more to neoclassical microeconomics than equilibrium theory and the generalizations concerning market behaviour like the law of demand. For example, Hausman correctly thinks that neoclassical micro includes partial equilibrium models and general equilibrium models.[5] He views these models as simply augmentations or applications of equilibrium theory (Hausman, 1992a, pp. 53–5). Hausman adopts a theory about economic models – it is the structuralist view – which will be discussed in detail in Chapter 7. On the structuralist view models themselves are definitions of kinds of systems, and the assumptions of a model, being open sentences, are without truth-value. So neither models nor their assumptions are scientific laws in light of Hausman's theory about economic models. For on the standard conception of laws discussed in section 4.1, laws are truths, and definitions are excluded from the category of laws. Hausman also rightly takes welfare economics to be an important part of neoclassical micro. But the accepted generalizations of welfare economics Hausman cites are normative claims like the Pareto principle 'A change is desirable if it makes some individual(s) better off without making anyone else worse off', and a couple of fundamental theorems of welfare economics which employ the normative concept of a Pareto optimum. But, as noted in section 4.1, normative claims are excluded from the class of scientific laws. So, outside of equilibrium theory and the generalizations about market behaviour, there is nothing in the conceptual structure of neoclassical micro as Hausman describes it that would support saying that economics fits the description the positivist condition (PC) says is necessary and sufficient for science. For, given Hausman's description of neoclassical micro, outside of equilibrium theory and the generalizations about market behaviour there are few if any accepted generalizations that might be scientific laws.

Let us now consider the question of whether Hausman takes the generalizations of equilibrium theory (PL1) to (PL10) to be scientific laws. As noted in the paragraph before last, if he does, then he is a naturalist about economics. Hausman's attitude toward the generalizations constituting equilibrium theory has changed over time. In his 1981 book *Capital, Profits, and Prices*, Hausman views these generalizations as qualified by vague *ceteris paribus* clauses. And he proposes four conditions that a generalization qualified by a *ceteris paribus* clause must meet in order for us to be justified in regarding it as a genuine scientific law. These four conditions are the lawlikeness, reliability, refinability and excusability conditions. (The reliability condition will be discussed in detail in section 4.4 below.) In *Capital, Profits, and Prices* Hausman (1981, p. 134) says 'Most of the basic assertions of equilibrium theory fail, however, to satisfy the excusability condition'. And from this claim Hausman infers the following conclusion:

> In my view all the basic generalizations of equilibrium theory should be regarded as qualified with ceteris paribus clauses. In some cases the qualified generalizations satisfy the four justification conditions. One can, I think, regard diminishing returns to a variable input and diminishing marginal utility as qualified laws. The other basic general statements of equilibrium theory cannot be regarded as qualified universal laws. (Hausman, 1981, p. 135)

We see that in 1981 Hausman thinks we lack good reason to regard the majority of the generalizations in equilibrium theory as laws. And so there is no basis for viewing the Hausman of 1981 as adopting naturalism about economics.[6]

However, in his 1992 book *The Inexact and Separate Science of Economics*, Hausman seems to view the ten generalizations of equilibrium theory as genuine scientific laws, though he has some qualms or reservations about doing so. Speaking of (PL1) to (PL10) above, he says:

> But everyday experience and introspection are sufficient to establish the conclusion that some of these laws, such as diminishing marginal rates of substitution and diminishing returns, are reasonable approximations. Without qualifications and a margin of error, they are false, but with these, they seem true, and economists have good reason to be committed to them.... Furthermore, each of the laws of equilibrium theory possesses *pragmatic*

virtues, for each plays an important role in making the theory mathematically tractable, consistent, and determinate.... So one finds a combined empirical and pragmatic basis for refusing to regard the basic propositions of equilibrium theory as disconfirmed. (Hausman, 1992a, p. 210, italics in original)

This passage is evidence that the Hausman of 1992 thinks that, suitably qualified with *ceteris paribus* clauses, *all* the lawlike generalizations of equilibrium theory are *true,* and therefore they are really laws. It might be objected that the last sentence of the passage just quoted only commits Hausman to viewing the generalizations of equilibrium theory as not disconfirmed, and this is not the same thing as viewing them as true. In response to this objection, let me quote Hausman:

Much of what I have written can be regarded as a defense of puzzling features of neoclassical economics. For I have maintained that the 'obvious falsehoods' upon which economic theory depends can be regarded as *qualified truths* and can be justifiably accepted and employed in some contexts. (Hausman, 1992a, p. 245, emphasis added)

In talking about the 'obvious falsehoods' of economic theory, Hausman is referring to the ten generalizations constituting equilibrium theory. And he certainly appears to be saying that these generalizations are true when qualified – presumably by *ceteris paribus* clauses. In his 1992 book Hausman endorses the lawlikeness, reliability, refinability and excusability conditions for our being justified in regarding a generalization as a law (Hausman 1992a, pp. 139–41). He also notes his own scepticism in *Capital, Profits, and Prices* about the generalizations of equilibrium theory meeting the excusability condition. But in the more recent book he appears to think these generalizations do fulfil *all* the four conditions for a qualified generalization being a law. He (1992a, p. 149) says 'In some contexts, it seems to me uncontroversial that the propositions of equilibrium theory employed do satisfy the above conditions [the four conditions just mentioned] ...' So, I am prepared to take Hausman in his early 1990s work to believe that the generalizations of equilibrium theory are hedged laws, and therefore he adopts naturalism about economics.

4.3   HAUSMAN'S DEFENCE OF NATURALISM

Hausman's naturalism about economics is constituted by the position that neoclassical microeconomics fits the description which the positivist condition (PC) says is necessary and sufficient for a discipline being a science. And Hausman is committed to this position because he believes the following propositions: (A) neoclassical micro includes a collection of derivative laws or approximate generalizations which are represented by the generalizations about market behaviour like the law of demand; (B) neoclassical micro includes a body of fundamental laws represented by (PL1) to (PL10); and (C) these fundamental laws, which constitute equilibrium theory, explain the derivative laws. The key proposition of the three is (B). It is the most controversial of the three and if Hausman can defend (B), then he would have gone a long way toward defending naturalism about economics. On the face of it, defending (B) would not seem to be a very promising endeavour. Hausman himself expresses a view shared by many which explains why:

> The fundamental theory of microeconomics and of general equilibrium models seems simultaneously sophisticated, successful, bursting with explanatory power, and full of false statements.... We know full well ... that businessmen do not always attempt to maximize their profits and that the preferences of consumers are not always transitive. (Hausman, 1992b, p. 51)

Many of the generalizations in equilibrium theory appear to be just false, and so they cannot all be laws. Proposition (B) would of course be erroneous if (PL1) to (PL10) are not all really laws.

But Hausman defends the claim that (PL1) to (PL10) are genuine laws. Central to his defence is a distinction that he borrows from J.S. Mill between exact and inexact sciences, and the correlative distinction between exact and inexact laws. In an exact science the laws – which are of course exact laws – specify *all* the causes on which the phenomena the science studies depend, whereas the inexact laws of an inexact science only delineate the *major or greater* causes of the phenomena the science studies (Mill, 1970, pp. 552–3). Following Mill, Hausman regards economics as an inexact science and its fundamental laws as inexact laws. Hausman considers four ways in which the concept of an inexact law might be analysed. The one he favours views inexact laws as qualified (explicitly or implicitly) by *vague ceteris paribus* clauses. Here is Hausman's own initial account of them:

> The *ceteris paribus* laws I am concerned with in this section and the next one are more problematic. Fundamental economic theory considers only some of the causes of economic phenomena. The basic claims of economics are true only under various *not fully specified conditions*. Without specifying the disturbing causes can one still make substantive claims concerning the 'greater' economic causes? What precisely is a vague *ceteris paribus* clause? What does

it mean to say that 'Ceteris paribus peoples' preferences are transitive'? (Hausman, 1992a, p. 134, emphasis added)

Hausman is saying here that the ten generalizations of equilibrium theory – 'the basic claims of economics' is the phrase Hausman uses in the quoted passage – are true only under various not fully specified conditions. But this is tantamount to affirming that these generalizations are true only when qualified (explicitly or implicitly) by *vague ceteris paribus* clauses. And a vague *ceteris paribus* clause excludes or rules out the presence of a not fully or completely specified list of disturbing factors.

To further clarify the concept of a vague *ceteris paribus* clause, it may be helpful to describe another kind of *ceteris paribus* clause which I will call a 'precise *ceteris clause*'. Felix Kaufman describes precise *ceteris paribus* clauses in the following passage:

> The *ceteris paribus* clause can be understood in two different ways. The *cetera* may consist of only a definite number of well-determined features.... Or, the factors to be subsumed under the clause may be left partly or completely undetermined. No possibility is excluded by a sentence to which such a clause is added, because we can always make an unknown factor responsible for the non-fulfilment of predictions made in terms of the law. (Kaufman, 1958, p. 84)

This is a good description of both kinds of *ceteris paribus* clauses. The second sentence of the quoted passage describes precise *ceteris paribus* clauses. Such a *ceteris paribus* clause subsumes a *fully* or *completely specified* list of influencing factors. As the third sentence of the passage suggests, the factors subsumed by the other kind of *ceteris paribus* clause are partially, or even completely, unspecified or undetermined. This of course is the vague *ceteris paribus* clause. The last sentence of the passage mentions a potential defect of vague *ceteris paribus* clauses, to wit, generalizations qualified by such clauses are threatened with empirical vacuity. For, we can all too easily blame a false prediction generated by such a generalization, not on the generalization, but on an unknown influencing factor subsumed or covered by the *ceteris paribus* clause. The generalization itself then becomes irrefutable by experience, and therefore empirically vacuous.[7]

It is vague *ceteris paribus* clauses that Hausman sees as (implicitly) qualifying the generalizations of equilibrium theory (PL1) to (PL10). For he thinks that neoclassical microeconomics delineates (some of) the greater or major causes of the economic phenomena it studies, with other causes lying outside the purview of neoclassical economics. And these other causes are in effect disturbing factors excluded by the *ceteris paribus* clauses qualifying (PL1) to (PL10), disturbing factors left unspecified or undetermined by neoclassical microeconomics itself.[8] However, vague *ceteris paribus* clauses raise several serious philosophical problems, a pair of which Hausman himself directly addresses. They are as follows. (1) How are we to analyse or give truth conditions for generalizations qualified by vague *ceteris paribus* clauses? And (2) under what conditions are we *justified* in regarding a generalization qualified by a vague *ceteris paribus* clause as a genuine law? It is especially important that we have an answer to question (2). As Hausman notes, we need to distinguish legitimate from illegitimate appeals to vague *ceteris paribus* clauses used to explain away apparent disconfirmations of generalizations. We could not reasonably invoke an implicit, vague *ceteris paribus* clause qualifying 'Crocodiles have feathers' to save this silly generalization from disconfirmation by an observation of a number of crocodiles without feathers. An answer to question (2) will allow us to distinguish legitimate from illegitimate uses of vague *ceteris paribus* clauses.

Hausman's answer to question (2) consists of his lawlikeness, reliability, refinability and excusability conditions alluded to in section 4.2 above. The reliability condition will be further discussed in section 4.4 below. Evaluating Hausman's naturalism about economics in the next section will be facilitated by setting out his answer to question (1). Hausman offers an analysis that is in fact applicable to both precise and vague *ceteris paribus* clauses, though it is the latter which are of particular interest here. The analysis affirms that the term '*ceteris paribus*' picks out different properties or propositions depending on the context in which the term is used. Hausman (1992a, p. 134) says 'Adapting this terminology, I suggest that *ceteris paribus* clauses have one *meaning* – "other things being equal," which in different contexts picks out different *propositions* or *properties*'. Hausman (1992a, p. 136) clarifies this by saying 'In my view "*Ceteris paribus* everything that is an F is a G" is a true universal statement if and only if in the given context the *ceteris paribus* clause picks out a property – call it "C" – and everything that is both C and F is G'. So, Hausman claims that a proposition of the form

(1) *Ceteris paribus* everything that is F is G

has the same truth conditions as the corresponding proposition of the form

(2) There is a property C such that everything that is C and F is G.

From now on when I speak of Hausman's analysis of *ceteris paribus* clauses, I will be referring to his view that (1) is equivalent to (2). Hausman's analysis in effect says that in the case of a true generalization of the form (1), there is a property – or perhaps better, a set of conditions – which, if added to the antecedent of the unqualified generalization 'Anything that is *F* is *G*', turns it into a *strict* (exact) law. A strict (exact) law is a law that is not qualified, explicitly or implicitly, by a *ceteris paribus* clause.[9] As Hausman (1992a, p. 137) himself says, 'All I am claiming is that when one takes an inexact generalization to be an explanatory law, one supposes that the *ceteris paribus* clause picks out some predicate that, when added to the antecedent of the unqualified generalization, makes it an exact law'. For Hausman, behind each law qualified by a *ceteris paribus* clause stands a strict law, known or unknown by us.

An important point about Hausman's analysis of *ceteris paribus* clauses needs to be made. Let us consider the law of demand formulated as follows:

(LD) *Ceteris paribus*, a good's own price and the quantity of the good demanded are negatively related.

At least often economists describe the quantity of a good *X* demanded in a market as a function of a *fully specified* list of independent variables. A fairly standard list is as follows: the price of good *X*, tastes of the consumers, the level of consumers' income, the prices of related goods like substitutes and complements and the number of consumers in the market. The *ceteris paribus* clause in (LD) then subsumes *just* the factors on this list; a change in any of these factors and only these factors is excluded by the *ceteris paribus* clause in (LD). (LD) frames a relationship between the price of good *X* and quantity of good *X* demanded when the independent variables just listed other than the price of good *X* are unchanging. Interpreted in this way, the *ceteris paribus* clause in (LD) is a *precise* one, as it excludes the presence of a fully specified list of disturbing factors.[10] Hausman's analysis of *ceteris paribus* clauses implies that (LD) is equivalent to this: there is a set of conditions *C* such that whenever *C* holds and the price of a good changes, then quantity of the good demanded changes in the opposite direction of the price change. And the *strict* law behind (LD) is something like this:

(LDs) Whenever prices of related goods like substitutes and complements, income of consumers, tastes of consumers and number of consumers are unchanging, *and* the good's own price changes, the quantity of the good demanded changes in the opposite direction of the price change.

Now in the case of a law like (LD) qualified (we are assuming) by a precise *ceteris paribus* clause, we should be able to actually state the strict law behind it, as we have been able to state (LDs).[11] But in the case of a putative law qualified by a *vague ceteris paribus* clause, it will not be possible to fully state a strict law standing behind the inexact law. For the disturbing influences subsumed under the vague *ceteris paribus* clause are partly or completely undetermined. Of course, Hausman's analysis does not require that we be able to actually state the strict law behind a law qualified by a vague *ceteris paribus* clause. It only requires that there be such a law, even if unknown to us.

But then a difficulty arises. Suppose that someone claims that a certain generalization G qualified by a vague *ceteris paribus* clause really is a law, and therefore true. Given Hausman's analysis, this claim entails that there is a property or set of conditions C which if added to the antecedent of G yields a strict law. But how are we to know that *there exists* at all such a property or set of conditions C? And if we do not know this, then we do not know that the original generalization G is itself a law, albeit an inexact one. At this juncture we will have to appeal to an answer to question (2) above. To answer the question of how we can know of the existence of the property or set of conditions picked out by a vague *ceteris paribus* clause, we would have to appeal to something like Hausman's lawlikeness, reliability, refinability and excusability conditions, which constitute his answer to question (2). Should generalization G fulfil the conditions specified by an acceptable answer to question (2), we can say that we are justified in viewing G as a genuine law. And from this proposition plus Hausman's analysis of *ceteris paribus* clauses, we can infer that the property or set of conditions C picked out by the vague *ceteris paribus* clause in generalization G really exists. In short, Hausman's analysis of vague *ceteris paribus* clauses needs to be supplemented with an answer to question (2). Without an answer to question (2), we would be always in doubt as to the existence of the properties or sets of conditions picked out by vague *ceteris paribus* clauses on Hausman's analysis of them.

We can now directly characterize Hausman's defence of his view that the ten generalizations of equilibrium theory – (PL1) to (PL10) above – are laws. His defence relies on (A) an account of the method of theory appraisal economists actually use which incorporates strategies for dismissing evidence that appears to disconfirm the generalizations of equilibrium theory, and (B) empirical and pragmatic grounds for thinking that, suitably qualified, the lawlike generalizations of equilibrium theory are true and therefore laws. One of the strategies alluded to in (A) employs Hausman's view that the generalizations of equilibrium theory are qualified by vague *ceteris paribus* clauses. He says:

> Many apparent difficulties with the 'laws' of economics can be met by arguing that they contain legitimate implicit *ceteris paribus* clauses.... Hedged, as they implicitly are, with *ceteris paribus* clauses, one can regard economic generalizations as laws despite apparent disconfirmations. No economist regards the generalization that consumer's [sic] preferences are transitive as falsified by a change in tastes. (Hausman, 1992b, p. 51)

So, a good deal of evidence apparently disconfirming generalizations of equilibrium theory can be dismissed by invoking their implicit *ceteris paribus* clauses. Below we will see how this and another strategy Hausman recognizes are incorporated into the method of theory appraisal he thinks economists in fact use.

What are the empirical and pragmatic grounds Hausman has for thinking the lawlike generalizations of equilibrium theory, suitably qualified, are true and therefore laws? In a section of *The Inexact and Separate Science of Economics* entitled 'Why believe equilibrium theory?', Hausman says:

> But everyday experience and introspection are sufficient to establish that some of these laws [the generalizations of equilibrium theory], such as diminishing marginal rates of substitution and diminishing returns, are reasonable approximations. Without qualifications and a margin of error, they are false, but, with these, they seem true; and economists have good reason to be committed to them. Furthermore, each of the laws of equilibrium theory possesses *pragmatic virtues*, for each plays an important role in making the theory mathematically tractable, consistent, and determinate. (Hausman, 1992a, p. 210, italics in original)

So, Hausman thinks (PL6) and (PL7) have the following empirical virtue: observation confirms their approximate truth within a certain domain. (Observation includes what Hausman refers to as 'everyday experience and introspection'.) And once these two generalizations are qualified with vague *ceteris paribus* clauses, they are true *simpliciter*, and therefore they are laws. Moreover, each of the generalizations of equilibrium theory has pragmatic virtues – Hausman lists mathematical tractability, consistency and determinateness – which afford reasons for believing them.[12] It is important to emphasize that Hausman regards pragmatic virtues as reasons for accepting a theory in the sense of believing it to be true, rather than merely reasons for using it, developing it, entertaining it, and the like. He (1992a, p. 219) says 'The educative function of expected utility theory provides good pragmatic reason for accepting it, unless there is a competitor that is much better supported by the evidence or is better able to guide choice'. And Hausman gives no indication that, in talking here of accepting expected utility theory, he means anything other than believing it to be true.

Hausman brings together the empirical and pragmatic grounds for accepting equilibrium theory as well as the strategy of invoking *ceteris paribus* clauses to explain away apparent disconfirmations, in his account of the method of theory appraisal which he thinks economists actually employ. He (1992a, pp. 221-2) calls it 'the economist's deductive method'. Here is a partial description of it set out as a number of methodological rules to be applied seriatim:

(R1) Formulate generalizations qualified with vague *ceteris paribus* clauses possessing empirical and pragmatic virtues, and which specify relevant causal factors (like seeking one's own material welfare).

(R2) Deduce from these generalizations *plus* suitable auxiliary assumptions – simplifications, statements of initial conditions, etc. – predictions about relevant phenomena.

(R3) Test the predictions.

(R4) If the predictions are verified, then regard the whole theoretical system – generalizations, statements of initial conditions, etc. – as confirmed; if the predictions are falsified, then compare alternative accounts of the failure on the basis of their relative empirical and pragmatic virtues.

To apply (R1) economists have *already* to possess generalizations of the sort the rule describes. The generalizations of equilibrium theory fill the bill. They are in Hausman's view qualified by vague *ceteris paribus* clauses, and they possess empirical and pragmatic good-making characteristics of theories as discussed above.

The economist's deductive method is a way of subjecting to empirical test generalizations that already have much going for them epistemically speaking. And the chances of an empirical test of generalizations of equilibrium theory leading to *rational* rejection using this method are *slight*. As Hausman himself says:

Since economists are typically dealing with complex phenomena in which many simplifications are required and in which interferences are to be expected, the evidential weight of predictive failure will be very small. It will rarely be rational to surrender a well-supported hypothesis because of predictive failure in circumstances as these. (Hausman, 1992a, p. 222)

As rule (R2) indicates, various auxiliary assumptions are needed to generate predictions from generalizations of equilibrium theory. These will include simplifications and *ceteris* is *paribus* assumptions, that is, assumptions affirming the *absence* of the disturbing factors subsumed under the vague *ceteris paribus* clauses qualifying generalizations of equilibrium theory. But these assumptions will typically be *less certain* than the generalizations of equilibrium theory under test. And this is so for two reasons: (A) economists are unable typically to perform controlled experiments and so cannot be assured disturbing factors are really absent; and (B) given the complexity of real world economic phenomena, the simplifications economists use in applying their deductive method may not be even remotely accurate. Therefore, in light of what Hausman (1992a, p. 207) calls 'the weak-link principle', it will be rational to attribute predictive failure in a test situation, not to generalizations of equilibrium theory under test, but to the falsity of auxiliary assumptions. Attributing predictive failure to the falsity of a *ceteris* is *paribus* assumption is of course the strategy, which was discussed above, of invoking the vague *ceteris paribus* clauses qualifying the generalizations of equilibrium theory. Attributing predictive failure to the falsity of other kinds of auxiliary assumptions, such as simplifications, is an additional strategy for explaining away apparent disconfirmations of equilibrium theory. In sum, in using their deductive method, it is quite unlikely that economists would rationally be led to reject the generalizations of equilibrium theory. Hausman himself regards the economists' deductive method as justifiable or philosophically defensible (1992a, p. 206, p. 221). Hausman's viewing economists' reasonable belief in equilibrium theory as resulting from a method he regards as justifiable, affords a reason for taking the lawlike generalizations of equilibrium theory to be qualified truths and therefore hedged laws. And this is a reason additional to the empirical and pragmatic considerations which Hausman cites for thinking that the generalizations of equilibrium theory, suitably qualified, are true and therefore laws.

4.4 PROBLEMS WITH NATURALISM

Hausman's basis for regarding the ten generalizations of equilibrium theory as hedged laws (laws qualified by implicit or explicit *ceteris paribus* clauses) is, I think, inadequate. In addition, it is not reasonable to regard all of the generalizations of equilibrium theory as genuine scientific laws. These are the two claims this section will attempt to establish. If the attempt is successful, then Hausman's naturalism about economics is without warrant or credibility. For, as noted at the outset of section 4.3, the key claim of that naturalism is that (PL1) to (PL10) are all fundamental laws; and if they cannot all reasonably be said to be laws, then of course they cannot all reasonably be regarded as fundamental laws.

Recall that Hausman thinks that there are empirical and pragmatic reasons for accepting the generalizations of equilibrium theory. This is one of the two key aspects of his case for viewing equilibrium theory as a group of hedged laws. As noted in section 4.3, he thinks that observation confirms that the following generalizations are approximately true (true with a margin of error) in a certain domain:

(PL6) Individuals' marginal rates of substitution diminish, that is, an individual is willing to give up less of a commodity Y for a unit of a commodity X as the amount of Y the individual has relative to the amount of X he has decreases.

(PL7) As a firm uses more and more of a variable input holding constant or fixed other inputs, then, over the normal range of input use, the marginal product of the variable input declines.

Hausman may well be correct in saying that everyday experience and introspection indicate that (PL6) and (PL7) hold true in some range of real world cases, perhaps with a margin of error. But Hausman takes (PL6) and (PL7) to be true *simpliciter*, and therefore laws, only if they are qualified by vague *ceteris paribus* clauses.[13] And, given Hausman's analysis of *ceteris paribus* clauses set out in section 4.3 above, (PL6) and (PL7) so qualified are equivalent to the following:

(PL6a) There is a set of conditions C such that if C obtains, then an individual is willing to give up less of a commodity Y for a unit of a commodity X as the amount of Y the individual has relative to the amount of X he has decreases.

(PL7a) There is a set of conditions C such that if C obtains, then, as a firm uses more and more of a variable input over the normal range of input use, the marginal product of the variable input declines.

I do not see how everyday experience and introspection confirming the approximate truth of (PL6) and (PL7) in some real world cases can afford good evidence that (PL6a) and (PL7a) are true. For (PL6a) and

(PL7a) to be true, there actually have to exist the sets of conditions *C* alluded to in the two statements; if no such sets of conditions *C* exist, (PL6a) and (PL7a) are false. And (PL6) and (PL7) holding in some range of real world cases hardly seems sufficient evidence for saying that the sets of conditions *C* really do exist. And this is especially true since we do not even know all of what is encompassed by the sets of conditions *C*. For it is *vague ceteris paribus* clauses that are supposed to qualify (PL6) and (PL7), and the factors subsumed under such *ceteris paribus* clauses are at least partly undetermined. But then if everyday experience and introspection are insufficient to establish (PL6a) and (PL7a), they are also insufficient to establish *as laws* (PL6) and (PL7) qualified with vague *ceteris paribus* clauses. For again, (PL6) and (PL7) so qualified are equivalent to (PL6a) and (PL7a) respectively, given Hausman's analysis of *ceteris paribus* clauses. In sum, Hausman's *empirical* reasons for thinking that (PL6) and (PL7) are approximately true in a certain domain do not justify thinking that these two statements, suitably qualified, are genuine hedged laws.

Hausman might reply by saying that observation does establish that (PL6) and (PL7) hold in a range of real world cases with a margin of error. And we just attach vague *ceteris paribus* clauses to cover the partly undetermined disturbing factors that in some real world cases cause (PL6) and (PL7) to break down. After all, the laws of economics do not specify all the causes of the phenomena the discipline studies – it is an inexact science. In response to this, the observations affording evidence for

(A) (PL6) and (PL7) – unqualified by *ceteris paribus* clauses – hold in a range of real world cases

are altogether insufficient to establish or justify

(B) (PL6a) and (PL7a) are true.

Evidence that supports (A) does not automatically support (B). And this is the case because the evidence that supports (A) – introspection and everyday observation – seems quite insufficient to establish the existence of the sets of conditions *C* alluded to in (PL6a) and (PL7a). But recall that, given Hausman's analysis of *ceteris paribus* clauses, (PL6a) and (PL7a) are equivalent to (PL6) and (PL7) *qualified with* vague *ceteris paribus* clauses. So the evidence that supports (A) does not support saying that (PL6) and (PL7) qualified with vague *ceteris paribus* clauses, really are true and therefore laws. Hausman cannot, then, correctly say that evidence for (A) is automatically evidence for the truth of the propositions resulting from attaching vague *ceteris paribus* clauses to (PL6) and (PL7).

Hausman thinks the approximate truth in some real world cases of some of the other generalizations of equilibrium theory is confirmed by observation. For instance, Hausman thinks that the approximate truth of (PL5) in a certain domain – he calls (PL5) 'consumerism' – is confirmed by observation. He (1992a, p. 216) says 'Introspection provides evidence that consumerism is a significant causal factor affecting economic phenomena....' But the same kind of argument used in the previous paragraph could obviously be marshalled to show that everyday experience and introspection are insufficient to establish the other generalizations of equilibrium theory as genuine laws qualified by vague *ceteris paribus* clauses.

As indicated in section 4.3, Hausman thinks that each of the generalizations of equilibrium theory has *pragmatic* virtues that afford reason for accepting them. But Hausman's position on this matter is of dubious merit. There is a tradition in the philosophy of science that distinguishes pragmatic virtues of theories or hypotheses from virtues that are connected with the truth or falsity of the theories. Bas Van Fraassen nicely describes the distinction as follows:

> Briefly, then, the answer is that the other virtues claimed for a theory are *pragmatic* virtues. In so far as they go beyond consistency, empirical adequacy, and empirical strength, they do not concern the relation between the theory and the world, but rather the use and usefulness of the theory; they provide reasons to prefer the theory independently of questions of truth. (Van Fraassen, 1980, p. 88, italics in original)

Among pragmatic virtues Van Fraassen lists mathematical elegance, simplicity, great scope or generality, completeness in certain respects, usefulness in unifying our account of otherwise disparate phenomena, and being explanatory (Van Fraassen, 1980, p. 87). So, Van Fraassen thinks the possession of any of these virtues by a hypothesis is *not* any reason at all for thinking the hypothesis is *true*, but rather a reason for taking some other stance toward the hypothesis. There may be some disagreement over some of the particular virtues Van Fraassen views as pragmatic. Some may see the simplicity of a hypothesis as a reason for thinking it is true, and so not a mere pragmatic virtue. But Van Fraassen is surely correct in taking some virtues of a hypothesis to be connected with truth or falsity, whereas other virtues of a hypothesis are independent of questions of truth. Internal consistency is a virtue of a hypothesis that is connected with truth and falsity, since its absence in a hypothesis is a conclusive reason for thinking the hypothesis is false. But mathematical tractability is a virtue of a hypothesis that is not connected with truth or falsity. That a hypothesis is mathematically tractable is surely no reason at all for thinking the hypothesis is true, nor is the fact that a hypothesis is not mathematically tractable any reason for thinking it false.

Hausman's distinction between empirical and pragmatic virtues of a theory or hypothesis cuts across the traditional truth related/pragmatic virtues distinction philosophers like Van Fraassen make. Empirical virtues for Hausman include such truth related features as being supported by observation and predictive success. Hausman's pragmatic virtues would better be called 'non-empirical virtues', as they are unconnected with questions of the relation of a hypothesis to empirical evidence or data. Some of the non-empirical virtues Hausman lists, such as consistency, are connected with questions of truth, whereas others, such as mathematical tractability and determinateness, are not. But here a serious problem arises for Hausman. Recall that he thinks that each of the ten generalizations of equilibrium theory have pragmatic or non-empirical virtues which he takes to be reasons for *accepting* them, that is, believing them to be true. Yet *not one* of the non-empirical virtues Hausman cites is clearly evidence of or a sign of truth. To be sure, internal consistency is one of Hausman's non-empirical virtues, and it is a feature connected with truth and falsity in a way described in the previous paragraph. But internal consistency is not any evidence of truth – though again, an absence of internal consistency is conclusive evidence of falsity. The statement 'The Earth is flat' is internally consistent. But of course, this fact is not the slightest grounds for thinking the statement is true. And other non-empirical virtues Hausman cites, such as having an educative function, simplicity, mathematical tractability and giving sharper advice, are either not signs of truth at all, or the claim that they are, as in the case of simplicity, is controversial and requires justification which Hausman does not provide. The upshot of all this is that, supposing each of the ten generalizations of equilibrium theory does possess the non-empirical virtues Hausman thinks they do, this still does *not* clearly afford any reason or evidence at all for thinking these generalizations truly describe the way the world is, whether or not they are qualified with vague *ceteris paribus* clauses.

It seems, then, that Hausman's effort to describe empirical as well as pragmatic or non-empirical reasons for the ten generalizations of equilibrium theory being hedged laws, is not at all successful. And this negatively impacts the other part of his basis for viewing these generalizations as hedged laws. The other part in question is the method of theory appraisal – the economist's deductive method – that Hausman thinks economists in fact employ. Recall that Hausman's account of this method views it as relying on the weak-link principle, which says that when an entire theoretical system generates a false prediction, one should pin the responsibility for predictive failure on the least certain hypotheses in the theoretical system. And Hausman thinks that the auxiliary hypotheses – *ceteris* is *paribus* assumptions and simplifications especially – needed to derive predictions from generalizations of equilibrium theory, are typically *less certain* than these generalizations. And in part this is so because the generalizations of equilibrium theory are *already* credible given the empirical and pragmatic reasons for accepting them independent of their being tested by the economist's deductive method. But, as I have argued, the empirical and pragmatic reasons in question do not afford any grounds for taking the generalizations of equilibrium theory as genuine laws qualified with vague *ceteris paribus* clauses. As a result, in the context of testing these generalizations by the economist's deductive method, the suitably qualified generalizations of equilibrium theory will be *as uncertain as* the auxiliary assumptions that need to be added to these generalizations to generate checkable predictions. But in this case, the weak-link principle will be of no use in preserving generalizations of equilibrium theory in the face of predictive failure. In sum, the economist's deductive method is not really of any use in propping up equilibrium theory in the face of predictive failures. So, even if the economist's deductive method is justifiable or philosophically defensible, it does not afford a reasonable basis for viewing the generalizations of equilibrium theory as genuine hedged laws.

But there is also a serious drawback attaching to the economist's deductive method. As Hausman characterizes it, it is not philosophically defensible. The central problem in this connection is with rule (R4). For convenience let me restate (R4) here:

(R4) If the predictions (of a theoretical system which includes one or more generalizations of equilibrium theory) are verified, then regard the whole theoretical system as confirmed; but if the predictions prove incorrect, then compare alternative accounts of the failure on the basis of their relative empirical and pragmatic virtues.

The trouble is with what comes before the word 'but'. That part of (R4) presupposes what might be called 'the simple hypothetico-deductive (HD) method of testing scientific theories'. According to this, testing a hypothesis or theory H consists simply in deducing one or more predictions from *H* (together with suitable auxiliary assumptions), and then checking to see whether the predictions are correct or incorrect. The test is successful and *H* is confirmed if the predictions prove correct; otherwise the test is unsuccessful and H is disconfirmed (at least if the auxiliary assumptions used in constructing the test are held true). And this is all there is to the testing and confirmation of scientific hypotheses on the simple HD method. (R4) seems clearly to assume the simple HD method. But the simple HD method is a *false* theory of testing and confirmation.[14] As a result, the economist's deductive method as stated is not justifiable.

This completes the argument for the inadequacy of Hausman's basis for viewing the ten generalizations of equilibrium theory as hedged scientific laws. But I believe that a case can be made that the claim that these generalizations are all hedged laws, is without warrant. The case relies heavily on one of Hausman's own conditions for a generalization qualified with a vague *ceteris paribus* clause being justifiably regarded as a law. In *The Inexact and Separate Science of Economics*, Hausman's defence of equilibrium theory does not rely on his lawlikeness, reliability, refinability and excusability conditions to argue for his claim that the generalizations of equilibrium theory *are* genuine hedged laws. However, as I pointed out in section 4.2 above, in *Capital, Profits, and Prices*, Hausman appeals to these conditions to argue for the position that we are *not* justified in taking all the generalizations of equilibrium theory to be hedged scientific laws. The position I will argue for here is the same as the one Hausman adopts in *Capital, Profits, and Prices*. But whereas Hausman's argument in *Capital, Profits, and Prices* for this position appeals to the excusability condition, my argument will emphasize the reliability condition.

Terence Hutchinson is one economic methodologist who tries to describe conditions for the legitimate or justified use of *ceteris paribus* clauses in economics. He says:

> We suggest that the ceteris paribus assumption can only be safely and significantly used in conjunction with an empirical generalization verified as true in a large percentage of cases but occasionally liable to exceptions of a clearly describable type. (Hutchinson, 1984, p. 46)

The first of the two conditions Hutchinson suggests here is similar to Hausman's reliability condition alluded to toward the end of section 4.2 above. Hausman expresses this condition as follows:

> Second, the *ceteris paribus* law must be *reliable*. In some class of cases, after

ignoring the *ceteris paribus* clause or allowing for *specific* interferences, the scientist should rarely need to explain away apparent disconfirmations. Reliability is a statistical requirement. A generalization such as *'ceteris paribus all F's are G's'* is reliable only if (perhaps after making allowances for specific interferences) almost all F's are G's. The evidence for reliability will typically be sample frequencies. (Hausman, 1992a, p. 140)

Let me express the reliability condition in terms of the following single proposition:

(RC) We are justified in regarding *'Ceteris paribus all F's are G'* as a scientific law only if we know that 'All F's are G' is true in a very high percentage of cases in which the already determined factors subsumed by *'ceteris paribus'* are absent or unchanging.

To clarify, suppose *'ceteris paribus'* in *'Ceteris paribus all F's are G'* subsumes just two already determined factors F1 and F2. (If the ceteris paribus clause is a precise one, F1 and F2 are the only influencing factors it subsumes; but if it is a vague *ceteris paribus* clause, then there are additional but as yet undetermined factors subsumed by the clause.) (RC) says that we are entitled to regard *'Ceteris paribus all F's are G'* as a genuine law only if 'All F are G' is true in a very high percentage of cases in which F1 and F2 are absent or unchanging. The rationale for (RC) should be pretty obvious, given that laws, even of the hedged variety, must be truths.[15]

I will argue that the majority of the generalizations constituting equilibrium theory do not meet the reliability condition (RC). As Hausman notes, (PL1) to (PL10) of equilibrium theory can be telescoped into the single generalization that individuals are rational (Hausman, 1992a, p. 30). Let us express this as

(PL1-4) Individuals are rational.

(PL1-4) affirms that real world individuals have preferences which conform to (PL1) to (PL3) and make choices conforming to (PL4). Is evidence available that (PL1-4) satisfies the reliability condition (RC)? To support a 'Yes' answer, an examination needs to have been conducted of real world cases in which the determined or known disturbing factors excluded by the vague *ceteris paribus* clause implicitly qualifying (PL1-4) are absent. What are these disturbing factors? In his textbook presentation of standard neoclassical micro theory, Walter Nicholson identifies a number of them:

> This *ceteris paribus* (other things being equal) assumption is invoked so as to
> make the analysis of choices manageable within a simplified setting.... but all
> economic analysis of utility-maximizing choices will usually be based on some
> form of the *ceteris paribus* assumption.... Not only must we hold 'tastes'
> constant but we must hold constant such quantifiable items as the individual's
> consumption in some future time periods, the number of hours worked (this
> amounts to holding income constant), and the amount of income saved.
> (Nicholson, 1978, p. 58)

So let us consider the class of real world individuals for whom the
disturbing factors Nicholson lists – tastes, hours worked, and so on – are
not changing. Have economists turned up good evidence of some sort
that 'Individuals are rational' is true for a very high percentage of the
members of this class? I myself have never seen such evidence in the
writings of economists with which I am familiar, nor any reference to
such evidence. Why do economists, in developing the theory of consumer
choice, make the assumptions that are included in (PL1-4)? The reasons
they often give invoke such properties as intuitive appeal, obviousness,
and plausibility. For example, in developing consumer choice theory in
his intermediate micro text, Edwin Mansfield (1979, p. 47) says 'Although
not all consumers may exhibit preferences that are transitive, this
assumption [of (PL2) which is part of (PL1-4)] certainly seems to be a
plausible basis for a model of consumer behavior'.[16] But plausibility,
intuitive appeal and obviousness do not constitute good evidence that
(PL1-4) is true for a very high percentage of individuals whose tastes,
hours worked, etc. are not changing. It might be claimed that everyday
experience and introspection furnish good evidence that (PL1-4) is true
for a very high percentage of the individuals in question. But this claim
is hardly persuasive. How large was the sample of real world individuals
who were the objects of everyday experience and introspection? How was
the sample selected? Was it a random sample? What was the percentage
of individuals in the sample who conformed to (PL1-4)? Without answers
to such questions, the claim that casual observation provides good
evidence that (PL1-4) fulfils condition (RC) is without any real
credibility.

Moreover, appeals to plausibility and the like are completely unable
to remove a legitimate doubt as to whether (PL1-4) does meet (RC). As
a matter of fact, there is pretty solid evidence that (PL1-4) is *false* as a
description of real world individuals. (PL1-4) is of course a conjunction
of (PL1), (PL2), (PL3) and (PL4). But (PL1) is false. Often real world
individuals face options without having full or complete information
about those options.[17] And in such situations the individuals sometimes

do not have complete preferences. For they do not have enough information to form a preference for one of the options over the other or to be indifferent between them (Hausman and McPherson, 1996, p. 28). (PL2) is also false. Amos Tversky did experimental studies using Harvard undergraduates to test the hypothesis of transitive preferences. He (1969, p. 40) says 'The empirical studies showed that, under appropriate experimental conditions, the behavior of some people is intransitive. Moreover, the intransitivities are systematic, consistent, and predictable'. And Tversky (1969, p. 31) is careful to inform us that the intransitivities people exhibit '... are observed even in the absence of systematic changes in the decision maker's taste ...'. So there is good evidence that (PL1) and (PL2) – and therefore (PL1-4) – break down not infrequently in the real world. This raises a serious doubt as to whether (PL1-4) is true for a very high percentage of individuals whose tastes, hours worked, etc. are not changing. Such a doubt cannot be allayed by thin appeals to plausibility or everyday experience and introspection. It seems to me, then, that there is not anything like adequate evidence to say that (PL1-4) meets condition (RC) for being a law. Therefore, regarding (PL1-4) as a genuine hedged law is not justified.

Hausman calls (PL5) 'consumerism'. Essentially it says that individuals' preferences, which are expressed in their choices, are always or only for larger rather than smaller commodity bundles, at least up to some point of satiation. As Hausman (1992a, p. 32) says 'Consumerism identifies options with commodity bundles and implies that choices are based on nothing but essentially greed'. Stated this way, the proposition that there are no interdependencies between the preferences of different individuals, is implied rather than explicitly expressed in (PL5)'s formulation. And (PL5) as just stated also implies that commodities or bundles of commodities are the exclusive objects of individuals' preferences. As Hausman readily admits, (PL5) is clearly false as a description of the real world. In the real world individuals' preferences are not exclusively defined over commodity bundles, and they are often interdependent. The satisfaction or frustration of the preferences of *others* are among the objects of some preferences of many of us. Husbands often prefer that certain of their wives' preferences are satisfied, some people prefer that their enemies' preferences are thwarted, and so on. Still, Hausman does apparently take (PL5) qualified with a vague *ceteris paribus* clause as a genuine hedged law; it does identify an important causal factor operating in economic behaviour (Hausman, 1992a, p. 216). However, it is hard to see that (PL5) satisfies condition (RC) for being a law. Presumably the vague *ceteris paribus* clause implicitly qualifying (PL5) is supposed to rule out or exclude changes in individuals' tastes, hours worked, and so on – the same disturbing factors excluded by the *ceteris paribus* clause qualifying (PL1-4). But it seems quite doubtful that (PL5) unqualified by a ceteris paribus clause holds true for a very high percentage of individuals whose tastes, hours worked, etc. are unchanging. Again, quite a few individuals have preferences whose objects are not commodities, and are not interdependent of the preferences of others. So, very good evidence needs to be marshalled to establish that (PL5) does meet condition (RC). Where is such evidence? I have never seen it, nor any reference to it.

I might add that Hausman's way of viewing (PL5) seems rather different than economists' own attitude toward the proposition. In the formulation of (PL5) in section 4.2 above, it is a conjunction whose first and second conjuncts are, respectively, as follows:

(PL5a) Individuals' preferences are defined only over commodity bundles.
(PL5b) There are no interdependencies among individuals' preferences.

Economists are no doubt well aware that these propositions are false. Yet they typically assume (PL5a) and (PL5b) in articulating consumer choice theory. But this may well be because (PL5a) and (PL5b) restrict the objects of individual preferences to quantifiable options, and thus the theory of consumer choice can be developed in a simple and mathematically tractable way. It is not that economists are committed to the truth of (PL5a) and (PL5b), or even committed to the truth of these two propositions when qualified by *ceteris paribus* clauses. The third conjunct of (PL5) as formulated in section 4.2 says this:

(PL5c) Up to some point of satiation, individuals prefer more of a commodity to less.

Economists are committed to the truth of (PL5c). But they tend to regard it as a consequence of a definition of a commodity. Henderson and Quandt (1980, p. 9) say 'By definition, a commodity is an item of which the consumer would rather have more than less'. And definitions and consequences of definitions are not scientific laws. So, economists' way of regarding (PL5) does not really square with Hausman's construal of it as a scientific law qualified by a *ceteris paribus* clause.

(PL6), which says that individuals' marginal rates of substitution decline, is often commended by economists on the basis of its intuitive appeal. Walter Nicholson says:

> The assumption of a diminishing marginal rate of substitution is both analytically important and accords well with an intuitive notion that people are progressively less willing to consume more and more of a commodity as they acquire more of it. An individual's psychic rate of trade-off between commodities depends on how much of these commodities he or she is currently consuming. (Nicholson, 1978, p. 63)

No doubt (PL6) does have intuitive appeal, in part it is the same sort of intuitive appeal as the so-called law of diminishing marginal utility it has largely supplanted in articulations of consumer choice theory. But even holding constant the determined or known factors that are subsumed by the vague *ceteris paribus* clause Hausman supposes qualifies (PL6), there are grounds for wondering how frequently (PL6) is true for real world individuals. William Baumol has drawn our attention to types of real world individuals who have an *increasing* marginal rate of substitution (MRS) of one good for another. Baumol says:

> Actually, this sort of shape of indifference curve [concave to origin] can occur also in region I, where it characterizes the behavior of an addict or collector (the more of either commodity he has, the more urgently he wants even more of it). If addiction to zabaglione were to characterize its consumption, we move toward point Z^* [the point where satiation in good Z sets in] additional units of this item will become very valuable and additional C comparatively worthless, i.e., the consumer will be willing to trade a small addition in Z for a great loss in C. (Baumol, 1977, p. 200)

Addicts and collectors seem common enough in the real world. And Baumol's view of such people as having increasing MRS's as they increase consumption of a good they are addicted to or collect, seems very plausible. But then this makes somewhat pressing the question of whether (PL6), unqualified by a *ceteris paribus* clause, is true for a very high percentage of real world individuals whose tastes, hours worked, etc. are unchanging. For (PL6) to be real hedged law, the answer must be 'Yes'. And I have not seen in the writings of economists good evidence, nor reference to such evidence, that (PL6) does fulfil condition (RC) for justifiably being taken to be a law. Pointing to the intuitive appeal or plausibility of (PL6) is no substitute for answers to questions like the following. Have unbiased samples of individuals been examined to see whether they conform to (PL6)? What were the percentages of individuals in the samples who conformed to (PL6)? So the claim that (PL6), even qualified by a *ceteris paribus* clause, is a genuine law seems unjustified.

I will be brief in the treatment of (PL7) to (PL9) of equilibrium theory. Economists largely seem to believe that (PL7) truly describes the way the world is. Walter Nicholson (1978, p. 185) says 'Nevertheless, the basic observation that the marginal productivity of labor (or any other input) declines when *all other inputs* are held constant is still recognized by economists as an empirically valid proposition' (italics in original). Earlier in this section I argued that Hausman's empirical and pragmatic reasons for taking (PL7) to be true when suitably qualified with a *ceteris paribus* clause, are inadequate.[18] But I will not pursue the argument any further here, and leave open the question of whether (PL7) meets the conditions, such as the reliability condition, for justifiably taking a generalization to be a genuine hedged law.

(PL8) states that firms' production functions exhibit constant returns to scale. Economists have conducted empirical studies of production functions in different industries and different countries. They often assume that production functions are of the Cobb–Douglas form, and, using econometric techniques, they estimate the parameters in the Cobb–Douglas production function. One often cited estimate of a Cobb–Douglas production function for the railroad industry in the USA. affords evidence that the railroad industry is characterized by *increasing* returns to scale (Pindyck and Rubinfeld, 1992, p. 193). And if an *industry* production function exhibits increasing returns to scale, it can be inferred that *each firm* in the industry has a production function that exhibits increasing returns to scale.[19] So, there is some empirical evidence that disconfirms (PL8). On the other hand, an empirical study that is sometimes cited provides evidence that is 'consistent with' the hypothesis that in most industries there are constant returns to scale (Maroney, 1967, p. 49). But this same study examined 18 manufacturing industries in the USA. And in five of the industries examined, the regression results afford evidence that the industry production function exhibits increasing returns to scale (Maroney, 1967, pp. 46–7). And thus we can say that there is evidence that individual firms in these industries – food and beverages, furniture, printing, chemicals, and fabricated metals – have production functions exhibiting increasing returns to scale. In sum, what evidence there is bearing on (PL8) seems rather on the inconclusive side. And there does not appear to be anything like adequate evidence available for saying that (PL8) holds for a very high percentage of real world firms. (I cannot tell what influencing factors Hausman takes to be subsumed by the vague *ceteris paribus* clause that is supposed to qualify implicitly (PL8).) In sum, (PL8) does not appear to fulfil the reliability condition (RC) for justifiably regarding a generalization as a genuine hedged law.

(PL9) affirms that business firms seek to maximize profits. This is a highly controversial element of equilibrium theory – it has often been criticized and perhaps equally often defended. A well-known criticism of (PL9) presented some 50 years ago is Richard Lester's. Lester sent questionnaires to business firm managers in the southern USA asking about unit costs, adjustments the firm would make to a given change, and so on. Lester's interpretation of the results of his survey included two claims: (A) in deciding how much labour to hire, managers do not equate marginal revenue product (MRP) of labour and marginal factor cost (MFC) of labour, and (B) variations in employment of labour are the result of actual and anticipated changes in orders for the products produced by the firms (Lester, 1947, p. 138). Claim (A) especially appears incompatible with (PL9). For if firm managers seek to maximize profits, then they would be expected to hire labour hours up to the point where the MRP of labour equals the MFC of labour, which (A) denies is what in fact happens. Lester's questionnaire approach and his interpretation of the results were trenchantly criticized, especially by Fritz Machlup. And (PL) remains controversial. But one thing that I have never seen in the literature defending (PL9) is good evidence that a very high percentage of real world firm managers attempt to set output (or inputs) at the level at which profits are at a maximum.[20] Have unbiased samples of real world firm managers been examined? What were the percentages of managers in the samples whose goal is to maximize profits? I know of no available answers to such questions. It certainly seems that (PL9) does not meet the reliability condition (RC) for justifiably regarding a generalization qualified by a *ceteris paribus* clause as a genuine scientific law.

Finally we come to (PL10), the last of the generalizations of equilibrium theory. (PL10) affirms that markets clear or come to equilibrium quickly. Apparently many economists believe that (PL10) is false. Walter Nicholson (1978, p. 321) says 'Many economists believe that markets are usually out of equilibrium'.[21] And (PL10) is in fact false. Quite a few real world markets do not clear because of interferences from outside the market, interferences that economists themselves study. As of 1 October, 1996 the Federal Government in the USA increased the minimum wage from $4.25 to $4.75 per hour, and it is scheduled to rise to $5.15 per hour in 1997. This places a price floor in markets for low skilled labour in various parts of the USA thereby preventing those markets from coming to equilibrium at all. Rent control, which exists in a number of cities in the USA and Europe, inserts a price ceiling in markets for rental housing preventing those markets from coming to equilibrium. Some neoclassical economists emphasize transactions costs in explaining why markets do not *quickly* come to equilibrium. Walter Nicholson says:

> In explaining why markets do not adjust immediately to changing conditions, economists have tended to stress *transactions costs*. Bringing suppliers and demanders together is not so simple a process as the Marshallian diagram suggests: There may be significant costs involved. Such costs not only consist of the direct costs of finding a 'place' in which to transact business, but, more important, they also include the costs to participants of gaining information about the market. For demanders, all prices are not perfectly known. Rather they must invest some time in search procedures that permits them to learn market prices. (Nicholson, 1978, p. 321)

So, (PL10) does not correctly describe the way the world is. Not infrequently, markets either do not go to equilibrium at all, or they do not do so quickly.

Admittedly, in developing *theoretical* or unapplied models of different kinds of markets – a perfectly competitive product market, a monopsony labor market, and so on – neoclassical economists typically analyse or show how equilibrium prices and quantities are established in these markets. And in doing comparative static analysis at the theoretical level – comparing an old and a new equilibrium position – neoclassical economists frequently assume that the market under analysis promptly moves to the new equilibrium. Yet these facts about theoretical neoclassical models hardly provides any warrant for saying that (PL10) correctly describes the way *real world* markets always or even usually work. Moreover, even at the level of unapplied theory, neoclassical economists do not always assume or establish that markets go to equilibrium. Consider the well-known cobweb model of price determination in a competitive market. When demand for the product is relatively inelastic, over time the market price actually *diverges* more and more from the equilibrium or market clearing price (Nicholson, 1978, pp. 318–21).

There is, then, good reason to regard (PL10) false. Hausman wishes to see (PL10) as qualified by a vague *ceteris paribus* clause. (He does not appear to say what determinate or known factors, if any, are subsumed by this *ceteris paribus* clause.) Does (PL10) so qualified meet the reliability condition (RC)? I have never seen answers to such questions as the following. Have unbiased samples of real world markets been examined to see whether or not they come promptly to equilibrium? What are the percentages of markets in the samples that quickly clear?

Moreover, given the fairly substantial number of real world markets that do not clear, or do not clear quickly, it seems doubtful that a very high percentage of real world markets do fit (PL10). Thus, (PL10) does not appear to meet the reliability condition (RC) for justifiably regarding a generalization as a genuine hedged law.

4.5 CONCLUDING REMARKS

Recall from the start of section 4.3 that the key proposition of Hausman's naturalism about economics is (B) neoclassical microeconomics includes a body of fundamental laws represented by (PL1) to (PL10). It has been argued that Hausman's own case for (PL1) to (PL10) being hedged laws is inadequate, even though his case is the best one extant. And it has also been argued that the majority of the generalizations (PL1) to (PL10) are not justifiably regarded as genuine hedged laws at all. As a result, (B) is without warrant or rational foundation, and so is Hausman's naturalism about economics. Hausman's naturalism cannot be credible or rationally grounded when its central proposition is without credibility.

With the failure of Hausman's naturalism about economics, we remain without a basis for seeing economics as fulfilling the positivist condition (PC) for a discipline being a science. (The positivist condition is stated in section 4.1 above.) For I know of no articulation and defence of naturalism about economics that even equals Hausman's in terms of its initial promise. And this in turn negatively impacts the form of the 'Is it science?' approach to economics that assumes the positivist condition and then asks the following query:

(QN) Does economics fit the description which the positivist condition (PC) claims is necessary and sufficient for a discipline being a science?

In order for this form of the 'Is it science?' approach to shed real light on economics, naturalism about economics would have to be credible or rationally grounded. Naturalism about economics just is the claim that 'Yes' is the answer to (QN). If we cannot justifiably accept naturalism about economics, then the 'Is it science?' approach to economics that assumes the positivist condition and asks (QN) is unable to supply us with a positive, illuminating characterization of economics. The outcome of pursuing this approach leaves us pretty much in the dark about what economics is all about, as long as naturalism about economics remains unjustified.

That we do not have a rationally grounded version of naturalism about economics is not the only drawback of the form of the 'Is it science?' approach to economics that assumes the positivist condition. As noted in section 4.2 above, macroeconomics is characterized by dissensus rather than consensus. As a result, there is not a sizeable number of broadly accepted macroeconomic generalizations that might count as scientific laws. And since the disagreement among macroeconomists – especially between Keynesians and new classicals – is at the level of theory, there seem to be few if any widely accepted generalizations that could count as fundamental laws. In this event the positivist condition (PC) is of little use in helping us understand the nature of macroeconomics. If a branch of economics lacks a stock of accepted generalizations, that branch simply fails to fit the description (PC) claims is necessary and sufficient for a discipline being a science. (PC) describes a science as a discipline which includes a stock of *accepted* generalizations some of which are fundamental laws that explain uniformities unearthed by the discipline. Thus, the form of the 'Is it science?' approach that assumes the positivist condition (PC) and asks question (QN), offers little by way of illumination of macroeconomics, a large and important part of economics.

The argument of this chapter supports the conclusion that the form of the 'Is it science?' approach to economics that assumes the positivist condition (PC) and asks question (QN) has so far failed to shed real light on economics. But there is a weak resemblance between economics and a discipline which does fit the description which (PC) claims is necessary and sufficient for science. Any discipline which fits this description must, among other things, include a corpus of scientific laws. And economics does contain generalizations that are genuine laws. An important example is the law of demand formulated as follows:

(LD) *Ceteris paribus*, a good's own price and the quantity of the good demanded are negatively related.

As indicated in section 3.4, there is a substantial amount of empirical evidence for the truth of (LD). Or to put the point another way, there is a substantial amount of evidence that (LD) meets the reliability condition (RC) for justifiably regarding a generalization as a hedged law. In a very high percentage of cases in which the known factors subsumed by the *ceteris paribus* clause in (LD) – consumers' income, tastes of consumers, etc. – are unchanging, changes in a good's own price and quantity of the good demanded move in the opposite direction. This claim is supported by casual observation of what happens when business firms have sales, and numerous negative number estimates of own price elasticities for different goods using multiple regression analysis with real world market data.[22] Another economic law is Engel's law which affirms the following:

(EL) As households' incomes rise, the proportion of total expenditures devoted to food declines.

This generalization has been confirmed in hundreds of studies across different countries (Nicholson, 1978, p. 96). (EL) is a lawlike generalization. Take some real world household whose income has not increased. (EL) implies the counterfactual 'If this household's income had increased, then the proportion of its expenditures devoted to food would have declined'. And since it is true as well, (EL) qualifies as a law on the standard philosophical conception of scientific laws. However, the number of economic generalizations that can justifiably be regarded as scientific laws is not especially large.[23] And the generalizations which are laws, such as the law of demand and Engel's law, are clearly empirical or phenomenological laws rather than fundamental laws. So the resemblance is weak indeed between economics and a discipline fitting the description the positivist condition (PC) claims is necessary and sufficient for a science.

NOTES

1. Mill is willing to say that a discipline D is an actual science as long as the phenomena it studies are subject to laws, whether or not the practitioners of D have discovered any of these laws. But if the practitioners of D have not discovered any of the laws to which D's phenomena are subject, Mill would say that D is not a science available in practice (Mill, 1970, p. 553). I want to avoid Mill's way of talking here, as it seems rather peculiar. Instead, I will speak of a science as actually existing only when it is available in practice in Mill's sense. So, in my usage, a discipline D is not a science if the laws to which its phenomena are subject remain entirely undiscovered.

2. Some philosophers have argued that fundamental scientific laws like Newton's law of gravitation are false viewed as descriptions of the real world. See Cartwright, 1983, pp. 54–73. On the standard philosophical conception of laws, this position would imply that the fundamental laws so-called are not really laws, or they would have to be reinterpreted as something other than descriptions of the way the world is. Another possible response would be to acknowledge the falsity of fundamental laws, and develop a conception of laws allowing for false laws. But in this monograph I will adopt the standard philosophical conception according to which laws are true. As will be clear from later chapters, I do not think that the concept of a law is of much use in making sense of what economics is about.

3. Hausman's explicitly stated reason for focusing on neoclassical microeconomics does

not invoke the positivist condition (PC). He (1992a, p. 1) says 'This book will be concerned only with contemporary microeconomic theory and general equilibrium theory. These theories are the best known of economic theories, the theories that have most influenced work in the other social sciences, and the theories which have been most discussed by philosophers, economists, and other social theorists'.

4.   See Hausman, 1992a, p. 30, p. 43, p. 51. Several comments. (A) As Hausman (1992a, p. 18) notes, (PL3) is redundant when the number of options over which preferences are defined is finite. With a finite number of options, complete and transitive preferences – which are postulated by (PL1) and (PL2) – are automatically continuous. And in Hausman's formulation of the fundamental laws in *Capital, Profits, and Prices*, (PL3) is omitted. See Hausman, 1981, pp. 108–9. (B) (PL6) does not appear on the list of fundamental laws in *Capital, Profits, and Prices*. Instead what appears is the law of diminishing marginal utility (PL6') the marginal utility of a commodity falls as an individual consumes more of it. But whether (PL6) or (PL6') appears on the list matters little. For the theory of consumer choice – which consists of (PL1) to (PL6) – can be stated so that (PL6) is derived from (PL6'). See Nicholson, 1978, pp. 66–9. (C) I have stated (PL6) a bit differently than Hausman does. Suppose a two commodity case and that the quantity of commodity X is on the horizontal axis with the quantity of commodity Y on the vertical axis. Imagine a single indifference curve for some individual of the usual convex shape drawn in the first quadrant. The marginal rate of substitution (MRS) is the maximum amount of Y the individual is prepared to give up for an added unit of X (with the individual staying on the same indifference curve). The principle of diminishing MRS says that the MRS falls as the individual moves down the indifference curve, i.e., as the amount of Y he has decreases relative to the amount of X he has. Hausman (1992a, p. 30) labels (PL6) 'Diminishing marginal rates of substitution'. But his formulation of (PL6), unlike mine, actually describes what happens moving back up the indifference curve.

5.   Hausman includes Leontief input–output models as a type of general equilibrium model (Hausman, 1992a, p. 55). But input–output analysis of the type Leontief developed is not really a form of general equilibrium analysis at all. This point is nicely and succinctly made by Alpha Chiang, 1974, p. 123.

6.   Hausman does regard himself in *Capital, Profits, and Prices* as presenting a naturalistic account of economics (Hausman, 1981, p. 201). But Hausman's concept of naturalism is different than the one I use here. Naturalism about economics in Hausman's sense is the claim that (A) the general goals, methods and logical structure of economic theories are the same as those of the natural sciences (Hausman, 1981, p. 199). But naturalism in my sense is the claim that (B) economics fits the description which the positivist condition (PC) claims is necessary and sufficient for a discipline being a science. Claim (A) may be true, and yet (B) could be false. Indeed, this is just the position to which Hausman is committed in *Capital, Profits, and Prices*.

7.   A standard mark of empirical vacuity is irrefutability by experience. A classic criticism of the use of *ceteris paribus* clauses in economics which uses notions such as irrefutability is Terence Hutchinson's (Hutchinson, 1984, pp. 40–46). But Hutchinson's discussion is bedevilled by philosophical errors (Rosenberg, 1976, pp. 134–7). And the concepts of empirical vacuity and irrefutability are quite problematic. As Quine has taught us, just about any statement can be held true come what may in experience as long as we are willing to make drastic enough adjustments in the truth-values we assign to other previously accepted statements. This is so because of holism or the Duhem–Quine thesis, which says that statements are not for the most part empirically testable taken singly but only in fairly large batches. But then how are we to see any

distinction between refutable and irrefutable individual statements? Quine replaces a sharp distinction with a sort of continuum. As Quine and Ullian (1978, p. 79) say, 'Properly viewed, therefore, Virtue V [refutability] is a matter of degree ... The degree to which a hypothesis partakes of Virtue V is measured by the cost of retaining the hypothesis in the face of imaginable events. The degree is measured by how dearly we cherish the previous beliefs that would have to be sacrificed to save the hypothesis. The greater the sacrifice, the more refutable the hypothesis'. It is consistent with Quine's position to say that any accepted statement *S* would become about as irrefutable as you could get should we *always* decide to make adjustments in other beliefs to preserve *S* in the face of apparently disconfirming evidence. And a statement that is irrefutable to this degree could be said to be empirically vacuous. This account of empirical vacuity reflects rather than contradicts the Duhem–Quine thesis.

8. Hausman believes that neoclassical microeconomics includes a methodological commitment to economics as a separate science (Hausman, 1992a, pp. 95–6). To regard economics as a separate science is to take it as concerned with a domain in which a small set of causes predominate. And equilibrium theory identifies the predominant causes in the domain that economics is concerned with; in particular, (PL5) (which Hausman labels 'consumerism') and (PL9) define key causal factors at work in the domain of economics. Hausman thinks that the commitment of neoclassical micro to economics as a separate science is unreasonable. It reflects both an unjustifiable dogmatism, and leads economists to neglect *important* causes of economic behaviour not specified or defined by equilibrium theory (Hausman, 1992a, pp. 256–7, p. 280). So, Hausman does not view as mere *minor* causes the disturbing influences unspecified by economics yet whose presence is excluded by the vague *ceteris paribus* clauses qualifying (PL1) to (PL10).

9. To avoid confusion, we need to be careful about terminology here. As Hausman uses the term, an inexact law is a law qualified by a vague *ceteris paribus* clause (Hausman, 1992a, p. 128). Thus, a law like the law of demand qualified by a precise *ceteris paribus* clause is *not* an inexact law. But in the sense of 'strict law' I introduce here – which I think is the same as Hausman's use of 'exact law'– the law of demand is *not* a strict law either. For it is qualified by a *ceteris paribus* clause. The law of demand is a non-strict law interpreted as qualified by a precise *ceteris paribus* clause.

10. Hausman apparently would dissent from this claim. He (1992a, p. 134) says 'Although the *ceteris paribus* clauses attached to derivative laws [like the law of demand] introduce no *additional* vagueness, they inherit the vague qualifications attached to the laws of equilibrium theory'. As I interpret Hausman here, he is saying that the *ceteris paribus* clause attached to the law of demand subsumes *both* a fully specified list of factors like the prices of other goods, tastes, buyers' income, and so on, *and* the partly undetermined list of factors subsumed by the *vague ceteris paribus* clauses qualifying the generalizations of equilibrium theory. If true, this would make the *ceteris paribus* clause in (LD) a vague one. But why does Hausman think the unspecified factors subsumed by the vague *ceteris paribus* clauses qualifying (PL1) to (PL10) are also subsumed by the *ceteris paribus* clause in (LD)? Here is a possible answer. As noted above, Hausman believes that the law of demand is one of the generalizations about market behaviour explained by (PL1) to (PL10). And perhaps he also accepts the following principle: if a generalization *G* qualified by a *ceteris paribus* clause is explained by a theory which includes generalizations with vague *ceteris paribus* clauses attached, then the *ceteris paribus* clause in *G* must subsume at least the same factors as do the vague *ceteris paribus* clauses in the theory. However, it is hardly obvious that this principle is true, especially if generalization *G* has evidential support – as is the case with the law of

demand – quite independent of the theory which explains G.

11. Does this mean that, given Hausman's analysis, laws qualified by precise *ceteris paribus* clauses fit the logical empiricist conception of laws treated above in section 3.4? No, as such laws are still qualified by *ceteris paribus* clauses, and, on the logical empiricist conception, genuine laws are unqualified by any *ceteris paribus* clauses. Do the strict laws standing behind laws qualified with precise *ceteris paribus* clauses fit the logical empiricist conception? Not necessarily. Recall that on the logical empiricist conception, a generalization that is not a law may be improvable in the direction of a law, and at the end of this process of improvement is the finished law. But, though I did not say so in section 3.4, the concepts used in the finished law must, on the logical empiricist conception, be drawn from a *closed theory*. As Donald Davidson (1986, p. 219) says 'I suppose that most of our practical lore (and science) is heteronomic. This is because a law can hope to be precise, explicit, and as exceptionless as possible only if it draws its concepts from a comprehensive closed theory'. But (LDs), the strict law behind the law of demand, does not employ concepts drawn only from a closed theory (a theory the events in whose domain interact with each other but not with events outside that domain). And thus (LDs) would still not count as a law on the logical empiricist conception of laws.

12. Hausman does not give a complete list of those good-making characteristics of theories which he regards as pragmatic. But others he cites are simplicity, ease of use, gives sharper advice, and has an educative function.

13. Hausman describes some of the disturbing factors excluded by the vague *ceteris paribus* clauses he takes to implicitly qualify (PL6) and (PL7). In the case of (PL7) one of the factors excluded is explicitly cited in the above formulation of the generalization, to wit, changes in the other inputs (Hausman, 1992a, p. 135). If Hausman really wants (PL7) to be qualified by a vague *ceteris paribus* clause, then explicit reference to other inputs being held constant in (PL7) should be removed – it is covered by the *ceteris paribus* clause. One of the factors subsumed by the vague *ceteris paribus* clause implicitly qualifying (PL6) is tastes of individuals (Hausman, 1992a, p. 133).

14. For supporting argument for this contention in the context of a discussion of economic methodology, see Rappaport, 1986a, pp. 49–52. I find puzzling Hausman's viewing the economist's deductive method as philosophically defensible. He is as aware as anyone of the defects of the simple HD method of testing and confirmation (Hausman, 1992a, pp. 305–6). So, why does he view the economist's deductive method so tolerantly, despite its assuming the simple HD method? Hausman does say that his account of the economist's deductive method is simplified. So perhaps he thinks a more sophisticated account of the method is feasible. But the fact is that, as Hausman describes it, the economist's deductive method assumes the false simple HD method. And it is not at all clear that a more sophisticated account of the economist's deductive method would make it apparently so easy to preserve the generalizations of equilibrium theory in the face of predictive failure.

15. Suppose that in *more* than 100% minus a very high percentage of real world cases in which F1 and F2 are absent, F's are *not* G. This would support saying that '*Ceteris paribus* all F's are G' is false and so not a law. Of course, the *ceteris paribus* clause could be invoked by blaming the breakdown of 'All F's are G' in the real world cases examined on the presence of *unknown* disturbing factors subsumed by '*ceteris paribus*'. But this would push '*Ceteris paribus* all F's are G' in the direction of empirical vacuity. It may also violate the excusability condition (EC). (EC) says that it is justifiable to regard '*Ceteris paribus* all F's are G' as a law only if, in all but a few real world cases in which 'All F's are G' breaks down, scientists are able to identify the specific

disturbing factors causing the breakdowns.

16. Hausman and McPherson note that economists regard the theory of consumer choice as both a theory of actual choice and a theory of rational choice that sets a standard for assessing choice. The fact that consumer choice theory is a theory of rational choice partly explains economists' firm embrace of it. Hausman and McPherson (1996, p. 41) say 'A defender of the standard theory [of rational choice] might then go on to claim that, although not perfectly correct, the standard theory of choice must be a good first approximation because a theory that portrayed choice as irrational would typically reveal opportunities for exploiting this irrationality. Since people will learn not to be exploited, acting on such a theory would undermine it'.

17. Consumer choice theory is usually developed on the assumption that individuals have full or complete information about the options open to them (Nicholson, 1978, pp. 83–4). But (PL1), (PL2) and (PL3) are not restricted to situations of certainty or full information. In fact, these three propositions are axioms of expected utility theory, which is the standard economic theory of choice under uncertainty (or better, choice in risky situations).

18. Some methodologists doubt that (PL7) can be supported at all by casual observation as Hausman seems to think. Mark Blaug (1985, p. 78) says 'Pseudoscientific or not, it is important to keep in mind that most of the classical economists regarded the law of diminishing returns as a simple generalization of everyday experience, whereas modern economists define it to be a statement about what would happen if one were to increase the amount of one input while holding all the others constant; the modern definition cannot be verified by glancing at the real world'.

19. I owe enlightenment on this point to Thayer Watkins of the economics department at San Jose State University.

20. Hausman regards (PL9) as implicitly qualified by a vague *ceteris paribus* clause. I am not at all sure what any of the influencing factors are that Hausman takes to be subsumed by this *ceteris paribus* clause. Economists do recognize the existence of not-for-profit firms such as some hospitals, schools, and some labour managed firms (Nicholson, 1978, pp. 276–7). But a *ceteris paribus* clause attached to (PL9) cannot be said to exclude the presence of motivations other than to maximize profits, except on pain of making (PL9) empirically vacuous.

21. If (PL10) is not really accepted as true by economists, then it is not clear what point there is to naturalists about economics like Hausman defending its status as a hedged law. Recall that naturalism about economics says that the *accepted* generalizations of economics include a group of phenomenological laws and a corpus of fundamental laws which explain the phenomenological laws.

22. Of course, (RC) is only one necessary condition for justifiably regarding a generalization as a genuine hedged law. But (LD) also meets the other conditions. One is the lawlikeness condition which says that a generalization G qualified by a *ceteris paribus* clause is a law only if G is lawlike. But (LD) is lawlike as it supports counterfactual conditionals such as 'If the prices of cars had fallen sharply in the Silicon Valley during September 1996, then, *ceteris paribus*, the quantity of cars demanded would have risen'. And (LD) also satisfies the excusability condition which is stated in note 15 above. When 'A good's own price and the quantity of the good demanded are negatively related' breaks down in real world cases, economists are usually able to explain the breakdown in terms of a change in one or more of the factors – consumers' income, tastes of consumers, etc. – that are subsumed by '*ceteris paribus*' in (LD).

23. Harold Kincaid (1996, pp. 232–7) uses the term 'the laws of supply and demand' to

refer to a rather motley group of microeconomic generalizations. These include (A) the law of demand, (B) the generalization that changes in the price of a good cause same direction changes in the quantity of the good supplied, and (C) the comparative static generalizations that tell us what happens to *equilibrium* price and quantity when the demand curve or the supply curve *shift*. An example of (C) is 'If the demand curve shifts out (demand increases)' and the supply curve does not shift, then equilibrium price and quantity both increase. Kincaid apparently regards (A) to (C) as genuine scientific laws, and I agree with him that (A) is a law. However, Kincaid apparently overlooks the fact that (B) and (C) are only applicable to competitive markets, that is, markets in whom there are numerous buyers and sellers each of whom is a price taker. For instance, Kincaid (1996, p. 238) says '... there is no reason to think that the laws of supply and demand hold only for agricultural commodities. There is extensive data showing that firms are generally price and cost sensitive in the ways we would expect according to the law of supply'. Kincaid uses 'the law of supply' to refer to (B) above. Yet (B) is not applicable to firms generally, as there is *no* firm supply curve or industry supply curve in markets where firms are not price takers (Mansfield, 1979, p. 288; Nicholson, 1978, p. 349). And in the majority of real world product markets, firms are not price takers. So (B) is no scientific law correctly describing the behaviour of firms generally. The generalities collected under (C) are often called 'the laws of supply and demand' by economists. But it is not at all clear that they afford true descriptions of the real world as genuine laws must. And this is for the same reason that (PL10) is false. Recall that (PL10) affirms that markets clear or come to equilibrium quickly. As indicated above, this is false as a description of the real world. Not infrequently markets do not go to equilibrium at all. So if the demand curve shifts out in a real world competitive market yet the supply curve does not shift, the equilibrium price rises. Yet the actual market price may not move to equilibrium at all, due to the existence of a price ceiling in the market or some other cause.

5. Is Economics a Galilean Science?

5.1 GALILEAN SCIENCE AND THE ABSTRACTIONIST DEFENCE

The special content version of the 'Is it science?' approach to economics that assumes the positivist condition fails to illuminate economics. Yet there is another form of the 'Is it science?' approach to economics that also makes a discipline being a science conditional upon its having a certain kind of content which should be explored. This form of the special content version of the 'Is it science?' approach is inspired by the conception of science associated with Galileo and his study of terrestrial motion in the first half of the seventeenth century.[1] According to this conception, a scientist assumes away one or more factors operating in a real world system of some kind, and then formulates a hypothesis or theory interrelating other more important or key variables operating in systems of the kind in question. The more important or key variables are abstracted from the various other factors with which they are always entangled in the real world. The hypotheses and theories interrelating the key variables may be called 'ideal' in that they are about cases that do not exist in the real world but only in idea. The Galilean conception regards a discipline as a genuine science if its accepted hypotheses and theories are to a substantial degree ideal hypotheses or theories which *correctly* interrelate the variables with which they are concerned. Let us use the term 'Galilean science' to refer to a discipline that meets this condition, and let us call the condition itself 'the Galilean condition'. There is a form of the special content version of the 'Is it science?' approach to economics that, assuming the Galilean condition for science, asks whether or not the accepted theories of economics are to a substantial extent ideal hypotheses correctly interrelating key economic variables. The primary aim of this chapter is to find out if this form of the special content version of the 'Is it science?' approach sheds real light on economics, an aim which will be realized in an indirect fashion.

Economics has long been criticized for relying excessively on unrealistic assumptions such as 'Firms maximize profits', and 'Firms employ homogeneous factors'. The critics view heavy reliance on such assumptions as defeating any claim economics has to afford much in the way of knowledge of real world economic phenomena. Some economists and economic methodologists attempt to justify the reliance of economics on unrealistic assumptions by appeal to the notion of abstraction. In Chapter 1 of a recent principles textbook, William Baumol and Alan Blinder say:

> Economic theory *does* make unrealistic assumptions; you will encounter many of them in the pages that follow. But this propensity to abstract from reality results from the incredible complexity of the economic world.... Abstraction from unimportant details is necessary to understand the functioning of anything as complex as the economy. (Baumol and Blinder, 1994, p. 11)

By making these remarks in their opening chapter, Baumol and Blinder are perhaps trying to get beginning economics students to be tolerant of unrealistic assumptions they will encounter in studying economics. And so it would be unwise to place too much philosophical weight on Baumol's and Blinder's remarks.

But the point about abstraction and unrealistic assumptions made by Baumol and Blinder has been used to construct a serious reply to the charge that economists rely excessively on unrealistic assumptions. Consider Uskali Mäki's remarks in a fairly recent methodological essay:

> Now that we have an idea of kinds of unrealisticness and types of assumptions, we can better understand a line of thought that may be used for justifying unrealistic elements in economics. Consider Galileo's law first. It is unrealistic in that it is partial. It is unrealistic also in involving assumptions that are mostly false.... The situation is similar in economics. Unrealistic peripheral assumptions help isolate what are believed to be the fundamental relations from the less relevant ones or the major causes from the minor causes of the phenomena studied. As Oliver Hart puts it, '[t]hese models, since they concentrate on one issue, tend to make simplifying and hence often unrealistic assumptions about everything which is not the central focus.... Any theory, if it is to get anywhere, must abstract from many (even most) aspects of reality.' ... The core assumptions are supposed to capture, in pure form, the 'essential features' or the 'more fundamental structure', while the peripheral assumptions, such as negligibility and early-step assumptions, are there to help see the essence of the matter undisturbed by eliminating the actual disturbances or complications. (Mäki, 1994a, p. 246)

By approvingly quoting Hart, Mäki in effect affirms the claim of Baumol and Blinder that abstraction eventuates in unrealistic assumptions, and abstraction is necessary for theory formation in economics. But Mäki goes beyond Baumol and Blinder. The process of assuming away less central or minor factors has as its product unrealistic assumptions. And Mäki says that this process enables the economist, or the physicist, to characterize the relations among the more fundamental or major factors which have been abstracted from the messy, complicated real world situations of the kind that are initially of interest. The goal of discovering the interrelations among the fundamental or important factors of interest to economists requires abstraction from reality, and thus justifies making the unrealistic assumptions abstraction necessarily produces.[2] Let us refer to the line of thought I have just ascribed to Mäki 'the abstractionist defence'.

The abstractionist defence incorporates elements of the Galilean conception of science. The defence sees economists as (A) abstracting key or important variables from the other factors with which they are attended in the real world, and (B) formulating hypotheses or theories about the relations among these important variables. That the practitioners of a discipline do (A) and (B) is a necessary condition for the discipline satisfying the Galilean condition for science. The abstractionist defence exploits elements of the Galilean conception of science in the service of justifying economists making the unrealistic assumptions they do. However, as presented by Mäki or anyone else to date, the abstractionist defence fails to rebut those who criticize economics for its heavy reliance on unrealistic assumptions. And the reason for the failure of the defence is also grounds for saying that economics does not satisfy the Galilean condition that a discipline is a science if its accepted generalizations are to a substantial degree ideal hypotheses or theories correctly interrelating the variables with which they are concerned. It will prove useful first to bring out the reason why the abstractionist defence is a failure. It is then a short step to showing that economics does not satisfy the Galilean condition for science. This indirect approach to evaluating the special content version of the 'Is it science?' approach that assumes the Galilean condition will enable me to make my evaluation of this special content version more meaningful by connecting it with the unrealistic assumptions issue.

5.2   ABSTRACTION, PARTIAL REPRESENTATION AND IDEALIZATION

It is not fruitful to proceed further without clarifying the notion of abstraction and several related concepts that are crucial to the discussion here. A particular real world situation, or kind of real world situation, can be represented in a variety of ways – a verbal description, a map, a diagram, and so on. In the representation one or more aspects of the real world item represented is omitted while other aspects are included in the representation. This process of omission and selective inclusion is abstraction from reality. A map of the streets of San Francisco omits some small streets and includes other larger streets; Galileo describes the behaviour of bodies falling to Earth omitting the factor of air resistance but including the variable acceleration. Both the cartographer and Galileo abstract in the sense described. The process of abstraction has two different types of products. One is *partial representation*, while the other is *idealization*. A partial representation is just that; it is a representation of some sort – a verbal description, a map, etc. – that does not convey or identify all the aspects of what it is about or refers to. It is a purported partial account of the facts about something.[3] A map of the streets of San Francisco omits some small streets, and so it is a partial representation. Partial representations are found in economics. An economist develops a simple Keynesian income–expenditure model. In the model, equilibrium real GDP is determined by the level of aggregate expenditure AE. A key component of AE is planned investment I. The economist assumes that

(1) I is affected by the interest rate and expectations of firm managers about the future profitability of investment projects.

But the economist may regard (1) as a partial representation of the variables affecting I. He may also view changes in output or income as an independent variable affecting I, even though changes in output is not mentioned in (1). Note that partial representations are often true or accurate. A representation need not be complete or exhaustive to be accurate. 'San Francisco has several buildings over 30 storeys' is true, though the statement does not convey many features of the city. (1) is correct, even though the interest rate and firm managers' expectations are not the only variables affecting I.

Idealization, the other type of product of abstraction, is common in science, and it typically works like this.[4] A scientist omits a factor or variable operating in all real world situations or systems of a kind K, and formulates a hypothesis – call it an 'ideal hypothesis' – about the relation between *other* factors operating in all real world instances of K. As Charles Wallis (1994, p. 411) says, '... mainstream idealization most often idealizes from factors operant upon all real world systems in all cases so as to capture a real relation between other factors also operant in all real world systems all of the time'. Note that the *omitted* variable does have an effect in all real world instances of K, though often the effect may be minor or negligible. But in the process of constructing the ideal hypothesis, the scientist *assumes* that the omitted variable has no effect at all or simply does not exist. Let us call this assumption an 'idealizing assumption'. An idealizing assumption is *false* as a description of the real world, and it is believed to be false by the scientist. (The connection between the ideal hypothesis and the true/false distinction will be treated below.) I will use the term 'idealization' to refer to both idealizing assumptions and the ideal hypotheses built upon them. For example, Galileo studied the behaviour of bodies falling to Earth. In the course of his enquiries he ignored or omitted the factor of air resistance. This is tantamount to saying that Galileo assumed the hypothesis

(H1) Air resistance has no effect on falling bodies.

(H1) is a way of stating Galileo's idealizing assumption. Another way of stating it would be 'Air resistance does not exist'. Of course, he knew that (H1) is *not* true generally of bodies falling to Earth in the real world. Under (H1), Galileo devised a number of hypotheses to describe the motion of falling bodies. One is

(H2) All bodies fall at a constant acceleration.

This is one of Galileo's ideal hypotheses. So, Galileo stripped away the factor of air resistance at least initially in his study of falling bodies, selectively including other variables like acceleration. The issue of this process of abstraction is the idealizing assumption (H1), and the ideal hypothesis (H2). Both (H1) and (H2) are idealizations in the sense used here.

Generally, an idealizing assumption assumes the non-existence of an aspect of a real world situation of some kind, and the assumption is used in constructing a hypothesis or theory. An ideal hypothesis or theory is a hypothesis, or a theory, built upon, or including, one or more idealizing assumptions. Together idealizing assumptions and ideal hypotheses or theories comprise the class of idealizations.[5] This description makes idealizations quite distinct from partial representations, the other kind of product of abstraction. A partial representation neglects to mention something that is present. But an idealization either (A) assumes the non-existence of something that is present, or (B) interrelates a number of factors or variables on the assumption of the non-existence of certain other factors. I have used 'idealizing assumption' to refer to idealizations of type (A), and 'ideal hypotheses or theories' to denote idealizations of type (B). A map of the streets of Boston may omit a number of small streets, and thus is a partial representation. But the map does not assume – or the cartographer does not assume – that the small streets do not exist. Nor does the map express relations among the streets it includes on the assumption that the small streets omitted do not exist. Maps are not normally idealizations. Sentence (1) above, which lists some key variables affecting *ex ante* investment, is also a partial representation, but not an idealization. It is not an idealization because it does not fit description (A) or (B). Note that (1) does not say that investment is affected by the interest rate and expectations of firm managers on the assumption that some other factors do not exist.

Though there are partial representations that are not idealizations, it would be difficult to give an example of an idealization that is not a partial representation. For it would be difficult if not impossible to give *any* description of something that is literally complete or exhaustive. And so it is hard to see that any idealization could be regarded as a literally complete characterization of something. Also, there may well be similarities between partial representations and idealizations. For example, both reduce complexity in an obvious way. But the fact that they are similar hardly entails that there is no distinction between partial representations and idealizations. There is a real distinction here as is indicated by my general descriptions, as well as the examples supplied of partial representations that are not idealizations.

A standard way of forming an idealizing assumption is to take to some *limit*, such as zero, a magnitude that does not assume that limiting value in the real world. The idealizing assumption here is that the magnitude in question assumes the value at the limit. For example, consider the following passage from a physics text prefacing the formulation of the law for the period of a simple pendulum:

> If you hang an apple down a stairwell at the end of a long thread and set it swinging with a small amplitude, the apple seems to move back and forth in a simple harmonic motion. We idealize this problem to that of a *simple pendulum*, which is a particle of mass m suspended from an inextendable,

massless string of length L ... (Halliday and Resnick, 1988, p. 313, italics in original)

In the second sentence, the authors in effect assume

(H3) The mass of the string or rod suspending a pendulum bob is zero.

Of course, in the real world there are no massless strings or rods which suspend pendulum bobs. But (H3) is an idealizing assumption which takes the mass of a pendulum's connecting rod to a limit, to wit, zero, which it never reaches in the real world. Or, to take an economic example, the model of perfect competition in microeconomics is typically developed by starting out with a variety of assumptions that define a perfectly competitive market (Henderson and Quandt, 1980, p. 136). One of these assumptions is

(H4) Buyers and sellers have perfect information.

Of course, in the real world it is never true that each buyer and each seller has complete or perfect information. But (H4) is an idealizing assumption which in effect increases the information buyers and sellers do have up to a limit, to wit, complete information, which it never reaches in the real world.

An additional point is crucial here. There are two methods for empirically *testing* ideal hypotheses and theories which are variants of essentially the same approach. What I will call the 'direct method' is this. A scientist finds, or creates, a real world situation in which the factor or factors *omitted* from the ideal hypothesis have a *negligible* effect. Suppose that such a real world situation is found or created. The scientist can derive a *prediction* about this situation from the ideal hypothesis under test, plus the assumption that in the situation at hand the omitted factor has a negligible effect. (As I am using the term 'prediction', predictions may record the occurrence of data already known to exist, or may predict data whose occurrence has yet to be ascertained; in other words, predictions may be *ex post* or *ex ante*.) Following Alan Musgrave (1981, pp. 235–8), let us use 'negligibility assumption' to refer to the assumption that in the real world situation the omitted factor has a negligible effect.[6] Should the prediction be verified, this would confirm or afford evidential support for the ideal hypothesis; but should the prediction prove false or inaccurate, this would disconfirm or provide evidence against the ideal hypothesis. (This is over simplified in light of the falsity of the simple hypothetico-deductivist account of testing and confirmation; but it will do for present purposes.) The availability of suitable and *true* negligibility assumptions is essential for the confirmation or disconfirmation of ideal hypotheses and theories on the direct method.

The second method for testing ideal hypotheses, which I will call the 'indirect method', works like this. A scientist finds, or creates, a series of real world cases in which (A) the factor omitted from the ideal hypothesis – the factor assumed away by the idealizing assumption – has less and less of an effect as we move through the series of cases, though perhaps still a non-negligible effect; and then (B) the scientist determines whether or not the observed outcomes in the series of cases get closer and closer to the outcome predicted by the ideal hypothesis were the omitted factor to have *no effect*. If the observed outcomes in the series of cases do get closer and closer, this would provide evidence *for* the ideal hypothesis. But if the observed outcomes do not get closer and closer to the outcome predicted by the ideal hypothesis were the omitted factor to have no effect, then this would afford evidence *against* the ideal hypothesis. The indirect method is really parasitic on the direct method. To see this we need only ask why the observed outcomes getting closer and closer to the outcome predicted by the ideal hypothesis were the omitted factors to have no effect, would be evidence for the ideal hypothesis. The answer is that the observed outcomes getting closer and closer is evidence that were the ideal hypothesis tested using the *direct method,* the test results would confirm the hypothesis. Testing an ideal hypothesis by the indirect method confirms or disconfirms by indicating the likely results of testing by the direct method.

It is worth emphasizing that I have only been describing the methods of empirically testing ideal hypotheses and theories. My discussion in no way purports to characterize *all* the kinds of arguments that might be given for or against ideal hypotheses. For example, one way to argue for an ideal hypothesis would be to deduce it from a broader theory that is acceptable, a style of argument which does not appeal to the results of testing the ideal hypothesis.[7] In addition, it is important not to confuse ideal hypotheses with laws or hypotheses qualified by *ceteris paribus* clauses. That there may be ways of testing *ceteris paribus* laws that have not been mentioned here, does *not* entail that there are ways of empirically testing ideal hypotheses other than the direct and indirect methods.

Let me buttress what I have just said by showing that ideal hypotheses are distinct from laws or generalizations qualified by *ceteris paribus* clauses. The discussion will also serve to further sharpen the idea of an ideal hypothesis. Let us consider the law of demand, an economic generalization qualified by a *ceteris paribus* clause. It can be expressed as follows:

(LD) *Ceteris paribus*, a good's own price and the quantity of the good demanded are negatively related.

As noted in section 4.3 above, '*ceteris paribus*' in (LD) subsumes a variety of factors such as consumers' level of income, the prices of related goods like substitutes and complements and the number of buyers in the market for the good. In stating (LD), the force of the *ceteris paribus* clause is to assume that the factors subsumed by the clause are unchanging. A *ceteris paribus* law like (LD) frames a relation between an explicitly identified independent variable, the good's own price in the case of (LD), and a dependent variable, quantity demanded in (LD). But the relation is framed on the assumption that the potentially disturbing factors subsumed by the *ceteris paribus* clause are not changing.

Recall that an *idealizing assumption* assumes away an influencing factor operating in *all* real world situations of a kind *K*; the factor assumed away *always* has an effect, however minor, in real world situations of kind *K*. And the *ideal hypothesis* frames a relationship that is supposed to hold in the absence of the factor assumed away. But the factors subsumed by a *ceteris paribus* clause do *not always* operate in real world cases in which the dependent variable changes. For example, often the quantity of a good demanded changes and yet the number of buyers in the market has not changed at all; some independent variable other than the number of buyers has caused the change in quantity demanded. Yet the number of buyers is a factor subsumed by the *ceteris paribus* clause in (LD). The inference is that the factors subsumed by a *ceteris paribus* clause are *not* strictly analogous to the factors assumed away in the case of framing an ideal hypothesis. The factors subsumed by a *ceteris paribus* clause do not always play a role in causing changes in the dependent variable, whilst the factors assumed away in constructing an ideal hypothesis always have some effect in real world cases of the relevant kind. So the idealizing assumptions on which ideal hypotheses are built are not equivalent to *ceteris paribus* clauses. And the fact that ideal hypotheses are built on idealizing assumptions is no warrant for taking such hypotheses to be qualified by *ceteris paribus* clauses in the manner of the law of demand (LD).[8] This should reduce any temptation to assume that any method for testing a *ceteris paribus* law that is not equivalent to the direct or indirect methods, is automatically also a method for testing an ideal hypothesis.

5.3 TWO KINDS OF UNREALISTICNESS AND HYPOTHETICAL TRUTH

Evaluating the abstractionist defence requires some conceptual apparatus additional to that provided in the previous section. Let us start with the term 'unrealistic' as applied to assumptions or statements in economics or elsewhere. One sense of this term is described by Ernest Nagel in a paper published some years ago when he (1973, p. 133) says 'A statement can be said to be unrealistic because it does not give an "exhaustive" description of some object, so that it mentions only some traits actually characterizing the object but ignores an endless number of other traits also present'. Obviously unrealistic statements in this sense are the same as what I called 'partial descriptions' in section 5.2 above. But there is another sense of 'unrealistic' in which it is not co-extensive with 'partial description'. This other sense is employed by Daniel Hausman in characterizing the position of those who criticize economics for its unrealistic assumptions. Hausman says:

> The fundamental theory of neoclassical economics is too 'unrealistic.' If taken literally and without qualification, the basic 'laws' of economics are simply false. It is not true that all businessmen always attempt to maximize profit or that individuals are never satisfied. (Hausman, 1992b, p. 100)

As applied in this passage to generalizations of neoclassical microeconomics, 'unrealistic' is a synonym of 'false'. Thus, in one sense of 'unrealistic', let us use 'unrealistic$_p$' to express it, the term refers to partial descriptions or representations. But in another sense, 'unrealistic' denotes statements or assumptions that are false, are untrue descriptions of the world. Let us use 'unrealistic$_f$' to express this sense. Of course, a statement that is unrealistic$_p$ may be false, in which case it is also unrealistic$_f$.

Let us connect up the distinction between the two sorts of products of abstraction, partial representations and idealizations, with the distinction just drawn between the two kinds of unrealisticness. Partial representations are all unrealistic$_p$, but there are *true* partial descriptions that are not unrealistic$_f$. These are quite common in economics. Consider the following economic truths:

(1) When the Federal Reserve System (FED) purchases US Treasury debt, the reserves of banks increase.

(2) Persistent growth in the money supply in excess of the growth in real GDP is a cause of inflation.

Being true, (1) and (2) are not unrealistic$_f$. However, they are unrealistic$_p$. (1) omits mention of any effect of an increase in bank reserves on the money supply or interest rates such as the federal funds rate, omits mention of FED goals in purchasing Treasury securities, and so on. (2) neglects to mention causes of inflation other than excessive money growth, omits mention of real world examples of inflations caused by excessive money growth like the post World War I German hyperinflation, and so on. Idealizing assumptions are all unrealistic$_f$ in that they are false of the real world. But what of ideal hypotheses and theories which are built upon or include idealizing assumptions? Are ideal hypotheses and theories unrealistic$_f$? Ernest Nagel is correct when he (1973, p. 135) says '... nor are they [ideal hypotheses and theories] literally false of anything; their distinguishing mark is the fact that when they are strictly construed, they are applicable to nothing actual'. There are no real world instances of the cases which ideal hypotheses and theories are about. Since such hypotheses and theories are not even about real world cases, they are not false descriptions of the real world. But we could *interpret* an ideal hypothesis or theory as being about the real world, in which case it would be unrealistic$_f$ given that the factors it omits do have an effect, and sometimes a non-negligible one, in all the real world cases of the relevant sort. Galileo's ideal hypothesis

(H2) All bodies fall to Earth at a constant acceleration

does not truly describe the behaviour of a feather dropped from a tower in a brisk wind. And (H2) is false when interpreted as a description of the behaviour of all bodies in the real world.

However, there is a sort of *truth* of which ideal hypotheses and theories are capable. It is *hypothetical truth*, a notion employed by nineteenth century economic methodologists like J.E. Cairnes. Cairnes explains the notion as follows:

> But he [the economist] can never be certain that he does not omit some essential circumstance, and indeed, it is scarcely possible to include all: it is evident, therefore, that, as is the case in those deductive physical sciences to which I have alluded, his conclusion will correspond with the facts *only in the absence of disturbing causes*, which is, in other words, to say that they represent not positive but hypothetic truth. (Cairnes, 1965, p. 64, italics in original)

Thus, to say that an ideal hypothesis or theory H is *hypothetically true*, is to say that were the factors omitted in the construction of H somehow entirely removed from the real world, H would be a true description of the world. Cairnes's hypothetical truth is simply what would be ordinary truth were certain disturbing factors absent from the world.[9] Galileo's hypothesis that bodies fall with a constant acceleration is an example that proves the point. Were air resistance entirely removed from the world, feathers and billiard balls would fall to Earth with the same constant acceleration, *viz.*, approximately 32 feet per second each second. Of course, an ideal hypothesis or theory can be *hypothetically false*. Suppose an ideal hypothesis H. Imagine that, were the factors omitted in framing H removed from the world, H would be a false description of the world. In this case H is hypothetically false.

Much discussion of the issue of unrealistic assumptions in economics has been bedevilled by the lack of an adequate conceptual apparatus within which to discuss the issue. As a result, distinctions get blurred, mistaken inferences made and the like.[10] The discussion here of abstraction, partial representations, idealizing assumptions, ideal hypotheses, the two kinds of unrealisticness and hypothetical truth provides a useful conceptual framework for evaluating the abstractionist defence, and thereby the special content version of the 'Is it science?' approach to economics that assumes the Galilean condition for science.

5.4   THE FAILURE OF THE ABSTRACTIONIST DEFENCE

Let us use the conceptual apparatus that has been developed to formulate the abstractionist defence in a perspicuous way. Essentially the defence appeals to the necessity of abstraction in economics to defend the discipline's substantial reliance on unrealistic assumptions. Abstraction is necessary to study complex, real world economic phenomena, and abstraction eventuates in unrealistic assumptions. But the abstractionist defence is not of much interest if it is taken as a defence of unrealistic$_p$ assumptions in economics. We can all readily agree that economics, like any discipline, must contain unrealistic$_p$ statements, as no one could reasonably expect a discipline to afford literally exhaustive descriptions of the phenomena with which it is concerned. Recall the passage quoted from Hausman some paragraphs back in which he characterizes the position of those who criticize economics for its unrealistic assumptions. In this passage Hausman says, 'The fundamental theory of neoclassical economics is too "unrealistic." If taken literally and without qualification, the basic "laws" of economics are simply false'. As this quote makes clear, the critics of economics object to the discipline's reliance on false and therefore unrealistic$_f$ statements. Thus, the abstractionist defence must be taken to be a defence of unrealistic$_f$ assumptions in economics if it is to be of genuine interest.

Recall that abstraction results in two different types of products. One is partial description or representation, while the other is idealization, that is, idealizing assumptions and ideal hypotheses. Let us use 'partializing abstraction' to refer to abstraction resulting in partial representation that is not an idealization; and let us use 'idealizing abstraction' to denote abstraction that eventuates in idealization. Now the abstractionist defence could not reasonably hope to be a successful defence of unrealistic$_f$ assumptions in economics if it is interpreted as appealing to partializing abstraction. For partializing abstraction may result in partial descriptions that are in fact unrealistic$_f$ (false). But how could an appeal to the need for abstraction be an adequate defence of a partial representation which is false or inaccurate? Suppose that a person makes a map of the streets of San Francisco which is a partial representation in that it omits many smaller streets, and the map also does *not* accurately represent the location and relation of streets that it does include. If criticized, this map could not be defended on the ground that abstraction is needed to make a map of the streets of San Francisco useful for the average visitor to the city. A need for abstraction can justify the *omission* of things from a partial representation, but it cannot be an adequate defence of *inaccuracy or falsehood* in a partial representation (that is not an idealization). Inaccuracy or falsehood cannot be justified by a need to omit or provide less than a complete description.

It is not clear that those who have used the abstractionist defence to justify unrealistic$_f$ assumptions in economics have always realized that they cannot appeal to *partializing* abstraction. (Indeed, as note 10 to this chapter indicates, some who use the abstractionist defence have not realized this fact.) But, as argued in the preceding paragraph, appealing to partializing abstraction cannot justify unrealistic$_f$ (false) assumptions. Thus, the abstractionist defence must be interpreted as appealing to *idealizing* abstraction, if it is to have even the slightest chance of successfully defending economists' reliance on unrealistic$_f$ assumptions. But how are we to understand the abstractionist defence when interpreted in this manner? The following line of thought provides the answer to this question:

> To acquire knowledge of complex, real world economic phenomena, idealizing abstraction is frequently necessary. Economists must often extract a few key variables from the messy, complex real world and analyse their interrelations,

assuming away less important circumstances with which these key variables are entangled in reality. Idealizing abstraction generates the idealizing assumptions of economics which are unrealistic$_f$. It also indirectly issues in ideal hypotheses and models, these being unrealistic$_f$ when interpreted as being about the real world. It is the ideal hypotheses and models that purportedly express the interrelations among key economic variables, and can express economic knowledge. Thus, unrealistic$_f$ assumptions are needed to acquire knowledge of real world economic phenomena.

From now on I will use 'the abstractionist defence' to refer to this line of thought. It is worth noting that it is quite similar to Mäki's version of the abstractionist defence set out in section 5.1 above.

Does the abstractionist defence succeed in rebutting those who criticize economics for its unrealistic$_f$ assumptions? It does not. The critics in question do not condemn economics because it contains any unrealistic$_f$ assumptions whatever. Rather the critics believe that the *specific* unrealistic$_f$ assumptions or statements economics contains are the problem. For example, critics of neoclassical microeconomics have objected to its assumption that firms hire an amount of an input like labour at which marginal revenue product of the input equals marginal factor cost of the input. (Of course, this assumption is implied by profit maximization.) They have argued that this assumption is unrealistic$_f$ (false), and so neoclassical theory fails to provide understanding of the behaviour of real world firms in the hiring of labour.[11] The abstractionist defence does nothing to remove this type of substantive concern about the unrealistic$_f$ assumptions of economics. And I will now show that the abstractionist defence really does fail.

It is certainly *not* true that a *sufficient* condition for economics or any other discipline providing knowledge of real world phenomena that it merely include ideal hypotheses or theories. For instance, not just any ideal hypothesis in physics would be a contribution to knowledge of physical phenomena. Suppose that Galileo, assuming away air resistance, had hypothesized that

(H5) Bodies fall to Earth with a constant velocity.

This is an ideal hypothesis. But (H5) would not advance our knowledge of bodies falling to Earth, as (H5) is hypothetically false. Were air resistance absent from the world, bodies would fall with a constant acceleration, not a constant velocity. I submit, then, that a necessary condition for an ideal hypothesis or theory H contributing to knowledge of the real world, is that H be *hypothetically true*. Let us call this 'the hypothetical truth condition'. Of course, it is analogous to the familiar requirement that if it is known that *P*, then it must be that *P* is true, that is, that truth is a necessary condition for knowledge.

The hypothetical truth condition can be used to construct an argument for the failure of the abstractionist defence. Here is the argument – call it 'Argument A'.

(P1) In order successfully to rebut the position of those who criticize economics for its unrealistic$_f$ assumptions, the abstractionist defence would have to provide, or tell us where to find, good evidence that the ideal theories of economics are hypothetically true.

(P2) But (a) the abstractionist defence does not direct our attention to *any* evidence for the hypothetical truth of ideal theories in economics, and (b) as economics has in fact developed, there is *insufficient* evidence that the ideal theories of economics are hypothetically true.

So, (C) the abstractionist defence not only does not succeed in answering the critics in question, but, given the present state of economics, it does not appear that it could succeed.

Premise (P1) is an application of the hypothetical truth condition. The rationale for (P1) is that the critics of economics claim that the presence of unrealistic$_f$ assumptions in economics calls into question any claim of the discipline to afford *knowledge* of the real world. The abstractionist defence itself represents the unrealistic$_f$ assumptions of economics as being included in its ideal theories. And, by the hypothetical truth condition, ideal theories furnish knowledge of the real world only if they are hypothetically true.

Clause (a) of premise (P2) is obviously true. Just look at the abstractionist defence as formulated a few paragraphs back. It does not even acknowledge the hypothetical truth/hypothetical falsehood distinction, much less direct our attention to the location of evidence of the hypothetical truth of ideal economic theories. Clause (b) of premise (P2) is certainly not obviously true. But a good case can be made for clause (b).

As noted previously, ideal theories and hypotheses are capable of empirical test. The two methods of testing such theories are described above, *viz.*, the direct method and the indirect method. It is reasonable to say that an ideal theory or hypothesis that have been confirmed through testing by either method is probably hypothetically true; confirmation by test results using either method would afford evidence of the hypothetical truth of the ideal theory tested. But an ideal theory that has been disconfirmed in repeated testing using either method is probably false; disconfirmation by test results is evidence of hypothetical falsity of the ideal theory tested. Economics certainly does appear to contain a variety of ideal theories or models. Prominent examples are the model of a perfectly competitive market, the model of individual choice in situations involving risk (expected utility theory), the theory of consumer choice (constituted by (PL1) to (PL6) of section 4.2 above), the classical model of international trade, and what Hausman (1992a, pp. 168–9) calls 'abstract general equilibrium theories'. (Abstract or Walrasian general equilibrium theories include all the commodities in an economy, and address the question of whether there can be a set of prices which clear all markets in a perfectly competitive economy simultaneously.) The classical model of international trade includes such idealizing assumptions as 'Factors of production are perfectly mobile between industries within each country' and 'Factors cannot move between countries engaged in trade'. (Recall that ideal theories are built on or include one or more idealizing assumptions.) I have some qualms about classifying expected utility theory as an ideal theory, because it is not easy to be confident about what its idealizing assumptions are. But one good candidate is the compound lottery axiom, which in effect assumes away such real world factors as the pleasure gamblers typically get from gambling (see Henderson and Quandt, 1980, pp. 53–4). The theory of consumer choice is developed on the idealizing assumption that consumers have perfect information. Abstract general equilibrium theories include such idealizing assumptions as that agents have perfect information, an idealizing assumption shared with the model of a perfectly competitive market.[12]

However, there is an important disanalogy between ideal economic theories and ideal hypotheses in physics. Various ideal hypotheses in physics have been tested by the direct method, and the test results have *confirmed* them. For instance, consider again Galileo's ideal hypothesis

(H2) Bodies fall to Earth at a constant acceleration.

Physicists have tested (H2) by dropping a billiard ball and making a strobe photograph of its fall. (Air resistance of course has a negligible effect on a billiard ball falling to Earth over a short distance.) Measurements on the photograph show that the acceleration of the ball is indeed constant. (H2) has been confirmed by the direct method, and is (probably) hypothetically true. But economics is not in the position of physics. One important ideal economic theory that has been subjected to empirical test is expected utility theory. But the tests results have apparently *disconfirmed* expected utility theory. Early experiments which produced disconfirming evidence were done by Sarah Lichtenstein and Paul Slovic. Lichtenstein and Slovic (1971) predicted that pairs of gambles could be constructed such that people would choose one member of the pair and yet place a higher monetary value on the other member of the pair. This phenomenon is called 'preference reversal'. Lichtenstein and Slovic conducted actual experiments and the predicted effect was observed, and subsequent experiments produced the same result. But people exhibiting preference reversal is not consistent with expected utility theory.[13] So, there is in fact evidence that expected utility theory is hypothetically *false*. This circumstance is part of the argument for clause (b) of premise (P2) of Argument A.

The rest of the case for clause (b) of premise (P2) appeals to the fact that little or no effort has been made by economists to test *ideal* economic theories by either the direct or indirect methods.[14] Of course, some ideal economic theories do generate false predictions. For instance, the classical model of international trade makes the following prediction (see Husted and Melvin, 1990, pp. 81–2):

(1) Countries will specialize completely in producing goods that they export, and will not produce at all the goods that they import.

(1) is obviously not a correct prediction of what happens in the real world in countries which conduct trade with each other. The USA both produces and imports wine. That the classical model of trade generates false predictions like (1) does *not* show that the model is hypothetically false. Galileo's ideal hypothesis (H2) stated above makes false predictions about the behaviour of feathers dropped from towers in a brisk wind, and yet (H2) is hypothetically *true*. To empirically test for the hypothetical truth of the classical trade model, the direct or indirect methods would have to be used. And, to my knowledge, neither method has ever been used to test the classical trade model. But the fact that the model has not been tested in an appropriate way, means that there is a *lack* of evidence for its hypothetical truth via empirical testing. The model of a perfectly competitive market is another ideal model in the same situation. This is a very important model in economics. The model is employed in establishing important results in welfare economics, such as the theorem that, under suitable conditions, an economy with only perfectly competitive markets attains a Pareto optimum. Also, the model of perfect competition is used as a framework for understanding real world markets of various kinds such as markets for agricultural commodities. But the model of perfect competition has not been subjected to empirical test by

either the direct or the indirect methods. Nor have abstract or Walrasian general equilibrium theories been subjected to empirical test using either of these methods. Indeed, it is a well-known complaint about Walrasian general equilibrium theories that they are not testable at all.

It might be said that my position here is mistaken, because the indirect method has in fact been used to test and confirm ideal economic models. Specifically, the indirect method has been used to test those numerous ideal economic models which assume that perfect information is possessed by economic agents. The way this has happened is as follows. A market is informationally efficient if the prices in the market always fully reflect all available information. Empirical work has been done which can be summed up by the following statement:

(OR) As the quantity and quality of information available to consumers in various markets has improved, these markets get closer and closer to being informationally efficient.

For instance, a well-known study done a number of years ago of markets for eyeglasses indicated that the improved information provided by advertising of eyeglasses, when legally allowed, results in consumers paying lower prices for eyeglasses, thereby reflecting the improved information (Benham, 1972). Now, the objection continues, the ideal economic models which assume perfect information predict or imply that markets are informationally efficient. Thus, my objector concludes, as we get closer and closer to perfect information, the observed results that (OR) records come closer and closer to the outcome predicted by ideal economic models, like the model of perfect competition, that assume perfect information. This means that the indirect method has in effect been used to test ideal models that assume perfect information, and the models have been *confirmed*.

But the line of thought just described is not credible. I will assume for the sake of argument that (OR) is true. But for one, in his study of the eyeglasses market, Lee Benham, the economist who did the study, did *not* say that he regarded his study as confirming, by the indirect or any other method, *any* of the ideal economic models which assume perfect information. Benham's avowed purpose was just to adjudicate between two competing views about the effects of advertising on prices of products (see Benham, 1972, p. 337, pp. 351–2). Secondly and more importantly, (OR) simply does not constitute confirming evidence by the indirect method of an ideal economic model like the model of perfect competition. Suppose that in real world markets buyers somehow manage to acquire perfect information. Suppose further that these real world markets are also informationally efficient thereby verifying

(2) Markets are informationally efficient.

(2) is supposed to be implied by the ideal models that assume perfect information. The objection in the preceding paragraph is committed to saying that (2) turning out to be true under perfect information would confirm the ideal models assuming perfect information. If the observed results (OR) records really do confirm by the *indirect method* the ideal models assuming perfect information, then markets actually being informationally efficient when buyers do have perfect information should directly confirm the ideal models in question. But surely this circumstance would provide no such confirmation of these ideal models. How could (2) turning out to be true under perfect information simultaneously confirm or provide evidential support for *all* the ideal models that assume perfect information? Just because (2) is true under perfect information would hardly seem enough to confirm, all at the same time, the model of perfect competition, the theory of consumer choice, the classical model of trade, abstract equilibrium theories, and so on. These models make particular and to some extent quite different assumptions. And (2) is not sufficiently connected in a specific enough way with the assumptions of the ideal models in question so that (2) turning out to be true under perfect information would confirm these assumptions. For instance, the model of perfect competition assumes that firms seek to maximize profits. But (2) turning out to be true under complete information would hardly confirm this assumption. I conclude that the objection set out in the preceding paragraph fails to show that ideal economic models which assume perfect information have been tested and confirmed by the indirect method. And so the objection fails to establish that the indirect method has been used to test and confirm ideal economic models.

It has been argued that clause (b) of premise (P2) of Argument A is correct. The argument has appealed to the fact that at least one prominent ideal economic theory, to wit, expected utility theory, has been disconfirmed by empirical test, *and* the fact that little has been done by economists to test their ideal economic theories. This pair of facts does afford support for thinking that there is insufficient evidence for the hypothetical truth of ideal economic theories, which is what clause (b) of premise (P2) affirms. It is possible to provide at least a partial explanation for the scant amount of empirical testing of ideal economic models. Daniel Hausman suggests the following:

The claims of economics are particularly difficult to test, and economists have been particularly loathe to test them. As the third criticism above alleges, testing plays a comparatively smaller role in economics than it does in many of the natural sciences.... Economists do little testing for three reasons.... Second, economists are generally unable to do controlled experiments. Since it is generally impossible to escape the disturbances and the mess of real economic circumstances, it is extremely difficult to get informative results. (Hausman, 1992b, pp. 101–2)

Hausman can be interpreted as saying that it is difficult if not impossible to find or create real world situations in which the factors *omitted* in the framing of ideal economic theories have a *negligible effect*. This is how I interpret his talk of it being 'impossible to escape the disturbances and the mess of real economic circumstances'. But since *true* negligibility assumptions are required for testing ideal theories by the direct method, we should then expect that economists would do little testing of their ideal theories using that method. The obstacle to testing in economics which Hausman notes also may make it difficult to test ideal economic models using the indirect method. Using this method requires finding or creating a series of cases in which the factors omitted from the ideal theory have less and less of an effect. But if, as Hausman notes, it is 'impossible to escape the disturbances and the mess of real economic circumstances', then it may not be possible to find or create a series of cases of the sort required for the application of the indirect method.

5.5 ECONOMICS AND GALILEAN SCIENCE

The previous section establishes that the abstractionist defence does not successfully rebut those who criticize economics for its unrealistic assumptions. And the reason for the failure of the defence is essentially the fact that there is insufficient evidence that the ideal theories of economics are hypothetically true. This same fact also spells failure for the form of the 'Is it science?' approach to economics that assumes the Galilean condition. This form of the 'Is it science?' approach leads to no positive characterization of economics which tells us what the discipline is about.

Recall that the Galilean condition says that a discipline is a genuine science if its accepted hypotheses or theories are to a substantial degree ideal hypotheses or theories which correctly interrelate the variables with which they are concerned. In light of the concept of hypothetical truth elucidated in section 5.3, we can rephrase the Galilean condition to say that a discipline is a genuine science if its accepted hypotheses or theories are to a substantial degree ideal hypotheses or theories that are hypothetically true. This confers a clear sense on the term 'correctly interrelate' used in the original formulation of the Galilean condition. A discipline that meets the Galilean condition is a Galilean science, and a discipline that fails to fulfil the Galilean condition is not a Galilean science. Again, there is insufficient evidence that the ideal theories of economics are hypothetically true. Thus, as economics has so far developed, there is no reason to say that the discipline meets the Galilean condition for science; and therefore an adequate basis is lacking for regarding economics as a Galilean science. This in turn supports saying that the form of the 'Is it science?' approach to economics that assumes the Galilean condition for being a science leads to no positive account of the discipline that illuminates it for us.

Three varieties of the 'Is it science?' approach to economics have been discussed in detail. One variety lays down some methodological rule a science must meet, and then attempts to determine whether or not economics conforms to the rule. A second variety claims that to be a science, a discipline must include a corpus of scientific laws some of which are fundamental laws. And the third variety of the 'Is it science?' approach stipulates that a discipline is a science if its accepted hypotheses or theories are to a substantial extent hypothetically true ideal hypotheses or theories. It has been argued in this as well as the previous two chapters that economics cannot be said to meet any of these three standards for being a science. As a result, the 'Is it science?' approach fails to shed any real light on economics; the 'Is it science? approach certainly seems to be a dead end.

NOTES

1. The conception of science associated with Galileo stems from a methodological tradition developed at the University of Padua in the sixteenth century. As J.W.N. Watkins (1965, p. 51) says 'At Padua, during the sixteenth century, a conception of scientific method had been worked out which Galileo and Harvey, and afterwards Hobbes, adopted.'
2. Mäki (1994a, pp. 246–7) says that sometimes unrealistic assumptions are justified by the fact that they serve the goal of increasing formal tractability, that is, make proofs easier to state and follow.
3. Mäki (1994b, pp. 150–1) discusses what he calls 'omissions,' which resemble partial representations in my sense. Though Mäki says that omissions are truth-valueless, whereas many partial representations in my sense do have a truth-value.
4. For a good, brief account of idealization in mainstream science, see Wallis, 1994.
5. Sometimes an idealization is defined as a hypothesis which is incompatible with central, deeply entrenched claims of the discipline to which the hypothesis belongs (Rosenberg,

1976, p. 132). But this definition is not altogether helpful without a criterion for determining whether or not a claim is a central, deeply entrenched part of its discipline. Also, the definition has the unattractive result that an idealization cannot itself be one of the central, deeply entrenched claims of its discipline, except on pain of making the set of such claims internally inconsistent.

6.   As Mäki (1994b, pp. 154–7) notes, negligibility assumptions are quite distinct from idealizing assumptions. The latter are *false* viewed as descriptions of the real world. But negligibility assumptions are often *true* descriptions of the real world. Suppose that a physicist wants to test Galileo's ideal hypothesis (H2) by dropping a billiard ball from a tower. The physicist would make the negligibility assumption that (NA) air resistance has a negligible effect on a billiard ball falling to Earth over a short distance. And (NA) would be true.

7.   Hempel (1966, pp. 38–9) gives the example of deducing the law for freely falling bodies on the Moon from Newton's theory of gravitation plus some additional true premises.

8.   Some philosophers have viewed scientific laws as generalized conditionals of the form 'For any x, if x is F then x is G' which are exceptionless truths about the world. This is a narrow variety of the standard philosophical conception of law treated in section 4.1 above. Let us call it the 'universal generalization conception of laws'. It has been suggested (Giere, 1988, pp. 38–40; Wallis, 1994, pp. 414–5) that on the universal generalization conception, an ideal law like the law for the period of a simple pendulum must be qualified by provisos which are included in the law's very content. A proviso describes some condition that has to be *absent* for an ideal law to be applicable to this or that real world situation, and this condition is *not* idealized from in framing the law. Without qualification by provisos, an ideal law so-called is false, and therefore cannot be a genuine law on the universal generalization conception of laws. To express the ideal law, the perhaps indefinitely many provisos qualifying an ideal law can be subsumed under a single *ceteris paribus* clause attached to the law (though empirical vacuity threatens here). Thus, developing the universal generalization conception of laws leads to seeing ideal laws as a special kind of *ceteris paribus* law. It would take me too far afield to fully deal with this challenge to my attempt to make the distinction between ideal hypotheses and *ceteris paribus* laws like the law of demand. But the line of thought just set out does not succeed in collapsing the distinction. For ideal hypotheses, such as Galileo's hypothesis (H2), do not purport to be exceptionless, generalized conditionals truly describing the real world. So ideal hypotheses need not be construed as qualified by endless provisos, or a single *ceteris paribus* clause subsuming such provisos, in order to preserve some putative status as laws on the universal generalization conception of what a law is.

9.   Uskali Mäki (1994b, pp. 163–4) notes that Cairnes himself thought that the fundamental premises of economic theory, such as 'Individuals maximize utility', are positively true, not hypothetically true. According to Cairnes, it is the conclusions of economic theory which are hypothetically true, since the fundamental premises only take account of some of the causes of real world economic phenomena. But since ideal hypotheses and theories are *false* when interpreted about the real world, it is hard to see how economic ideal hypotheses could be positively true. Hypothetical truth is the best we could hope to get in the realm of ideal hypotheses and theories. Cairnes himself may not have viewed the fundamental premises of economics as ideal hypotheses in the sense used here. Instead he may have adopted a modal view of economic theory. And on the modal view, the fundamental premises of unapplied economic models are indeed positively true. The modal view is treated in Rappaport,

1989 and in Chapter 7 below.

10. Donald McCloskey provides an example of what I am talking about. In his attractive book on price theory, McCloskey relies on the usual assumption that firms maximize profits, which he regards as unrealistic$_f$ (1985b, pp. 237–8). McCloskey defends this unrealistic$_f$ assumption by appeal to the analogy of a map of Baltimore which he says is unrealistic because it leaves out much detail. But McCloskey is blurring the distinction between being unrealistic$_f$ and being unrealistic$_p$. Accurate maps are normally unrealistic$_p$ rather than unrealistic$_f$. As a result, his analogy is unpersuasive. He cannot legitimately defend relying on an unrealistic$_f$ assumption by appeal to the usefulness of an unrealistic$_p$ representation such as a map.

11. A well-known source of this criticism is Lester, 1947.

12. An early and interesting ideal economic theory is J.H. von Thünen's model of agricultural land use. For a brief discussion of this model, see Ekelund and Hébert, 1990, pp. 318–20.

13. I borrow here from Hausman, 1992a, Chapter 13; and Heap, *et al.*, 1992, pp. 43–4. In his illuminating treatment of preference reversal, Hausman suggests that preference reversals violate either the expected utility theory assumption of the transitivity of preferences, or an assumption called 'procedure invariance'. Hausman also notes that some economists have claimed, though not plausibly, that the compound lottery axiom not holding in the experiments caused the people involved to exhibit preference reversals. This is in effect to claim that the direct method was not after all used in testing expected utility theory since what is assumed away by the compound lottery axiom has to have a *negligible effect* in the situations used to test expected utility theory if indeed it is the direct method that is used.

14. It might be thought that some of the assumptions of ideal models are tautologies which could not be refuted by empirical test. For example, an ideal model like the model of perfect competition includes tautologous assumptions such as (A) If firms maximize profits, then they set output at a level at which marginal revenue MR equals marginal cost MC. But this line of thought misconstrues economic models. The assumption or axiom about the firm's goal included in the model of perfect competition is (B) Firms maximize profits. It is not true that (A) is an axiom of the model. But in developing the model of perfect competition, an economist will *infer* from (B) that (C) Firms set output at a level at which MR equals MC. The line of thought in question confuses axioms of a model with the corresponding conditionals of inferences made in developing the model. (A) is the conditional corresponding to the inference from (B) to (C). For a discussion of economic models relevant to the point here, see Rappaport, 1986b, p. 250.

6. Economic Models (I)

6.1 MODELS, MINI-THEORIES AND GLOBAL THEORIES

I suggest that we replace the failed 'Is it science?' approach to economics with an account of economics that places models at the centre of economic thinking. In the Introduction (Chapter 1) it was noted that Gibbard and Varian claim that much economic theorizing is investigating models. No less an economist than John Maynard Keynes also emphasized the role of models in economics. He says 'Economics is a science of thinking in terms of models joined to the art of choosing models which are relevant to the contemporary world'.[1] I agree with the central role Gibbard, Varian and Keynes accord models in economic thinking. More precisely, much economic thinking is the construction or formulation of models and/or their utilization in various cognitive activities such as explanation. For this characterization of economics to be at all illuminating, much more needs to be said about economic models and their uses. In this chapter I will begin to describe the nature of models, a task that will be continued in Chapter 7. Also, the use of models in several key cognitive activities economists engage in will be discussed in this chapter. Chapter 8 will focus on the key role of models in constructing explanations of real world economic phenomena. Finally, some have claimed that the excessive formalism of contemporary economics is bound up with the role of models in economic thinking. This chapter will conclude by arguing that the centrality of models in economics is not responsible for any excessive formalism in contemporary economics.

There are different kinds of items recognized as models by economists themselves, and we need to identify the kind of model that is relevant here. The claim that much economic thinking is the construction and/or use of models is not true for every kind of model. In econometrics the term 'model' is often used as an abbreviation for 'regression model'. Consider

$$C = a + bY + U \qquad (6.1)$$

with C being aggregate consumption spending, Y aggregate disposable income, and U an error or disturbance term. Equation (6.1) is a regression model. Given the presence of the error term in equation (6.1), the relationship between C and Y that it specifies is stochastic rather than exact or deterministic. (Multi-equation regression models contain more than one equation; but some of these equations contain error terms as well.) Regression models are not of interest here. The economic models of interest here specify exact rather than stochastic relations among the variables or factors involved in the models. There is another kind of model in econometrics that is also not germane here. An econometrician may wish to estimate the parameters a and b in equation (6.1) using some set of data. The econometrician would likely use the ordinary least squares (OLS) technique for estimating the values of a and b in the situation from which the data are drawn. The OLS estimates of a and b are the best linear unbiased estimates as long as certain assumptions hold. These assumptions taken together are called 'the classical linear regression model' (Kennedy, 1992, pp. 42–7). This model includes such assumptions as that the error terms in regression models like equation (6.1) are normally distributed, and that there is no correlation between independent variables like Y in equation (6.1) and error terms. So, sometimes the term 'model' is used to refer to assumptions that have to hold for a certain econometric technique to generate the best or optimal estimates of parameters like a and b in equation (6.1). But models in this sense are not of interest here. The models much economic thinking is the construction and/or use of, are not of the kind the classical linear regression model instantiates.

The models that are of interest here include the supply/demand model, the Tiebout model (to be discussed below), the model of a firm's behaviour in the short run in perfect competition, the classical model of international trade, Walrasian or abstract general equilibrium models, the model of a monopoly firm's pricing behaviour and Keynesian income–expenditure models. What can be said in a general way about the nature of the kind of economic model that is of interest here? Ronald Rubin and Charles Young (1989, p. 63) define models by saying 'Generally speaking, a model is a simplified representation that we can use to gain an understanding of the object or system it represents'. Economists themselves sometimes describe their models in such terms (Baumol and Blinder, 1994, pp. 14–5). Calling a representation 'simplified' presumably means that it involves idealizing assumptions or partial representations in the senses of these terms described in section

5.2 above. Some simplified representations in this sense are ideal hypotheses or theories, while others are partial representations that are not ideal theories yet omit aspects of the object or system represented. Thus, describing economic models as simplified representations seems correct, yet it does not tell us a great deal. It just informs us that economists' models are either ideal theories, or partial representations that do not involve idealizing assumptions.

We can get the beginnings of a more illuminating account of economic models by relating them to an important distinction in the philosophy of science. It is the distinction between global theories and mini-theories. This distinction came into prominence with the emergence of the so-called globalist perspective in the philosophy of science in the early 1960s (McGuire, 1992, pp. 145–7). Globalists include Thomas Kuhn, Imre Lakatos, Paul Feyerabend and Larry Laudan. It would be a mistake to over-emphasize the extent of consensus among globalists; Larry Laudan for instance is sharply critical of both Kuhn and Feyerabend. But the globalists' dominant concern with scientific change typically leads them to distinguish global from mini-theories. Here is Laudan's own very useful preliminary account of the two kinds of theories:

> In the standard literature on scientific inference, as well as in common scientific practice, the term 'theory' refers to (at least) two very [sic] types of things. We often use the term 'theory' to denote a very specific set of related doctrines (commonly called 'hypotheses' or 'axioms' or 'principles') which can be utilized for making specific experimental predictions and for giving detailed explanations of natural phenomena. Examples of this type of theory would include Maxwell's theory of electromagnetism, the Bohr–Kramers–Slater theory of atomic structure, Einstein's theory of the photoelectric effect, Marx's labor theory of value, Wegener's theory of continental drift, and the Freudian theory of the Oedipal complex. By contrast, the term 'theory' is also used to refer to much more general, much less easily testable, sets of doctrines or assumptions. For instance, one speaks about 'the atomic theory,' or 'the theory of evolution,' or 'the kinetic theory of gases.' In each of these cases, we are referring not to a single theory, but to a whole spectrum of individual theories. The term 'evolutionary theory' for instance, does not refer to any single theory but to an entire family of doctrines, historically and conceptually related, all of which work from the assumption that organic species have common lines of descent. Similarly, the term 'atomic theory' generally refers to a large set of doctrines, all of which are predicated on the assumption that matter is discontinuous. (Laudan, 1977, pp. 71–2)

In the second sentence of this passage Laudan says that a theory is a very specific set of related doctrines, called 'axioms' or 'principles', usable to make predictions and construct explanations. With this remark Laudan is attempting to describe what I am calling 'mini-theories' (this term is actually Laudan's own). A slightly different way to describe a mini-theory which I prefer is that such a theory is a specific set of assumptions or axioms together with their logical and mathematical consequences. (Laudan's own account seems to exclude from a mini-theory the deductive consequences of the axioms of the theory, whilst on my account these consequences are included in the mini-theory.) In short, a mini-theory is a well-defined deductive system.[2] Note that a mini-theory can be expressed by means of different kinds of representations – sentences of a natural language, equations, graphs, and so on. Also, a mini-theory's assumptions and derived statements or theorems cannot be identified with a set of sentences of a particular language which formulates the mini-theory. The English sentence 'Firm managers seek to maximize profits' expresses an assumption of a number of mini-theories in neoclassical microeconomics. It is the statement or content expressed by the sentence 'Firm managers seek to maximize profits', not the English sentence itself, that is an assumption of the microeconomic mini-theories. The examples of mini-theories Laudan cites in the above passage count as mini-theories on my account. They are all examples drawn from the natural and social sciences. But mini-theories are also found in mathematics. Indeed, the most famous mini-theory of all is probably Euclidean geometry.

What are global theories? In the passage quoted above, Laudan suggests that a global theory is a spectrum of mini-theories which are historically and conceptually related. Laudan may appear to suggest that global theories – or, as Laudan prefers to call them, 'research traditions' – each include a single set of basic or core ideas that do not change over the entire history of the global theory, and a change in any of these ideas would result in a different global theory. In the quoted passage Laudan says that the atomic theory, which is a global theory or research tradition, includes mini-theories *all* of which reflect the idea that matter is discontinuous, suggesting perhaps that this idea partly defines the identity of the atomic theory. As is well-known, Kuhn and Lakatos have espoused philosophical theories about global theories. Kuhn calls them 'paradigms' (in one sense) as well as 'disciplinary matrices', while Lakatos calls them 'scientific research programmes'. Lakatos clearly thinks that a global theory has a set of unchanging basic principles or ideas, which he calls 'the hard core', that defines the identity of the theory. Kuhn too seems to think a global theory has some unalterable basic principles. A key element in any global theory or disciplinary matrix is a set of symbolic generalizations. For example, the symbolic generalizations in the global theory known as Newtonianism might include Newton's three laws of motion and the law of universal gravitation (Kuhn, 1970, pp. 182–3). Kuhn's discussion certainly suggests that the same set of symbolic generalizations in a disciplinary matrix partly constitutes its identity over the entire history of the matrix; any change in the set would mean that the disciplinary matrix is no longer the same. But Laudan does not really share this view I am ascribing to Kuhn and Lakatos. Laudan takes global theories to be more protean entities than do Kuhn and Lakatos. Laudan believes that at a given time, a global theory has a set of principles that define its identity at *that time*; to give up any of these principles at the time in question is to repudiate the global theory (Laudan, 1977, p. 99). Yet over the entire history of a global theory its basic principles or ideas typically change and it still remains the same global theory (Laudan, 1977, pp. 96–100). Laudan's attractive argument for this latter claim, which appeals to historical examples, purports to show that Kuhn and Lakatos are wrong to think that global theories include an unalterable set of basic principles or ideas constituting the identity of the global theory over its entire history. This disagreement between Kuhn and Lakatos on the one hand and Laudan on the other highlights the difficulty of obtaining even a minimal characterization of global theories which is free of controversy and yet sheds some light on their nature.

Let us return to Laudan's notion that a global theory is a spectrum of mini-theories. Global theories are in fact typically associated with a set of distinct mini-theories. For example, the theory of evolution or Darwinism is a global theory. In *The Origin of Species* Darwin himself states a mini-theory which is a version of the theory of evolution, though what the assumptions and derived statements of Darwin's own theory are has been a matter of controversy.[3] Subsequent to Darwin there have been versions of the theory of evolution which differ from Darwin's, an important example being the synthetic theory of evolution which incorporates Mendelian genetics. These other versions as well as Darwin's own version are mini-theories associated with the global theory which is the theory of evolution or Darwinism. Neoclassical microeconomics is a global theory. It is associated with a plethora of distinct mini-theories. As I will suggest below, the familiar models of neoclassical microeconomics – the model of firm behaviour in perfect competition, the model of the rational consumer, and so on – are all mini-theories. Laudan is correct, then, in thinking that a global theory is typically associated with a set of mini-theories which partly constitute it.

Are there other features of global theories which might serve to identify them? Laudan believes that global theories also include metaphysical and methodological principles. The metaphysical principles of a global theory consist of an ontology which Laudan (1977, p. 79) says '... specifies, in a general way, the types of fundamental entities which exist in the domain or domains within which the research tradition is embedded'. Laudan gives as an example the global theory in psychology known as behaviourism. Its ontology is that the only basic entities in the domain of psychology are publicly observable behaviours of organisms. Methodological principles included in global theories Laudan (1977, p. 79) describes as specifying '... certain modes or procedures which constitute the legitimate *methods of inquiry* open to a researcher within that tradition' (italics in original). For example, the global theory known as Newtonianism includes as an official methodological rule that only mini-theories or hypotheses inductively inferred from the empirical evidence are to be accepted. It does seem reasonable to say that *many* global theories incorporate a set of methodological rules (criteria for evaluating theories as acceptable, worth further development, unacceptable, and so on) as well as an ontology. Laudan's own historical examples support this claim. But, as Laudan himself acknowledges, not all global theories incorporate methodological rules and an ontology. Laudan (1977, pp. 105–6) cites a number of historically given global theories that arguably either lack an ontology or methodological rules. Finally, as suggested by the examples of global theories Laudan supplies in the passage quoted above, a global theory is usually associated with a set of general statements that are not comfortably regarded either as methodological rules or as part of an ontology. Examples include '$f=ma$', which is associated with the global theory Newtonianism, and the claim that all organic life is related, which is associated with Darwinism. Let us use 'global statements' to refer to such general statements. Global statements are in some sense accepted by adherents of the global theory to which they belong for whatever period of time they are included in the theory. But global statements associated with a global theory do not constitute a Lakatosian hard core, nor are they symbolic generalizations as Kuhn seems to understand them. A particular global statement might be modified or dropped from a global theory and it could still remain the same global theory. Moreover, a given global statement often appears in some form in at least several of the mini-theories included in the global theory (though it need not appear in all the mini-theories associated with the global theory). For example, the generalization 'Individuals are optimizers, that is, they act so as to maximize or minimize something perhaps subject to constraints', is a global statement associated with the economic global theory neoclassical microeconomics. This generalization is in some sense accepted by neoclassical economists. And it appears in various forms in numerous neoclassical models. For example, it appears in the form 'Firm managers seek to maximize profits' in a number of neoclassical models of business firm behaviour, such as the model of a monopolist's pricing and output decisions in the short run.

Obviously it is not easy to describe features of global theories in a way that is at all illuminating and free of difficulty. To sum up our brief discussion here, a global theory is typically associated with a set of mini-theories which partly constitute it. These mini-theories may be adopted by adherents of the global theory contemporaneously, or they may be adopted successively as the reigning mini-theory is replaced by another deemed better by the adherents of the global theory. Often, but not always, a global theory incorporates methodological rules and/or an ontology. Finally, global theories regularly include global statements as explained in the previous paragraph. How is a global theory connected to a mini-theory which it includes? Laudan talks of a global theory *inspiring or generating* constituent mini-theories. He cashes out these metaphors in terms of particular kinds of conceptual and historical connections between mini-theories and their parent global theories (Laudan, 1977, pp. 85–100).[4] But for us to pursue this matter any further here would carry us beyond the intended scope of the discussion.

It is now easy to connect economic models with the mini-theory/global theory distinction. As I suggested several paragraphs back, economic models are mini-theories. When an economist constructs or formulates a model, he makes a number of assumptions, and perhaps states one or more definitions. Then typically the economist derives additional statements of interest using logic and/or mathematics. The product of these activities is a set of statements organized into a deductive system. This product is the economic model. This description of economic models purports to accurately characterize the models actually found in the books and articles economists write, and the description can be verified by inspecting those books and articles.[5] And on this description, economic models are plainly mini-theories as these have been described above.

My account of economic models is not meant to apply only to the models produced by neoclassical, Keynesian or other mainstream economists nowadays. For instance, another global economic theory that has been important historically – more so outside economics than within the discipline – is Marxist economics. Marxist economics too includes models as I have described them. One Marxist model of capitalist or free enterprise economies is found in Marx's own work *Capital*. But other economists have developed models inspired by the global theory Marxist economics. For instance, John Roemer (1988, pp. 20–25) develops a model of an economy producing one good to illustrate the emergence of so-called exploitation in the Marxist sense of the term (the model includes a definition of exploitation). Marx's model in *Capital* and the model of Roemer's just alluded to fit my account of economic models. They are constructed by setting out assumptions and definitions, and then deriving other statements of interest. So these Marxist models are also mini-theories. My characterization of much economic thinking as the construction or formulation of models and their use in various cognitive activities such as explanation, may seem relatively uninformative in light of the account of economic models as mini-theories. My characterization is tantamount to saying that much economic thinking is the construction of mini-theories and their uses in various cognitive activities, and this may seem to say relatively little. But the account of economic models as mini-theories is just the beginning of my effort to flesh out my characterization of economics. It is the informativeness of the completed characterization that should be judged. Moreover, to say that much economic thinking is the construction and/or use of mini-theories does say something important about economics itself, and distinguishes it from disciplines such as history which are not in the business of constructing mini-theories, that is, sets of statements organized into deductive systems.

Since I have mentioned global theories, the reader may wonder what place they have in my account of economic thinking. There are global theories in economics, but it is often difficult to describe them in a way that is free of controversy.[6] And the problem of adequately characterizing particular global theories in economics intersects with the problem of whether different philosophical theories about global theories, such as Kuhn's and Lakatos's, are usefully applied to economics. To illustrate these points, in *General Equilibrium Analysis* Roy Weintraub applies Lakatos's account of global theories to a global theory he calls 'the neo-Walrasian research program'. Weintraub (1985, p. 109) cites six statements which he takes to constitute the hard core of the neo-Walrasian. In a critical discussion of Weintraub, Daniel Hausman objects to Weintraub's analysis on two related grounds – Hausman apparently equates neo-Walrasian economics with neoclassical microtheory. One ground is that there are important global statements (to use my terminology) associated with neoclassical microeconomics that are not shared by every neoclassical model or mini-theory. Some examples Hausman (1994b, p. 204) cites are 'Consumers' preferences are transitive' and the law of diminishing marginal productivity. These global statements are not cited by Weintraub. So, Weintraub's characterization of neoclassical microtheory is inadequate, given that it omits important elements of the theory it purports to describe. Secondly, Hausman thinks Weintraub is wrong to rely on Lakatos's account of global theories in trying to characterize neoclassical theory. For, a global theory may have no hard core at all in Lakatos's sense, or, as in the case of neoclassical microtheory, specifying the hard core affords a nearly empty account of the global theory in question. Hausman's criticisms of Weintraub nicely illustrate the interrelation between disputes about how to describe a given global theory and what philosophical theory is usefully relied upon to describe particular global theories.[7]

Fortunately, my purposes here do not require providing adequate accounts of particular global economic theories. It is particular models that economists construct and use; economists normally do not set out to develop global theories independently of particular models or mini-theories. And a given global theory is manifested in the particular economic models or mini-theories that it inspires or generates, manifesting just being the converse of the relation of inspiring. So, my claim that much economic thinking is the construction of models and their use in various cognitive activities, takes into account the effect or operation of global theories in economic theorizing. But my claim emphasizes the models themselves rather than the global theories which are manifested in the models.

6.2   SOME USES OF ECONOMIC MODELS

Philosophers often distinguish different cognitive activities scientists engage in which utilize mini-theories. Von Wright says the following:

> Scientific inquiry, seen in a very broad perspective, may be said to present two main aspects. One is the ascertaining and discovery of facts, the other the construction of hypotheses and theories. These two aspects of scientific activity are sometimes termed *descriptive* and *theoretical* science. Theory building can be said to serve two main purposes. One is to *predict* the occurrence of events or outcomes of experiments, and thus to anticipate new facts. The other is to *explain*, or to make intelligible facts which have already been recorded. (Von Wright, 1971, p. 1, italics in original)

As we saw in Chapter 3, it is a matter of ongoing controversy as to how well economic theories and hypotheses have fulfilled the predictive purpose which Von Wright cites. Though it is important for economics to generate correct predictions in some contexts, such as justifying policy proposals, economics is to a significant degree an explanatory enterprise. In Chapter 8 I will discuss the utilization of economic models in explaining real world economic phenomena. But there are cognitive activities other than predicting and explaining in which economic models are utilized. The remainder of this section is devoted to treating two such activities which are extremely important in economics. They are the resolution of conceptual problems and the resolution of normative problems. This section points towards a partial instrumentalism about economic models discussed in the next section.

The distinction between normative and positive claims is familiar to economists and economic methodologists, though the distinction is perhaps not a sharp one. And one can acknowledge the distinction without being committed to philosophically controversial theses such as that no set of positive claims ever entails a normative claim. Normative problems or questions take normative claims as their answers. To take a rather simple example, suppose the problem an economist is addressing is what should be done to combat the crime problem in the USA. Suppose that the (best supported) answer is 'More prison capacity should be constructed in the USA and more offenders put in jail'. As this answer is a normative claim, the problem it addresses is a normative one. Of course, it is consistent with the problem being normative that positive claims would be among the premises appealed to in an attempt to support the answer. Also, often a number of competing answers to a normative problem are offered by different parties, and addressing the normative problem requires determining which competing answer is the best supported one.

Conceptual problems are difficult to characterize. Roughly, conceptual problems are problems about the attribution of *modal* properties and relations. Modal *properties* may be seen as attributes of individual statements or propositions. Important examples are possible truth, possible falsehood, necessary truth and necessary falsehood. (Truth and falsehood themselves are not modal properties.) Modal *relations* are relations between two statements or two sets of statements. Important examples are entailment (implication), being consistent with, being inconsistent with and equivalence. Modal properties and relations are philosophically controversial. Some philosophers, such as W.V. Quine, argue that certain modal concepts like necessary truth are empty or lack a denotation. I will assume here that at least some modal concepts are meaningful and have a denotation. Now some problems or questions take as their answers (A) an attribution of a modal property to a statement, or (B) a claim that some modal relation obtains between two statements or two sets of statements. Any problem answered by (A) or (B) I will regard as a conceptual problem. Conceptual problems are common in philosophy. For instance, one question philosophers address in connection with freedom of the will is 'Is free-will compatible with determinism?'. This is a conceptual problem. Answering it requires determining whether or not the modal relation of being consistent with obtains between 'Humans have free-will' and 'Every event, including human actions, has a cause'. Conceptual problems are also important in science. Larry Laudan is one of the few philosophers of science to emphasize the role of conceptual problems in the evaluation of theories in scientific disciplines like physics. Laudan does not give the same account of conceptual problems that I have. But there is a good deal of overlap between conceptual problems in my sense and in Laudan's. For example, Laudan (1977, p. 46) cites as a conceptual problem a question Leibniz raised about Newton's theory, *viz.*, how could Newton's theory be reconciled with an intelligent deity who designed the world? This is also a conceptual problem in my sense. Answering it requires determining whether the modal relation of being consistent with obtains between Newton's theory and the view that an intelligent deity designed the world.

Economists often address conceptual problems, and they commonly utilize models to resolve these questions. I want to describe in some detail the actual use of an economic model by an economist to settle a conceptual problem. Doing so will illustrate and support the claim I have just made. The model I will examine is an important model in public sector economics which was included in a paper published by Charles Tiebout in 1956. The Tiebout model is a neoclassical microeconomic model which addresses a conceptual problem. Public or collective goods are often defined by economists as goods having one or both of two features: (A) it is impossible or at least not feasible to charge a price for them and exclude those who do not pay from consuming the goods; and (B) one or more persons enjoying or consuming the good does not reduce the quantity of the good available for others to consume. (A) is the non-exclusive feature of public goods, and (B) is the non-rivalness in consumption feature. National defence is a commonly cited example of a public good which pretty clearly has both (A) and (B). Economists claim that a system of private markets will fail to provide the quantity of a public good that people want. A cause of market failure in the case of public goods is the problem of preference revelation. In the case of a large number of potential consumers of a public good, each person has a motive to conceal his preference for a public good hoping that it will be provided by the others. Due to the non-exclusive feature (A), a given person will then be able to consume the good without having to pay for it. But the result of this free-riding behaviour by all is that the good will not be provided at all. This problem of preference revelation will also negatively impact the ability of the *national government* to adequately meet the demand for public goods. The problem is again figuring out exactly what the demand is. People have no motive for accurately revealing to government their true preferences for a public good. Charles Tiebout notes the difficulty of relying on the national government to provide the quantity of a public good people really want, and sets out the problem or question his model is intended to resolve in the following way:

> The current method of solving the problem [of how to force a consumer to reveal to government his true preferences for a public good] operates, unsatisfactorily, through the political mechanism. The expenditure wants of a 'typical voter' are somehow pictured. This objective on the expenditure side is then combined with an ability-to-pay principle on the revenue side, giving us our current budget. Yet in terms of a satisfactory theory of public finance, it would be desirable (1) to force the voter to reveal his preferences; (2) to be able to satisfy them in the same sense that a private goods market does; and (3) to tax him accordingly. The question arises whether there is any set of social institutions by which this goal *can* be approximated. (Tiebout, 1972, p. 515, emphasis added)

As the term 'can' in the last sentence of this remark indicates, Tiebout's paper is concerned with a conceptual problem in the sense explained in the previous paragraph. Tiebout's problem is 'Is it *possible* for there to be a set of social institutions in which people will reveal their true preferences for public goods, and for the approximate quantities of these goods people want to be provided?'. The short version of Tiebout's own answer to this problem is 'Yes', and his model explains and justifies this answer. (Note Tiebout's answer in effect attributes the modal property possible truth to the statement that there is a set of social institutions in which people will reveal their true preferences for public goods and the approximate quantities people want will be provided.)

Tiebout's solution to the problem he addresses emphasizes the role of local governments, as opposed to the national or central government, in the provision of public goods. This can be seen in the assumptions or axioms of the Tiebout model which are as follows (Tiebout, 1972, pp. 516–8):

(A1) Consumer-voters living under local governments are fully mobile and move to the community whose tax and expenditure package best satisfies their preferences for local public goods.

(A2) Consumer-voters have full knowledge of the tax and expenditure packages of the different local governments.

(A3) There are a large number of communities in which consumer-voters can choose to live.

(A4) The source of consumer-voter incomes provides no obstacle to their full mobility – for example, they might derive all their income from dividends on common stock they own.

(A5) There are no positive or negative externalities from the provision of public goods by the different local governments or communities consumer-voters can choose to live under.

(A6) A local community reaches its optimum size when its expenditure package for existing residents is provided at lowest average cost.

(A7) Communities below optimum size try to get new residents to lower costs, and communities at optimum size try to keep their population constant.

Given axioms (A1) to (A4), consumer-voters will reveal their preferences for public goods by moving to another community or staying put. Voting with one's feet provides the solution to the problem of preference revelation at the level of *local* government. The equilibrium state of the model obtains when no consumer-voter can better satisfy his preference for public goods provided by local government by moving to another community of less than optimum size. That is, once no consumer-voter can better satisfy his preference for public goods by moving to another community, no motive exists for further adjustment. Thus, when the Tiebout model is in equilibrium, consumer-voters come at least fairly close to getting the quantities of public goods they want insofar as local government can supply these.[8]

A number of the assumptions of the Tiebout model are quite unrealistic. Axioms (A1), (A2), (A4) and (A5) are pretty obviously false viewed as descriptions of the real world. But then Tiebout's purpose in developing the model was not to describe how the world in fact works.[9] Instead its purpose was to solve the conceptual problem described toward the end of the paragraph before last. Tiebout sums up his answer to this problem as follows:

> It is the contention of this article that, for a substantial portion of collective or public goods, this problem *does have* a conceptual solution. If consumer-voters are fully mobile, the appropriate local governments, whose revenue-expenditure patterns are set, are adopted by the consumer-voters. (Tiebout, 1972, p. 522, italics in original)

So, Tiebout's answer to the problem in question is given by

(TA) It is possible for there to be a set of social institutions in which people do reveal their true preferences for public goods and for the approximate quantities of these goods people want to be provided. The set of social institutions in which this possibility would be realized is a system of local governments or communities operating as described by the Tiebout model.

It should be fairly obvious how the axioms of the Tiebout model and the equilibrium condition determined by those axioms explain and justify (TA).

An additional point about the Tiebout model is worth making. Above I identified the Tiebout model as a neoclassical model. This identification is appropriate as the model is inspired by the global theory neoclassical microeconomics. As noted in section 6.1, a key global statement included in neoclassical microeconomics is

(GS1) Individuals are optimizers, that is, they act so as to maximize or minimize something perhaps subject to constraints.

Another global statement of neoclassical microeconomics is

(GS2) Individuals are able to rank alternatives from the most to the least desirable.

These global statements explain and justify the presence of a number of the statements in the Tiebout model. For instance, axiom (A1) says that consumer-voters move to the community whose tax and expenditure package best satisfies their preferences for local public goods. This implies that consumer-voters are able to rank tax and expenditure packages of different local governments from most to least desirable. This reflects (GS2). By saying that consumer-voters actually move to the community best satisfying their preferences for local public goods, axiom (A1) implies that consumer-voters choose the community whose tax and expenditure package they most prefer. Of course this reflects (GS1); by moving to the community best satisfying their preferences, consumer-voters are optimizing. No doubt global statements of neoclassical micro like (GS1) and (GS2) partly guided Tiebout in deciding what statements to include in his model as well as justified the choices he made in this regard.

The Tiebout model is hardly the only economic model devised to solve a conceptual problem. Indeed, one of the most widely discussed class of models are Walrasian or abstract general equilibrium (GE) models.[10] These trace their ancestry back to Léon Walras who constructed the first one. Walrasian GE models include all the goods in an economy, and are constructed especially to help solve the following problem: can there be a set or vector of prices which simultaneously clears all markets in a perfectly competitive economy?[11] But this is a conceptual problem in the sense explained above. The answer to it, economists have established, is 'Yes', which in effect attributes the modal property possible truth to the proposition that there is a vector of prices that simultaneously clears all markets in a competitive economy. GE analysis and the GE models it produces have been highly controversial. There is a fairly sizable literature generated by economists and economic methodologists on the character of GE analysis and GE models and their value in economics. Unfortunately, a certain amount of this literature assumes some dubious philosophical claim such as that to be of value, GE analysis would have to generate falsifiable implications about real world economic behaviour. In any case, the point I wish to emphasize here is that Walrasian GE models, like the Tiebout model, are constructed to resolve conceptual problems. I do not of course imagine that this remark settles all the legitimate philosophical problems that are raised by GE analysis and GE models. But the construction of economic models to solve conceptual problems is a salient feature of economic thinking.

Economists also construct and utilize models to answer normative problems. This use of economic models seems more widely recognized than their use in solving conceptual problems. For example, areas of neoclassical economics such as welfare economics, public finance and urban economics in part address normative problems and utilize models to help answer these normative concerns. An influential neoclassical model which addresses a normative problem is Gary Becker's model of optimal use of resources for crime control. Becker describes the problem he is concerned with as follows:

> The main purpose of this essay is to answer normative versions of these questions, namely, how many resources and how much punishment *should* be used to enforce different kinds of legislation? Put equivalently, although more strangely, how many offenses *should* be permitted and how many offenders *should* go unpunished? (Becker, 1976, p. 40, italics in original)

In order to answer this normative issue, Becker (1976, p. 42) says 'It is useful in determining how to combat crime in an optimal fashion to develop a model ...'. Becker's model is fairly complex and it is not feasible to present it in its entirety here. But the model includes a variety of assumptions. A couple of representative ones are

(B1) The amount of harm done by criminal acts increases with the number of crimes or offences committed.

(B2) The gain to offenders increases with the number of offences committed.

The model also includes definitions such as that the net cost or damage to society caused by criminal offences themselves is the amount of harm done minus the gain to offenders. And the assumptions of Becker's model also incorporate a key normative principle that the *optimal* values of the choice variables in the model – these include the probability of conviction and the punishment per offence – are those that minimize the total social loss in real income. (The total social loss includes variables in addition to the net damage caused by criminal acts.)

The general approach to crime control represented by Becker's model has influenced economists' thinking about particular policy issues connected with crime. For instance, in a widely discussed paper, Edwin Zedlewski adopts the approach of Becker's model. He says:

> Gary Becker first sketched an analytic framework for deciding upon optimal expenditure for crime control. By advancing the notion that the criminal justice system ought to minimize the 'net social harm' of crime, Becker recognized that while expenditures to reduce crime drained resources, crime imposed other costs upon a community. (Zedlewski, 1995, pp. 124–5)

Zedlewski argues that various policies *should* be adopted to combat the crime problem in the USA, including building more prisons and incarcerating more offenders. As the passage just quoted indicates, Zedlewski adopts the Becker style normative principle that the criminal justice system ought to minimize the net social harm or loss of crime. And Zedlewski arrives at actual dollar figures for various types of losses or costs from crime in the USA, including the cost of keeping an offender in prison for a year. Estimates of these costs or losses to society, plus the requirement that social losses from crime should be minimized, form the basis for Zedlewski's policy recommendations. Becker's model of optimal use of resources for crime control is a clear example of the construction and use of an economic model to address a normative problem in general terms. And Zedlewski's paper illustrates how an economic model devised to address a general normative issue in turn is utilized in the discussion of particular policy issues.

6.3 PARTIAL INSTRUMENTALISM

My emphasis on uses of economic models in the previous section may seem to amount to acceptance of *instrumentalism* about economics. And this may be taken to be inconsistent with the view that economics pursues truth, a view I endorsed in Chapter 2. In section 2.3 I defined instrumentalism as affirming that economists or other scientists do not put forward their mini-theories (models) and single hypotheses as even approximately true descriptions of the real world, but rather as convenient devices for serving various purposes.[12] On the other hand, realism holds that economists put forward or accept their mini-theories and hypotheses as true, or approximately true, descriptions of the real world. I have claimed that economists put forward some models for the purpose of resolving conceptual and normative problems. And in doing so, the economists do not put forward these models as true descriptions of reality. For instance, Charles Tiebout did not view the model bearing his name as even a close to true description of the real world. (This point applies to the model taken as a whole; Tiebout may well have regarded some of the component statements of his model, perhaps axiom (A3), as true of the real world.) So I have committed myself to a partial instrumentalism about economics, and the discussion of this section does indeed support this position. It is a *partial* instrumentalist position, since I have only said that *some* economic models are not put forward as true descriptions of the real world. As the next two chapters will show, economists also put forward some models and individual hypotheses as true, or at least approximately true, descriptions of reality. These models and hypotheses fit a realist view of economics.

My partial instrumentalism about economics does not in any way compromise the view that economics is in pursuit of truth, that is, a chief goal of economists is to acquire true beliefs. Indeed, even a complete instrumentalism about economics is compatible with viewing truth as a key goal of economic inquiry. To see this, it is necessary to recall the distinction invoked in section 2.3 between first-order mini-theories and second-order statements which are *about* first-order theories. The Tiebout model, Becker's model of crime control, a four sector Keynesian income-expenditure model, the model of short-run firm behaviour in perfect competition, and so on are first-order mini-theories. But second-order statements attribute some property to first-order mini-theories. Of particular relevance here are second-order statements of the form 'T is useful' or 'T is useful for such-and-such', where 'T' stands in place of terms referring to first-order theories and 'such-and-such' stands in place of descriptions of purposes like resolving a certain conceptual problem or generating predictions about the effects of minimum wage legislation. Second-order statements of these two forms are themselves true or false statements. According to my partial instrumentalism, economists are in pursuit of truth even when they put forward and endorse a model that is not supposed to be a true description of reality. It is just that in such cases, they do not come to accept as true first-order theories, but rather accept as true second-order statements of the form 'T is useful' or 'T is useful for such-and-such'. For instance, in his investigation of the conceptual problem his model was designed to address, Charles Tiebout did not come to accept his model as a true description of reality. But he did come to accept as true the second-order statement that the Tiebout model is useful for resolving the conceptual problem of whether there can be a set of social institutions in which people get approximately the quantities of local public goods they really want. Thus, my partial instrumentalism about economics squares quite well with viewing economists as seeking truths to believe or accept. It is just that the kinds of truths the partial instrumentalist has the economist accepting as true are different from the ones a thorough going realist would have economists accept as true.

Partial instrumentalism does leave us with a problem to which I am only able to give a partial answer. Economists would not regard just any model as of use to resolve a conceptual or a normative problem. How, then, do economists discriminate between good or genuinely useful models for resolving conceptual or normative problems, and models that are not suitable to be utilized to resolve such problems? Part of the answer is that economists rely upon the stock of global statements belonging to a global theory to which they adhere. More precisely, economists typically accept some global theory which provides a framework within which they conduct their inquiries. And they regard as a partial basis for a model M being a good or genuinely useful model for resolving a conceptual or normative problem that M includes in some form one or more global statements belonging to a global theory they accept. For example, consider again the following pair of neoclassical global statements:

(GS1) Individuals are optimizers, that is, they act so as to maximize or minimize something perhaps subject to constraints.
(GS2) Individuals are able to rank alternatives from the most to the least desirable.

In constructing a model regarded as useful for resolving a conceptual or normative problem, a neoclassical economist may rely upon (GS1) and

(GS2). As indicated above, this is what happened in the case of the Tiebout model. Axiom (A1) of the Tiebout model says in part that consumer-voters are able to rank tax and expenditure packages of different local communities. This is an implication of (GS2). And axiom (A1) also says that consumer-voters actually move to the community whose tax and expenditure package best satisfies their preferences. This is implied by (GS1). And that his model included in some form (GS1) and (GS2), was surely part of Tiebout's basis for regarding his model as being a good or genuinely useful model for resolving the conceptual problem it addresses.

Now of course economic methodologists may insist that the fact that a model *M* includes in some form accepted global statements can form part of a *good* or *adequate* basis for viewing *M* as a useful model for resolving a conceptual or normative problem, only if the global statements themselves are *worthy* of acceptance. It would be nice if we had an agreed upon, adequate set of criteria for appraising the epistemic worth of entire global theories. With such a set of criteria in hand, we could say that a particular global statement is worthy of acceptance if it belongs to a global theory which fulfils the criteria for the acceptability of such theories. However, no set of agreed upon, adequate criteria for assessing global theories is available. Globalists such as Kuhn, Lakatos and Laudan have set out criteria for evaluating global theories. But their proposed criteria are highly controversial.[13] And no one else has proposed an adequate set of criteria for appraising global theories which has secured general agreement.

Even in the absence of a complete set of criteria for determining the worth of global *theories,* something can still be said about what makes global *statements* worthy of acceptance. Global statements are generalizations, and there is a style of reasoning or argument that economists in fact sometimes use to justify acceptance of generalizations, including global statements. Consider the following passage from John Maynard Keynes:

> The fundamental psychological law, upon which we are entitled to depend with great confidence both *a priori* from our knowledge of human nature and from the detailed facts of experience, is that men are disposed, as a rule and on the average, to increase their consumption as their income increases, but not by as much as the increase in their income. (Keynes, 1964, p. 96)

A central concept in Keynesian macroeconomics is the marginal propensity to consume (MPC). It is defined as the change in consumption spending divided by the change in income for a small change in income.

(Nowadays, income in this definition is usually interpreted as disposable income, though Keynes himself construed income more broadly.) In the passage just quoted, Keynes states and strongly endorses the following generalization:

(GS3) The MPC for the aggregate of consumers in an economy exceeds zero but is less than one.

Keynesian macroeconomics is a global theory, though it has been a matter of controversy as to what its elements are.[14] But (GS3) is surely a global statement of Keynesian macroeconomics whatever its other ingredients are. Speaking of (GS3) Keynes (1937, p. 220) says 'This psychological law was of the utmost importance in the development of my own thought, and it is, I think, absolutely fundamental to the theory of effective demand as set forth in my book'. Moreover, as indicated in section 6.1, one mark of a global statement in economics is that it appears in some form in several or many specific models belonging to the relevant global theory. And (GS3) is regularly employed one way or another in particular Keynesian models from the simplest income–expenditure models to IS–LM models.

In the passage from Keynes quoted above, he says that (GS3) is warranted because it is supported 'both *a priori* from our knowledge of human nature and from the detailed facts of experience.' Keynes's distinction between being entitled to believe something *a priori* from a type of knowledge we have, and being entitled to believe something from the detailed facts of experience, is perhaps the distinction Kant draws our attention to in the following passage:

For it has been customary to say, even of much knowledge that is derived from empirical sources, that we have it or are capable of having it *a priori*, meaning thereby that we do not derive it immediately from experience, but from a universal rule – a rule which is itself, however, borrowed from experience. Thus we would say of a man who undermined the foundations of his house, that he might have known *a priori* that it would fall, that is, that he need not have waited for the experience of its actual falling. But still he could not know this completely *a priori*. For he had first to learn through experience that bodies are heavy, and therefore fall when their supports are withdrawn. (Kant, 1965, p. 43)

Kant is in effect acknowledging that we can be warranted in accepting a generalization 'All *F* are *G*' on the basis that (A) the generalization is confirmed by our observation, including introspective awareness, of a sample of cases in which *F* is instantiated (the generalization is, in Kant's language, derived 'immediately from experience'); or (B) the generalization is implied by one or more generalizations which themselves are confirmed by what we observe in samples of particular cases. I will say that if someone is justified in accepting a generalization on the basis of (A) or (B) or both, then he is justified in accepting it on the basis of *everyday experience*. Now in the passage quoted previously, I submit that we may interpret Keynes as saying that we are entitled to accept (GS3) because it meets both conditions (A) and (B). In short, Keynes attempts to justify acceptance of (GS3) on the basis of everyday experience. Keynes does not say what specific real world cases he or anyone else observed which confirm (GS3). Nor does he cite generalizations confirmed by observed cases which imply (GS3). But it is not hard to imagine generalizations which Keynes might have had in mind which imply (GS3). Two are 'Consumers in an economy typically include some high income people', and 'High income people do not normally spend on consumption 100% of additional income they receive; they save at least some of the added income'.

So economists sometimes seek to justify acceptance of global statements on the basis of everyday experience. Not every such attempt may be successful. For instance, the sample of observed cases relied upon in an effort to justify a generalization by appeal to experience may not be large enough, or it may not exhibit sufficient variety. But it is true that global statements can be warranted by the appeal to everyday experience. Inductive generalization from a suitable sample of observed cases is one way to justify a generalization, as is inferring a generalization from other statements which are themselves (unfalsified) inductive generalizations from suitable samples of observed cases. Several paragraphs back I raised the issue as to how economists determine whether a model is good or genuinely useful for resolving a conceptual or a normative problem. As indicated, part of the answer is that they rely on global statements belonging to a global theory which they accept. More fully, a partial basis economists have for regarding a model *M* as a good model for resolving a conceptual or normative problem, is that *M* includes in some form global statements belonging to a global theory they accept. But then global statements can form an *adequate* partial basis of this sort only if the global statements are themselves *worthy* of acceptance. And how can global statements become worthy of acceptance? The answer I have sketched here is that one way economists can justify their acceptance of global statements is on the basis of everyday experience in the sense explained above. And economists do in fact sometimes employ such a justification procedure to warrant acceptance of global statements, as the example of Keynes and (GS3) illustrates.[15]

A very important qualification to these claims about global statements must be made. The partial account of the justification of global statements I have given seemingly represents economists as accepting *as true* global statements which they justify by appeal to everyday experience. But this is not always the case. An economist may accept a generalization *G* in the sense, not of believing that *G* itself is true, but believing that *G* is what Hausman calls a 'rough generalization'. Hausman explains rough generalizations as follows:

> Mill suggests on several occasions that some of the laws of inexact sciences are rough generalizations, reasonably, but not perfectly reliable.... As I am using the term, a rough generalization is not a law, because it is not true. It is simply a generalization that faces some counterexamples, but not so many that one learns nothing from it. (Hausman, 1992b, p. 36)

A rough generalization is false as a description of the real world, as there are counterexamples to it. But it *is true* in a range, and perhaps a very large one, of real world cases. It is not uncommon for economists to view their generalizations as rough in the sense just explained. In their principles text Baumol and Blinder say the following about the so-called law of diminishing marginal utility:

> The assumption upon which this 'law' [of diminishing marginal utility] is based is plausible for most consumers and for most commodities. But, like most laws, there are exceptions. For some people, the more they have of some good that is particularly significant to them, the more they want. The needs of alcoholics and stamp collectors are good examples.... Similarly, the alcoholic who finds a dry martini quite pleasant when he first starts drinking may find one more to be absolutely irresistible once he has already consumed four or five. Economists, however, generally treat such cases of *increasing marginal utility* as anomalies. For most goods and most people, marginal utility probably declines as consumption increases. (Baumol and Blinder, 1994, p. 193)

So, Baumol and Blinder do not accept as true 'The more of a good a consumer has, the less will be the marginal utility of one more unit consumed', but they do believe (accept as true) that this generalization holds in a large range of cases. In other words, Baumol and Blinder accept the 'law' of diminishing marginal utility in the sense of believing that it is a rough generalization.[16]

Above I said that economists can justify acceptance of global statements on the basis of everyday experience; this is one way in which global statements can become worthy of acceptance. In light of what has just been said, the term 'acceptance' here can refer to acceptance of a generalization *G* in the sense of believing *G* is true, *or* it can refer to acceptance of *G* in the sense of believing only that *G* is a rough generalization. And acceptance of *G* in the latter sense can also be warranted on the basis of everyday experience in the sense explained previously. Supposing that *G* is a generalization, consider the following:

(1) *G* is true in a large range of real world cases.

(1) can be confirmed by observation of a sample of cases in which *G* itself mostly holds. And the fact that *G* holds with but a few exceptions in the sample of observed cases may well not *logically imply* (1), but only afford *inductive support* for (1). For, the person who affirms or accepts (1) may interpret the range of cases alluded to in (1) to be much more extensive than the cases included in the observed sample even if the sample is large. In addition, (1) could be implied or supported by generalizations which themselves are confirmed by what is observed in samples of particular cases. This is the second mode of justification on the basis of everyday experience described above.

The fact that economists may accept global statements only in the sense of believing them to be rough generalizations, does not affect the role I have accorded global statements in economists' determination of the utility of models in resolving conceptual or normative problems. I said that the fact that model *M* includes in some form global statements belonging to a global theory GT, is viewed by economists who accept GT as part of the basis for regarding *M* as of real use in resolving a conceptual or normative problem. A global statement GS can fulfil this role even if economists merely believe that GS is a rough generalization. Note that it is GS itself, *not* 'GS is a rough generalization', that in some form appears in model *M*. But that economists believe that GS is a rough generalization – true in perhaps a very large range of real world cases – still affords economists a partial basis for regarding a model *M* including GS as of real use in solving a conceptual or normative problem. That model *M* incorporates a global statement which economists believe to be a rough generalization, distinguishes *M* from other models whose assumptions they do not accept in any sense but which might be used to answer a conceptual or normative problem.

6.4 MODELS AND EXCESSIVE FORMALISM

A fairly large chorus of critics has charged economics with excessive formalism. The critics include some prominent economists. But even publications catering to the educated public at large have contained articles charging economics with excessive formalism. In an article published in *The Atlantic* Robert Kuttner says the following:

> The deductive method of practicing economic science creates a professional ethic of studied myopia. Apprentice economists are relieved of the need to learn much about the complexities of human motivation, the messy universe of economic institutions, or the real dynamics of technological change. In economics, deduction drives out empiricism. Those who have real empirical curiosity and insight about the workings of banks, corporations, production technologies, trade unions, economic history, or individual behavior are dismissed as casual empiricists, literary historians, or sociologists, and marginalized within the profession. In their place departments of economics are graduating a generation of *idiots savants*, brilliant at esoteric mathematics yet innocent of actual economic life. (Kuttner, 1985, p. 77)

In a more recent article in *The New Yorker*, John Cassidy has expressed similar criticisms of economics. Cassidy (1996, pp. 50–51) says '... economics has been transformed into an abstruse discipline that often appears to resemble a branch of mathematics'. Cassidy even goes so far as to suggest that the abolition of the Nobel Prize for economics might encourage economists to change their discipline 'to become more worldly'. What I am calling 'the charge of excessive formalism' claims that economists exhibit to an excessive or undesirably high degree the following pair of properties:

(P1) expending effort deducing theorems from assumptions or axioms which typically describe hypothetical or imaginary situations rather than actual economic phenomena;
(P2) fondness for the use of often esoteric mathematics which does not contribute to our understanding of real world economic phenomena.

So, the charge of excessive formalism says that economists spend an excessive or disproportionate amount of effort doing what is described in (P1). And they also exhibit an excessive fondness for often esoteric mathematics of little use in understanding the real world.[17]

A number of economists have directed this type of criticism at their discipline. In a well-known paper, Wassily Leontief (1985, pp. 273–4) says 'The mathematical-model-building industry has grown into one of the most prestigious, possibly the most prestigious branch of economics.... In the presentation of a new model, attention nowadays is usually centered on a step-by-step derivation of its formal properties'. But Leontief complains that economists typically show little interest in the question of whether the axioms or assumptions of their models truly describe the real world. He (1985, p. 274) says 'By the time it comes to the interpretation of the substantive *conclusions*, the assumptions on which the model has been based are easily forgotten. But it is precisely the empirical validity of these *assumptions* on which the usefulness of the entire exercise depends' (italics in original). Leontief (1985, p. 275) abbreviates this complaint by referring to economists' 'Continued preoccupation with imaginary, hypothetical rather than with observable reality ...'. He adds that this preoccupation has led economists to downgrade the value of empirical research and the task of finding new empirical facts or data. Instead economists have developed sophisticated econometric techniques to compensate for the meagre data base. But these techniques have not enhanced economists' understanding of the real world. Leontief (1982, p. 107) says '... the econometricians fit algebraic functions of all possible shapes to essentially the same sets of data without being able to advance, in any perceptible way, a systematic understanding of the structure and operation of a real economic system'. Leontief's remarks about his discipline clearly ascribe to it properties (P1) and (P2) in an undesirably high or excessive degree.

Donald McCloskey (1994, Ch. 10) has urged the charge of excessive formalism against his discipline. McCloskey seems to think that at least the presence in economics of property (P1) in an excessive degree flows from the investigation of models being centre stage in the discipline. McCloskey says this:

> The problem was brought into focus by the philosopher Allan Gibbard and the mathematical economist Hal Varian some time ago. 'Much economic theorizing,' they noted (without intent to damn it), 'consists not ... of forming hypotheses about situations and testing them, but of investigating economic models' (Gibbard and Varian 1979 [sic], p. 676). That's right. Economic literature is largely speculative, an apparently inconclusive exploration, as I say, of the hyperspace of assumptions A, A', A". (McCloskey, 1994, p. 141)

The passage from Gibbard and Varian which McCloskey quotes is the very same one that I have used to convey the positive view of economics elaborated in this monograph. At the beginning of section 6.1, I paraphrased Gibbard and Varian and elaborated on their point of view by saying that much economic thinking consists in the construction of models and their use in various cognitive activities. So it may be thought that what is responsible for economics being open to the charge of exhibiting property (P1) to an undesirably high degree, is that it does indeed fit my characterization of the discipline. After all, in the quoted passage McCloskey equates economics investigating models à la Gibbard and Varian with the discipline exploring imaginary situations rather than finding out about the real world. But is the centrality of models in economics really responsible for the discipline (allegedly) possessing property (P1) to an excessive degree? I think not, and I want to provide some support for this opinion.

I do not wish to deny that there is some merit in the accusation of excessive formalism. Too many economists have voiced the accusation in one form or another for there to be nothing to it. Leontief and McCloskey are just two examples. Thomas Mayer has written an entire book built upon the distinction between what he calls 'formalist theory' and 'empirical science theory' in economics. About formalist theory he says this:

> In formalist theory logical rigour and elegance play a much larger role than they do in empirical science theory. In its pure state formalist theory is a set of theorems. Results are rigourously derived from assumptions whose validity is, at least for the purposes of the particular theory, simply asserted.... Formalist economists use mathematics and logic as their exemplars. (Mayer 1993, p. 24)

Formalist theory certainly looks like it exhibits properties (P1) and (P2) to a very high degree. Much of Mayer's book is an effort to beat back what he regards as the harmful intrusion of formalist theory into domains, such as macroeconomics, that have hitherto belonged to empirical science economics. Economic inquiry in these domains exhibiting attributes (P1) and (P2) to a high degree *is* undesirable – this is where the charge of excessive formalism enters the picture for Mayer. And Mayer is not alone in levelling the charge of excessive formalism against work in particular areas of economics. In the context of summing up his discussion of the use of the mathematical theory of games in industrial organization, Franklin Fisher says the following:

> But in another sense, the reply exemplifies what is wrong with modern game theory as applied to industrial organization and especially to oligopoly. There is a strong tendency for even the best practitioners to concentrate on the analytically interesting questions rather than the ones that really matter for the study of real-life industries. The result is often a perfectly fascinating piece of analysis. But as long as that tendency continues, those analyses will remain merely games economists play. (Fisher, 1989, p. 123)

This passage explicitly ascribes to the study of oligopoly property (P2) cited in the charge of excessive formalism. For, the study of oligopoly is represented by Fisher as extensively using the mathematical theory of games without substantially advancing our understanding of real world industries.

Though there appears to be some merit in the complaint that economics exhibits excessive formalism, the central role of models in economics is not the culprit. That is, it is not the fact that much economic thinking is the construction and use of models that causes the discipline to exhibit properties (P1) or (P2) to a higher degree than might be desirable. To support this claim I will focus on (P1) and offer two partial explanations of economics exhibiting (P1) to a high degree. These explanations invoke causes other than the centrality of models in economics.

One aspect of economic inquiry emphasized in this chapter is the use of economic models to resolve conceptual problems. Axioms of models devised to deal with such problems often may not afford true descriptions of actual economic phenomena. For instance, most of the axioms of the Tiebout model do not truly describe the actual or real world. But this should not be a cause for concern. The Tiebout model was not constructed to describe actual economic phenomena, but rather to establish a certain *possibility* and thereby resolve a conceptual problem. It is unreasonable to criticize economic models devised to resolve conceptual problems for having assumptions that fail to truly describe the real or actual world but instead describe hypothetical situations. Such criticism assumes an inappropriate standard of evaluation for such models. But it might be said that economists spend a disproportionate amount of time in devising models to solve conceptual problems. The large amount of effort that has gone into developing Walrasian or abstract general equilibrium models might be cited in support of this. Thus, since models devised to solve conceptual problems typically include assumptions false of the real world, the result of all the time spent devising models to solve conceptual problems is that economics exhibits (P1) to a higher degree than might be desirable. However, this line of thought does not really represent economics exhibiting (P1) to an undesirable degree as due to the fact that models occupy centre stage in the discipline. Instead it represents it as due to the choices economists make about what problems to address. Economists choose to address a high proportion of conceptual problems. And of course the models they devise to address these problems have assumptions false of the real world. But it is the choice of problems, not the use of models *per se*, that leads to the heavy dependence on assumptions not true of the actual world. The centrality of models in economics is not itself to blame for the discipline exhibiting (P1) to a high degree.

As indicated in section 5.1, neoclassical microeconomics has especially been the target of the charge that economics exhibits property (P1) to an excessive degree. It is often expressed by saying that neoclassical microeconomics exhibits an excessive reliance on unrealistic$_f$ (false) assumptions. (See note 17 on the connection between attribute (P1) and unrealistic$_f$ assumptions.) But neoclassical economics' reliance on unrealistic$_f$ assumptions is *not* due to the fact that the investigation of models is centre stage in neoclassical microeconomics. In part it is due to the fact that many neoclassical microeconomic models belong to a class of theories which Brian Fay has called 'competence theories'. Fay makes an important distinction between competence theories and performance theories, a distinction which is a sort of generalization of Noam Chomsky's distinction between theories of competence and theories of performance in linguistics. Here is one of Fay's accounts of the distinction:

> Competence theories are those theories which seek to detail how an idealized, fully rational actor would act.... Or, to give another instance, much of Decision Theory is an attempt to articulate rules which would guide decisions trying to accomplish certain goals in a variety of different situations characterized by different degrees of uncertainty, costs and benefits, probability of outcomes, and so forth.... Performance theories try to do exactly what their name indicates, namely, explain the actual performance of people. As such, they are causal in character in that they try to pick out those events or conditions which are jointly sufficient and necessary to produce the behaviour in question. (Fay, 1984, p. 538)

A competence theory describes the behaviour of *rational* individuals. A performance theory identifies the causes or explanatory reasons for the behaviour of actual or real world individuals. (The term 'theory' in 'performance theory' should be taken to refer to single hypotheses as well as mini-theories in the sense described earlier in this chapter.)

An actual individual may be *guided by* a competence theory or the principles of rational conduct it includes. In this case a performance theory that explains the individual's conduct will have to make reference to the competence theory in question. For instance, suppose an individual S is in a situation in which he cannot assign probabilities to the outcomes of the alternative courses of action open to him, but he can describe and rank these outcomes from most to least preferred for each of the courses of action. S might then use the maximin rule to decide which course of action to adopt, adopting the action whose least preferred outcome is the best. This rule of course belongs to the theory of rational choice under uncertainty, which is a competence theory. A performance theory of S's conduct will then have to make reference to this competence theory. S's belief in the theory of rational choice under uncertainty is part of the cause of his behaviour. But even if actual choice is not guided by a theory of competence, the conduct of an individual may be *as if* it were guided by a given theory of competence, that is, the individual's outward behaviour is the same as would be exhibited by someone who *is* guided by the theory of competence in question. In this case we may say that the conduct of the individual *fits* or *conforms* to a given theory of competence, though it is not guided by that theory. Finally, in the real world the behaviour of individuals in part is at least sometimes caused by impulse, forgetfulness, ignorance of principles of probability and statistics, and the like. Factors of this sort may lead individuals to behave in ways that in fact contradict or violate a given theory of competence; their behaviour does not even conform to the theory. Of course, in such cases the theory of competence violated or contradicted will be *false* as description of the actual behaviour of the individuals in question.

Jon Elster (1989, p. 22) says 'Rational choice is instrumental: it is guided by the outcome of action. Actions are valued and chosen not for themselves, but as more less efficient means to a further end'. Neoclassical microeconomics adopts this highly plausible instrumental conception of rationality and further assumes that the end rational conduct is a means to the maximization or minimization of something. In section 6.2 I expressed essentially the same point by saying that

(GS1) Individuals are optimizers, that is, they act so as to maximize or minimize something perhaps subject to constraints

is a key global statement of neoclassical microeconomics. (GS1) is equivalent to saying that individuals act rationally, where rationality is understood as optimization. Above I noted that (GS1) appears in one form or another in many neoclassical microeconomic models. But then this makes such models theories of competence in the sense previously explained.[18] For example, the model of the behaviour of a monopoly firm in the short run found in microeconomics texts assumes that firm managers act so as to maximize profits. It is inferred that firm managers set the output of the firm where marginal revenue equals marginal cost, which is a necessary condition for maximizing profits. To set the price per unit of output, managers go up to the point on the firm's demand curve (which is the same as market demand in monopoly) above the profit maximizing quantity of output and charge the price at that point. This of course is to describe firm managers' conduct as rational; managers adopt the right means to the end of maximizing profit.

As indicated in the previous paragraph, real world individuals' behaviour is sometimes at least partly caused by impulse, forgetfulness, wishful thinking, ignorance of principles of probability and statistics, and so on. Thus, the behaviour of real world individuals might be expected sometimes to contradict neoclassical models. And this has in fact happened. In section 5.4 I cited the fact that the preference reversals exhibited by individuals in real world experimental situations contradicts expected utility theory, a central neoclassical model. The set of assumptions of expected utility are apparently false as a description of real world individuals' conduct. I submit, then, that part of the explanation for neoclassical microeconomics' heavy dependence on assumptions that are not always true of real world individuals, is that so many neoclassical models are competence theories. And, like competence theories generally, they describe *rational* conduct from which real world individuals sometimes deviate. It is not the centrality of models in economic thinking per se that is responsible for neoclassical microeconomics relying to a high degree on assumptions that are not true of the real world. It is in part the penchant of neoclassical economists for constructing models that are competence theories.[19] I hasten to add that I am not saying that real world individuals are not instrumentally rational. Individuals by and large are instrumentally rational. But real world individuals are not always rational. As a result, theories of competence, such as many neoclassical microeconomic models, are not true without exception when interpreted as describing the behaviour of individuals in the real world.

6.5   CONCLUDING REMARKS

This chapter has given a partial account of the nature and role of models in economics. The account is part of my effort to flesh out the view that much economic thinking is the construction and utilization of models in various cognitive activities. I have provided a characterization of the philosophical distinction between global theories and mini-theories, and claimed that economic models are mini-theories. Two cognitive activities of considerable importance in economics are the resolution of conceptual problems and the resolution of normative problems. This chapter has described in some detail the utilization of economic models in this pair of cognitive activities. One upshot of this discussion is that a partial instrumentalism about economics is justified. This says that some, but only some, economic models are not put forward as true, or close to true, descriptions of the real world, but rather as convenient devices for serving various purposes. I have argued that this partial instrumentalism does not at all compromise the view that economics is in pursuit of truth, a view defended in Chapter 2 above. But we are faced with the problem as to how economists distinguish between those models that are, and those models that are not, genuinely useful for resolving conceptual and normative problems. I suggested a partial answer to this problem which emphasizes the role of global statements economists in some sense accept in their determination that a model is of genuine use in resolving a conceptual or normative problem. Finally, it is a common complaint about contemporary economics that it exhibits excessive formalism. Some have suggested that it is the centrality of models in economics that is responsible for the excessive formalism. I have argued that whatever excessive formalist tendencies economics may be thought to exhibit is not due to the centrality of models in economics. Instead it is in part due to economists' choosing to address a high proportion of conceptual problems, and also to the fondness of neoclassical economists for constructing models that are competence theories.

NOTES

1. This passage is from a letter by Keynes to Roy Harrod. The letter is partially excerpted in Hausman, 1994a, pp. 286–7.
2. A mini-theory may also include one or more definitions, though these may not be sharply distinguished from the theory's assumptions in a given formulation of the theory.
3. Rosenberg (1989, p. 123) formulates a version of the theory of evolution that is at least similar to the version in *The Origin of Species*.
4. George Argyrous discusses in detail a particular case in which a global economic theory inspired mini-theories. The global theory is neoclassical economics and the mini-theories are the permanent income hypothesis (PIC) and the life cycle hypothesis (LCH). These similar mini-theories were devised to deal with the problem of accounting for data concerning income and consumption which the simple Keynesian consumption function was unable to account for, data such as that consumption is more stable than current income. Speaking of how the (PIC) and (LCH) approached this problem, Argyrous (1992, p. 237) says 'By posing the problem of savings and consumption in terms of maximization under constraint, researchers were able to import the techniques and apparatus that had already proven to be powerful analytical devices in microeconomics'. Argyrous is noting that the construction of the (PIC) and the (LCH) was in part guided and justified by the neoclassical global statement that economic agents are optimizers. Argyrous's remark illustrates the crucial heuristic and justificatory roles that global theories often play in the construction of mini-theories.
5. Hausman (1981, pp. 111, 139–41) correctly notes that economic models often include simplifications among their assumptions (though Hausman's own account of simplifications ties them too closely to the use of models to explain and predict real world phenomena). Simplifications are statements that are false if viewed as

descriptions of the real world, but serve some purpose such as increasing mathematical tractability or making essential principles stand out more clearly. For instance, an economist may develop a model about the expansion and contraction of transactions deposits in the banking system in the USA, and how the Federal Reserve System can affect these processes through open market operations. The model might well include the assumption that the M1 money supply contains no paper money and coins or travellers' cheques. This assumption is a simplification, since it is false as a description of the real world but allows the essential points about the Fed's impact on deposit expansion/contraction to stand out more clearly. The simplification just cited happens also to be an idealizing assumption in the sense described in section 5.2 above. In general, idealizing assumptions are a special kind of simplification. But not all simplifications are idealizing assumptions. For example, suppose an economist develops a model of demand for labour by business firms. To simplify the discussion, he or she may assume that the labour and product markets firms operate in are competitive. This is false as a description of the real world; many firms do not operate in competitive labour and product markets. Yet the assumption in question is not an idealizing assumption, as it does not take to a limit some magnitude which does not ever assume that limiting value in the real world. The frequent inclusion of simplifications in economic models does not affect my general account of them as mini-theories. Mini-theories can, and economic mini-theories frequently do, include simplifications among their assumptions.

6.   Globalists such as Lakatos are sometimes associated with the view that only global theories, not mini-theories, are the proper units of appraisal or assessment. For instance, Mark Blaug (1980, p. 143) says 'Lakatos begins by denying that individual theories [mini-theories] are the appropriate units of appraisal; what ought to be appraised are clusters of interconnected theories or "scientific research programmes" (SRP).' But in acknowledging the existence of global theories in a discipline, I am not granting that the sole appropriate unit of epistemic or cognitive appraisal is the global theory. In fact, in economics and elsewhere mini-theories are appropriate objects of appraisal. For instance, in a well-known article George Stigler criticizes the kinked demand model of oligopoly (Stigler, 1952). His objection is that the model fails to square with the empirical evidence of the behaviour of firms in various oligopoly industries. It would be unreasonable at best to *object* to Stigler's criticism by pointing out that it is directed at a mini-theory rather than a global theory.

7.   Hausman (1994b, pp. 205–10) follows his critique of Weintraub with a much richer account than Weintraub's of neoclassical microeconomics. But Hausman is not as careful as he might be to keep separate elements *within* neoclassical microtheory and *philosophical descriptions* of the theory. For instance, Hausman apparently includes within neoclassical microtheory the proposition that (C4) neoclassical microtheory provides a unified, complete yet inexact account of its domain. Hausman (1994b, p. 205) says that (C4) is generally accepted, and presumably this means by economists themselves. Yet (C4) looks more like a philosopher's description of neoclassical microtheory rather than part of the economic global theory itself. Furthermore, in *The Inexact and Separate Science of Economics,* Hausman's account of neoclassical microeconomics represents it as having the deductive structure of a mini-theory. Its axioms are the ten alleged laws of equilibrium theory set out in section 4.2. Theorems or derived statements include the generalizations about market behaviour like the law of demand. But this account misrepresents neoclassical microeconomics. It is a global theory which does not have the deductive structure of a mini-theory, though it does include many mini-theories which are deductive systems. The global statements of

neoclassical micro like 'Individuals are optimizers' occur in various specific neoclassical mini-theories or models. But these global statements are not themselves the axioms of a separate deductive system. They are just a loose assemblage of statements that are part of neoclassical microeconomics.

8. As Tiebout (1972, p. 520) notes, the Tiebout model being in equilibrium does not necessarily involve all preferences for local public goods being *completely* satisfied. Suppose a consumer-voter's first choice of a tax and expenditure package is in a community already at optimum size, and which he therefore cannot get into by axiom (A7). His second choice is a community at less than optimum size by one person, and so he moves there. Assume no other consumers can do better by moving to communities of less than optimum size. In this case the model is in equilibrium, and yet one citizen-voter is not completely or perfectly happy with the tax and expenditure package of his community.

9. But some economists have attempted to determine whether the Tiebout model does to some extent approximate what happens in the real world. The approach is to infer from the Tiebout model some statements which are capable of being tested against empirical data. The inferred statement is then tested with the aid of multiple regression analysis. Depending on the outcome of the regression, some conclusion is reached about the relevance of the Tiebout model to the real world. Wallace Oates (1969) made the first attempt to pursue this approach to the Tiebout model. The statement Oates claimed follows from the Tiebout model and which he checked against empirical data is this: a community's level of expenditure on public goods is positively correlated with local property values, and the level of local taxes is negatively related to local property values. Call this alleged implication of the Tiebout model 'the Oates implication'. Using a sample of New Jersey municipalities, Oates did a regression analysis which confirmed the Oates implication, and Oates concluded the Tiebout model is relevant to the real world. However, this conclusion is not warranted, as the Oates implication does not really follow from the Tiebout model. Edel and Sclar (1974, pp. 944–5) present an argument for the claim that the Oates implication is not implied by the Tiebout model.

10. Though I think Weintraub's reliance on Lakatos's theory about global theories is unfortunate, there is much of value in his book *General Equilibrium Analysis*. Weintraub (1985, p. 122) makes the suggestion that the term 'general equilibrium theory' should be avoided and instead we should use 'general equilibrium' as an adjective as in 'general equilibrium model'. I have adopted this sensible suggestion here.

11. In Chapter 1 of *General Equilibrium Analysis* Weintraub constructs a simple GE model which assumes the existence of an economy with just three goods. Commenting on the key problem the simple GE model addresses, Weintraub (1985, p. 3) says 'We want to know whether the choices that the agents make are even *potentially* consistent. The search for the existence of equilibrium prices is equivalent to a search for a mutually consistent set of decisions.' In a brief but useful treatment of GE analysis, Walter Nicholson (1978, p. 596) says 'The question posed by Walras is whether or not there exists a set of prices for which supply is equal to demand *in all markets simultaneously*' (italics in original). And it is clear from Nicholson's discussion that the question is not whether or not such a set of prices exists in the real world. Rather the question is whether or not all markets in a perfectly competitive economy *could* arrive at equilibrium prices simultaneously.

12. Instrumentalism has been understood in somewhat different ways by economic methodologists. For a description of three interpretations of instrumentalism by other

methodologists, see Rappaport, 1986a, pp. 44–7. None of these three interpretations is the same as the one I endorse here.

13. Kuhn's views about the appraisal of global theories are criticized by Laudan, 1996, pp. 89–99. Lakatos's views about the assessment of global theories incorporate Popper's unacceptable views on induction. Lakatos is criticized by Hausman, 1992a, Ch. 11. Laudan (1996, pp. 84–5) takes a global theory GTa to be more adequate than another global theory GTb provided that the mini-theories in GTa exhibit a greater degree of problem-solving effectiveness than the mini-theories in GTb. But Laudan's problem solving approach to the assessment of both mini-theories and global theories suffers from the drawback that it disconnects scientific inquiry altogether from the pursuit of truth about the real world. Laudan (1977, pp. 123–5) admits that the fact that a theory exhibits problem solving effectiveness implies nothing at all about its truth. As David Hull (1979, p. 462) says 'The feature of Laudan's analysis which is most likely to give them [philosophers] pause is the absence of any role for empirical truth in science'.

14. Disagreements about Keynes's own theory are in part disputes about the elements of the global theory Keynesian macroeconomics. For useful discussion of differing accounts of Keynes's views, see Blaug, 1985, pp. 654–72.

15. The appeal to experience to justify global statements is not uncommon among economists. Speaking of neoclassical global statements like (GS2) above, Lionel Robbins (1994, p. 89) says 'We do not need controlled experiments to establish their validity: they are so much the stuff of our everyday experience that they only have to be stated to be recognized as obvious'. Economic methodologists also sometimes appeal to experience in assessing economic generalizations. Speaking of the generalizations of equilibrium theory in his sense, Hausman (1992a, p. 210) says 'But everyday experience and introspection are sufficient to establish that some of these laws, such as diminishing marginal rates of substitution and diminishing returns, are reasonable approximations. Without qualifications and a margin of error, they are false, but, with these, they seem true; and economists have good reason to be committed to them.' Notice that Hausman does not say that experience warrants accepting *as true* any of the generalizations of equilibrium theory. He just regards experience as justifying viewing some generalizations of equilibrium theory as approximations, that is, statements that are false as stated yet true in a range of real world cases within a margin of error. Of course, Hausman believes that once the generalizations of equilibrium theory are qualified with vague *ceteris paribus* clauses, then they become laws and so are true. In section 4.4 I argued that experience is altogether insufficient to establish this belief of Hausman's.

16. A rough generalization is not a scientific law on the standard conception of laws set out in section 4.1. For rough generalizations are false, and laws are truths. That economists not infrequently accept their generalizations only in the sense of believing them to be rough generalizations, is an obstacle to viewing economics as a science in the manner of the positivist tradition described in section 4.1. Nor can economics be moved closer to a science meeting positivist standards by prefixing vague *ceteris paribus* clauses to the rough generalizations of economics. This manoeuvre, which is essentially Hausman's, was shown to be unsuccessful in section 4.4.

17. The charge of excessive formalism incorporates the accusation that economics relies excessively on unrealistic assumptions, which was treated at length in Chapter 5. Saying that economists expend too much effort deducing theorems from axioms which describe imaginary situations, rather than actual economic life, implies that these axioms are not realistic$_b$, that is, are false descriptions of the real world.

18. Theories of competence are not necessarily ideal theories in the sense described in

section 5.2. But the neoclassical models that are competence theories tend to be ideal theories. Expected utility theory, the theory of firm behaviour in perfect competition, the theory of consumer choice under conditions of certainty, *et al.* are at the same time both competence and ideal theories.

19. The fact that neoclassical economists exhibit a considerable, if not excessive, fondness for mathematics is partly due to their acceptance of (GS1) and their resulting penchant for constructing competence theories. As Alexander Rosenberg (1992, pp. 231–2) says 'Microeconomics is avowedly an extremal theory. Like these other theories [Newtonian mechanics and evolutionary biology], it asserts the system it describes maximizes a quantity – in this case, utility (or preference, etc.) instead of fitness or total energy. That is why it can be couched in the language of differential calculus.' Thus it is the extremal character of neoclassical microeconomics that in a large measure explains the widespread use of mathematical theories like calculus which contain sophisticated techniques for finding maximum and minimum values of functions.

7. Economic Models (II)

7.1 THE MODAL VIEW

The preceding chapter provided only a partial account of the nature of economic models. Two of the main points about models made in Chapter 6 are (A) economic models are mini-theories, that is, sets of assumptions or axioms together with their deductive consequences; and (B) the axioms of models typically include in some form global statements belonging to a global theory accepted by the economists constructing the models. But more needs to be said about the nature of models to complete the account begun in Chapter 6. Different views of economic models have been discussed by economic methodologists, one of which is the modal view. Daniel Hausman, a critic of the modal view, provides the following rough description of it:

> Instead they [economists] wish to interpret their models as making unrealistic claims (hence the use of the term 'ideal') about how things *would be,* were various complications absent. I shall call this view of economic models the 'modal model' view, since it interprets models as making *modal* claims about how things would be. According to the modal view, sentences like 'Entrepreneurs attempt to maximize profits' do not merely define predicates in models and make inexact claims in theories. Rather they state truths about certain *possible* economies. (Hausman, 1981, pp. 146-7, italics in original)

Let us provide a more precise account of the modal view. A model consists of a set K of assumptions together with their deductive consequences, *plus* a set of objects L whose behaviour is described by K. (Some models may include definitions in set K in addition to non-definitional assumptions and the theorems of the model.) The objects in L are *hypothetical* in that they would exist if the conditions conveyed by K were met in the real world. For example, the model of the short run behaviour of a firm in perfect competition is typically developed by presenting the definition of a perfectly competitive market, as well as setting out a number of assumptions or axioms. The axioms include such

statements as that firms' managers act so as to maximize profits, and
assumptions about the shapes of various cost curves of the firm. Using
logic and mathematics, theorems are generated from the axioms and the
definition of a competitive market. The model describes the behaviour of
hypothetical objects, that is, objects that would exist if certain conditions
were met. The model includes a set of firms, firm managers, etc. – this
is the model's set L – whose behaviour is characterized by the statements
of the model. These firms, firm managers, etc. are hypothetical. They
would exist if the conditions conveyed by the statements in the set K of
the model obtained in the real world.

What has been said so far about economic models holds for *theoretical*
models. The modal view in the form I am going to defend it here also
recognizes *applied* models. The distinction between the two kinds of
models is as follows. Often in developing a model, an economist is doing
so in abstraction from any particular real world situation, or any kind of
real world situation. Such a model is a theoretical model. For instance,
an economist may present the model of firm behaviour in the long run
in a perfectly competitive industry. He may begin by setting out the
definition of a perfectly competitive market and then state axioms of the
model. The economist then proceeds to generate theorems such as 'In
the long run a firm only makes a normal profit (its revenues just cover
all its costs)'. The economist is not applying the model to some particular
real world situation such as the wheat market in the United States. Nor
is he applying the model to a specific kind of real world situation, such
as agricultural markets in the United States and other countries. The
model in question would then be a theoretical model.

An applied model is a model that is being applied to a particular real
world situation, or a whole class of real world situations of some sort.
The following passage from Gibbard and Varian provides further
illumination about applied models:

> A model, though, may be applied to the world or, as we shall say, applied to
> a *situation*. It is then said what firms, what prices and the like are being
> modeled; the result we shall call an *applied model*. An applied model is
> stipulated by starting with a model and then giving its predicates particular
> extensions, its quantifiers particular domains, and the like – by providing an
> 'interpretation' in the logicians' sense.... However an applied model is
> presented, the difference between a [theoretical] model and an applied model
> is this: whereas a model speaks of entities of certain general kinds – prices,
> consumers, information, and the like – without saying which particular entities
> in the world they are, an applied model specifies the particular classes of
> entities it treats. The theory of the firm, for instance, is a [theoretical] model;
> when it is interpreted as talking about General Motors, the cars General

Motors produces, their prices, and the like, it is an applied model. (Gibbard and Varian, 1978, p. 667, italics in original)

Gibbard and Varian are suggesting that an applied model results from a theoretical model M by interpreting the variables and general terms in M in terms of a particular real world situation, or a specific kind of real situation.[1] To interpret a variable in model M in terms of a particular real world situation S, or a kind of real world situation Z, is to replace the variable with the corresponding variable whose values are *restricted to* magnitudes in S or particular situations of kind Z. For example, consider a Keynesian income-expenditure model whose axioms include the following consumption function:

$$C=a + MPC \cdot DY \quad a>0, \; 0<MPC<1 \qquad (7.1)$$

To interpret the variables 'C' and 'DY' in (7.1) and elsewhere in the model in terms of the American economy in, say, 1929, is to replace C and DY in the model – actually or merely mentally – with 'consumption spending in the American economy in 1929' and 'disposable income in the American economy in 1929' respectively. To interpret a general term in a model M in terms of a particular real world situation S, or a kind of real world situation Z, is to replace the general term with another one denoting *only* items in S or situations of kind Z. For example, to interpret the term 'firm' in the model of perfect competition in terms of the wheat market in the United States, is to replace 'firm' in the model with a term like 'American wheat farm'.[2]

On the modal view *only* theoretical models are about hypothetical objects. Various statements in an applied model are true or false statements about the particular real world situation, or class of real world situations, to which the model is being applied. For example, suppose that an economist applies the model of perfect competition to the wheat market in the USA. The axiom of the model 'Firm managers act so as to maximize profits' becomes a truth or a falsehood about *just* the firms in the American wheat market. It will be a truth provided that managers of wheat farms set their output level where marginal revenue equals marginal cost (and the second order condition for a maximum is also met). But theoretical models do *not* contain true or false statements about real world situations. They include *true* statements about *hypothetical objects*. I am not saying that non-definitional statements of a theoretical model *would* be true if certain circumstances obtained. The statements of a theoretical model *are* true. The point is worth emphasizing to avoid misunderstanding. A theoretical model in effect includes a domain or universe of discourse consisting of hypothetical objects – this is the set L mentioned earlier in this section. The statements of the theoretical model are interpreted in terms of the domain of hypothetical objects. For example, a term such as 'firm' in the theoretical model of perfect competition is interpreted as applying to firms among the hypothetical objects in the model's domain. It is stipulated or postulated that the axioms of a theoretical model afford a *true* description of the hypothetical objects in the model's domain or universe of discourse. Thus the truth of the axioms – and so the theorems or derived statements – of a theoretical model is quite actual; it is only the objects that these statements are about which are hypothetical.

Gibbard and Varian deny that the sentences used to formulate a model that is not applied have a truth value. They say this:

> Now although a model, as we use the term, is a story, it is not a story about any particular situation in the world. The theory of the firm, for instance, does not tell us which firms it is describing. The assumptions and derived statements of a model, then, are not themselves propositions that can be true or false, roughly true or wildly off the mark. (Gibbard and Varian, 1978, p. 667)

The second sentence in this passage does not, however, follow from the first. That a set of statements is not about objects in some particular situation in the real world, does not entail that the statements in the set lack a truth value. Gibbard and Varian appear to overlook the possibility that a set of statements can be about hypothetical objects which are not found in any particular situations in the real world, and that such statements can be true.

But how, one may wonder, can statements about hypothetical objects be true. W.V. Quine in effect provides the answer in an illuminating discussion of truth in set theory. Speaking of set theory, Quine says this:

> In set theory we discourse about certain immaterial entities, real or erroneously alleged, viz., sets, or classes. And it is in the effort to make up our minds about genuine truth and falsity of sentences about these objects that we find ourselves engaged in something very much like convention in an ordinary non-metaphorical sense of the word. We find ourselves making deliberate choices and setting them forth unaccompanied by any attempt at justification other than in terms of elegance and convenience. These adoptions, called postulates, and their logical consequences (via elementary logic), are true until further notice. So here is a case where postulation can plausibly be looked on as constituting truth by convention.... Insofar as we would epistemologize and not just mathematicize, we might divide postulation as follows. Uninterpreted

postulates may be put aside, as no longer concerning us; and on the interpreted side we may distinguish between *legislative* and *discursive* postulation. Legislative postulation institutes truth by convention, and seems plausibly illustrated by contemporary set theory. On the other hand discursive postulation is mere selection, from a pre-existing body of truths, of certain ones for use as a basis from which to derive others, initially known or unknown. (Quine, 1966, pp. 110-11, italics in original)

So, legislative postulation is simply deciding to take a statement as true – Quine cites elegance and convenience as two bases for making such a decision. Statements that become true *via* legislative postulation are true by convention. But, as Quine notes, statements that become true through legislative postulation are only true until further notice; their truth value is subject to revision.

Above I said that theoretical models contain true statements about hypothetical objects. The non-definitional assumptions of a theoretical model are interpreted as being about hypothetical objects in the set L that is included in the model. And these assumptions become *truths* through legislative postulation as Quine describes it. And of course, the truth of a model's assumptions, merely conventional though it may be, is transmitted to the theorems or derived statements of the theoretical model by the deduction of these theorems from the assumptions of the model. It might be asked how this account could be squared with feature (B) of economic models cited at the very start of this chapter. It is true that a global statement such as

(GS2) Individuals are able to rank alternatives from the most to the least preferred

is most naturally interpreted as being about real world individuals rather than hypothetical ones. This is the natural interpretation of (GS2) regarded simply as one of the global statements belonging to neoclassical microeconomics. But once a global statement like (GS2) is, as it were, inducted into a specific theoretical model it becomes reinterpreted as being about hypothetical objects in the set L that is part of the model. Although should the model be applied to a real world situation or class of real world situations, (GS2) as occurring in the model would be interpreted as being about some range of real world individuals.

Two final points need to be made to clarify what the modal view of economic models involves. It is very important to deflect a certain misunderstanding of the modal view, a misunderstanding which has led to a negative appraisal of the view by some. Consider the following passage from one of Hausman's discussions of the modal view:

> Many economists have regarded their theories as making claims about how things would be were various complications absent. I do not see any way of arguing that this view of economic models and theories is incorrect. I have, however, two qualms. First I am disposed toward metaphysical modesty. If one can thoroughly and sensibly understand economic theory without making reference to merely possible economies, so much the better. (Hausman, 1981, p. 147)

This passage implies that the modal view of economic models is committed to an ontology of possible or hypothetical objects. And this commitment is reason to reject the modal view. In response to this, the modal view carries *no* commitment whatsoever to an ontology of possible or hypothetical objects. The modal view says that theoretical economic models afford true descriptions of the behaviour of hypothetical objects. But this does not mean that the modal view is committed to the *existence* of hypothetical objects of any kind. To say that a model provides a true account of the behaviour of hypothetical objects of some sort, is to say that the model describes the behaviour of objects that *would* exist if certain conditions were met. This hardly implies that objects of the sort in question *do exist*. I can give a true description of a forest fire that would occur in the Santa Cruz mountains if certain conditions were met. But this does not mean that the fire exists or is occurring.

Even though the modal view of economic models is not committed to the existence of hypothetical or possible objects, it might still be thought that the modal view relies on or presupposes the possible worlds framework which some philosophers – David Lewis, Saul Kripke, *et al.* – have tried to develop to interpret ordinary modal discourse and provide semantics for modal logic. (Of course, many who adopt the possible worlds framework do not think that *there are* possible worlds, possible objects, and so on; only modal realists like David Lewis think this.) The modal view does say that theoretical economic models afford true descriptions of hypothetical objects. And, it might be said, what else is a hypothetical object but an object that exists in, or is an inhabitant of, a possible world? The conclusion that would be drawn is that the modal view is unattractive given its involvement with the problematic possible worlds framework. However, the line of thought just set out is not persuasive. To be sure, the modal view of economists' models uses the concept of a hypothetical object. As indicated above, this notion is explainable as follows:

(Df1) X is a hypothetical object iff if certain conditions were met in the real world, then X would exist.

The subjunctive conditional on the right side of 'iff' in (Df1) obviously does not contain a term expressing the concept of a (logically) possible world or kindred notions such as an inhabitant of a possible world. Of course, there is an analysis of subjunctive conditions, developed by David Lewis, Robert Stalnaker, *et al.*, which uses the possible worlds framework. A rough, informal version of this analysis applied to what follows 'iff' in (Df1) above is as follows (see Lewis, 1973, p. 1):

(2) 'If certain conditions were met in the real world, then X would exist', means that X exists in that possible world most like the actual world in which the certain conditions are met.

If (2) reflects how we are to understand subjunctive conditionals like the right side of (Df1), then the notion of a hypothetical object, and so the modal view, does presuppose the possible worlds framework. But the modal view's involvement with that framework would simply be a result of the *correct* analysis of subjunctive conditionals, which happens to use the possible worlds framework. And this involvement could hardly be seen as a defect in the modal view. On the other hand, there is no general agreement among philosophers that the possible worlds approach does represent the correct analysis of subjunctive conditionals. And if it should turn out that a possible worlds analysis of subjunctive conditionals is *not* correct, then the modal view's notion of a hypothetical object as defined by (Df1) would not presuppose the possible worlds framework. In sum, either the modal view presupposes the possible worlds framework, but this implies no defect in the modal view. Or the modal view does not involve the possible worlds framework at all, in which case it cannot be seen as unattractive because of a commitment to that framework.

7.2 TWO ALTERNATIVES TO THE MODAL VIEW

There are alternatives to the version of the modal view of economic models developed in the previous section.[3] The two competitors to the modal view worth discussing are the lawlike generalization view of models, and the structuralist view of models. Let us start with the former. The lawlike generalization view of economic models is an application of a view of scientific theories which is succinctly set out in the following passage from Hausman:[4]

> Few contemporary philosophers still accept the positivist view of scientific theories. Theories cannot be formalized in the way in which the logical positivist wished, and to view scientific theories as primarily formal or syntactic objects does not do justice to the way in which theories are constructed or used. Furthermore, the problems of relating theory to observation, in the form in which positivists posed them, are intractable. Many philosophers now settle for an informal construal of theories as collections of lawlike *statements* (not uninterpreted, purely syntactic sentences) systematically related to one another. (Hausman, 1994a, p. 12, italics in original)

Applying the view of scientific theories presented here to economic models gives us the lawlike generalization view of models. According to this view, an economic model is a systematically related set of statements including some lawlike general statements. Presumably the sort of systematization in question is deductive. So, on the lawlike generalization view, an economic model is a set of statements, including some lawlike generalizations, which are organized into a deductive system. Not all the statements in an economic model need be lawlike generalizations; for instance, a model may include simplifications which are not lawlike generalizations. (On simplifications see note 5 to Chapter 6.) But at least some of the statements in any economic model must be lawlike generalizations. Of course, given the standard philosophical conception of scientific laws set out in section 4.1, this means that should the lawlike generalizations in an economic model be *true*, then the model would contain scientific laws.

A crucial feature of the lawlike generalization view is that the lawlike generalizations included in any economic model are about *real world* objects. Or alternatively, the statements in any economic model are interpreted in terms of the real world; models are never interpreted in terms of a universe of discourse of hypothetical objects. For example, the model of the rational consumer familiar from microeconomic textbooks includes the statement

(3) Consumers have preferences that are transitive.

According to the lawlike generalization view, the general term 'consumers' in (3) denotes or refers to real world consumers such as you and me. A distinction between theoretical and applied models such as the modal view makes is not recognized by the lawlike generalization view. *All* economic models are applied in the sense that their terms are interpreted as denoting real world items, and their variables are regarded as expressing real world economic magnitudes.[5] As a result of this feature of models, the lawlike generalizations in economic models are true or false statements about the real world.

The second alternative to the modal view I want to discuss is the structuralist conception of economic models. The structuralist view that I will present and evaluate here is an application to economics of a composite of several versions of the structuralist view of scientific mini-theories adumbrated by various philosophers.[6] Daniel Hausman and D. Wade Hands are two prominent economic methodologists who have treated in detail the structuralist view of economic models. The structuralist view presented here is very close to the one Hausman accepts and the one Hands discusses, although Hands himself does not accept the structuralist view. According to the structuralist view, an economic model is a *definition* of a predicate. As Hausman (1992a, p. 78) says 'In summary, models are definitions of kinds of systems, and they make no assertions'. Since a predicate denotes or is true of systems of a particular kind, Hausman's description of models is effectively the same as the one I have just cited. For example, consider the following definition of a rational consumer:

(Df2) *S* is a rational consumer iff (A) *S* has preferences which are complete, transitive and continuous, and (B) *S* maximizes his utility, that is, *S* prefers no option (of those attainable) to the one he chooses.

(Df2) is a model according to the structuralist view. The clauses (A) and (B) on the right side of 'iff' are the assumptions or axioms of the model. Note that they are included in the definition which is the model. Clauses (A) and (B) are not true or false, being simply open sentences. The assumptions of an economic model as contained in the definition which is the model are without truth value.[7]

A *realization* of an economic model is an item which is denoted by the predicate defined by the model.[8] For example, suppose the economist Paul Samuelson in fact has preferences which are complete, transitive and continuous, and also maximizes his utility. In other words, Paul Samuelson satisfies the two axioms (A) and (B) of the model of a rational consumer. In this case Paul Samuelson is denoted by the predicate 'is a rational consumer', and so is a realization of the model. In addition, on the structuralist view, an economic model has a set of *intended applications,* which comprise the *real world* items which are intended to be (or which proponents of the model want to be) realizations of the model. The set of intended applications of a model is the set of real world objects or systems which are intended to be realizations of the model. For example, real world consumers such as Paul Samuelson, you and me may be among the intended applications of the model of a rational consumer which is (Df2) above.[9] A realization of a model need not be a real world item or system; it could be a hypothetical object or system in the sense described in section 7.1. But the set of intended applications of an economic model contains only real world objects or systems. Although a particular real world object or system that is a member of the set of *intended* applications of a model might turn out *not* to be a realization of the model.

On the structuralist view of economic models, how do such models get connected with the real world? It is by formulating *theoretical hypotheses* that economists link up models and reality. Hausman (1992a, p. 75) says 'The other crucial part is proposing *theoretical hypotheses*, which assert that the new term [for the kind of system the model defines] is true of some actual system' (italics in original). Letting P be the predicate defined by an economic model and X a real world object or system, 'X is P' is a theoretical hypothesis. For example, suppose I affirm that

(4) Paul Samuelson is a rational consumer.

This is a theoretical hypothesis, as it asserts that a particular real world object is denoted by the predicate 'is a rational consumer' which is defined by the economic model (Df2). So far only *singular* theoretical hypotheses have been described. But theoretical hypotheses can be *general*. Hausman (1981, p. 48) says 'In my view scientists *can* offer not only singular theoretical hypotheses ('The solar system is a classical particle system') but general theoretical hypotheses ('Everything is a classical particle system') (italics in original). So a singular theoretical hypothesis such as (4) above is about just one real world object or system, whereas a general theoretical hypothesis is about a whole class of real world objects. Suppose that I affirm that

(5) American consumers in the 1990s are rational consumers.

This is a general theoretical hypothesis. A general theoretical hypothesis is of the form 'All S are P', with P being a predicate defined by an economic model and S a general term denoting real world items of some kind.[10]

The distinction between the modal and lawlike generalization views of economic models should be fairly clear. On the latter, all economic models are about real world objects, whereas on the modal view only applied models concern real world phenomena. Theoretical models are about hypothetical objects. But the relationship between the modal and structuralist views of economic models is less clear cut. A key difference between the two is that the structuralist view identifies a model with a definition of a predicate which includes a set of axioms or assumptions lacking a truth value. But the modal view does not identify an economic model with a definition of a predicate. A theoretical model is identified with a set K of definitions and non-definitional assumptions together with their deductive consequences, plus a set L of hypothetical objects described by the statements in K. An applied model is identified with a set of definitions and non-definitional assumptions about real world objects together with their deductive consequences. Nor are the axioms of a theoretical or an applied model without truth value. But there are some similarities between the modal and structuralist views. The theoretical hypotheses associated with a given economic model on the structuralist view are rather analogous to the applied models corresponding to a given theoretical model on the modal view. Both the theoretical hypotheses and the corresponding applied models say something, whether true or false, about real world economic phenomena. Although a theoretical hypothesis is a single statement, whereas an applied model of the modal view is a whole group of statements organized into a deductive system.[11]

Does the structuralist view recognize anything analogous to the theoretical models of the modal view? The set of axioms included in the definition of the predicate which is the model does not fill the bill. For, on the modal view the axioms of a theoretical model – which are included in the model's set K – are *truths*, albeit about hypothetical objects. But the axioms included in the definition of a predicate which is an economic model on the structuralist view *lack* a truth value, unless a realization of the model is supplied. However, the structuralist view does recognize something which is similar to the theoretical models of the modal view. Suppose that we have a set of hypothetical objects which constitute a realization of an economic model, and so the axioms listed in the definition of the predicate given by the model become *truths* when interpreted in terms of the hypothetical objects in question. Obviously this set of truths *plus* the realization of the model in question are quite similar to a theoretical model as conceived by the modal view.

7.3   IN DEFENCE OF THE MODAL VIEW

I turn now to indicating some advantages of the modal view of economic models over the two rival positions set out in section 7.2. Let us first compare the merits of the modal view and the lawlike generalization view. One relative disadvantage of the latter view is that it is an application to economics of a conception of scientific theories that comes out of the positivist movement described in section 4.1. Recall that a salient aspect of the positivist movement is the view that science as a process is a search for laws, and science as a product includes a corpus of laws. Accordingly positivists often view scientific theories as deductively organized sets of statements which include laws, or at least lawlike generalizations. The twentieth century positivist May Brodbeck (1968, p. 10) says 'A theory is such a deductively connected set of laws'. The lawlike generalization view of economic models is simply an application to economics of this positivist conception of scientific theories. However, as we saw in Chapter 4, the attempt to shed light on economics from the positivist perspective has not been a success. In section 4.1 the positivist conception of science as a quest for laws was encapsulated in the positivist condition, according to which it is necessary and sufficient for a discipline being an actual science that it includes the laws to which the phenomena it studies are subject. (This condition was further spelled out in terms of the distinction between fundamental and phenomenological laws.) And it was argued in Chapter 4 that the best case extant for economics fulfilling the positivist condition – which is found in Hausman's methodological writings – is a failure.[12] That the lawlike generalization view of economic models comes out of an approach to understanding economics that has been tried yet failed, leads one to think that some alternative way of viewing economic models not tied to the positivist movement would be preferable. And the modal view of economic models certainly fits this description. The modal view does not afford a positivist style characterization of economic models. This is shown by the fact that it makes no use of notions like that of a lawlike generalization or a scientific law to describe economic models.

But there is a second relative drawback of the lawlike generalization view of economic models. There is a feature of economic theorizing which the modal view accounts for much better than does the lawlike generalization view. The feature I have in mind is that some economic models do not purport to describe any real world phenomena. I will call such models 'nondescriptive models'. Nondescriptive models might be defined within the structuralist view of models by saying that for such models the set of intended applications of the model is empty. And from within the modal view, a nondescriptive model could be defined as a theoretical model whose corresponding applied models economists do not generally regard as truly describing a particular real world situation or class of situations they are about.[13] I have tried to define nondescriptive models in a way that is neutral between the competing theories about models by simply saying that such models do not even purport to describe economic reality.

A clear example of a nondescriptive model is the Tiebout model discussed in detail in section 6.2. Recall that Tiebout's model was originally constructed to resolve a *conceptual problem*. The problem is this: Is it possible for there to be a set of social institutions in which people reveal their true preferences for public goods, and for the approximate quantities of these goods people want to be provided? The axioms of the Tiebout model, which are set out in section 6.2, emphasize the role of local governments in affording a solution to this problem. Specifically, the axioms and relevant theorems cited in section 6.2 explain and justify Charles Tiebout's answer to the conceptual problem which is as follows:

(TA) It is possible for there to be a set of social institutions in which people do reveal their true preferences for public goods, and for the approximate quantities of these goods people want to be provided. The social institutions in which this possibility would be realized are a system of local governments or communities operating as described by the Tiebout model.

This characterization of the Tiebout model makes clear that the model does not purport to describe real world economic phenomena of interest to economists. Axioms of the model such as (A1) and (A2) are *plainly false* as descriptions of the real world, and of course were recognized to be so by Tiebout himself. Instead the Tiebout model is designed to establish the *possibility* conveyed by (TA).

According to the lawlike generalization view of economic models, we would have to interpret terms such as 'consumer-voters' and 'local governments' in the axioms and theorems of the Tiebout model as referring to real world individuals and real world local governments or communities such as San Francisco, California and Florence, Italy. Recall that it is part of the way the lawlike generalization view was defined in section 7.2 that the view affirms that *any* economic model is about real world objects or systems. But then to interpret terms such as 'consumer-voter' in the Tiebout model as referring to real world individuals is necessarily to construe the model as *describing the real world* – of course, the Tiebout model so construed provides a *false* description of the real world. The reasonable general principle behind this claim is that if a set of largely descriptive or non-normative claims, such as the axioms and theorems of the Tiebout model, is interpreted as being about the real world, then the set of claims at least in part affords a description, whether true or false, of the real world. However, as indicated in the previous paragraph, the Tiebout model does not even purport to describe the real world. Yet the lawlike generalization view of economic models is committed to saying that the Tiebout model describes the real world (though the description it affords is false). In general, the lawlike generalization view of economic models commits us to saying of a given nondescriptive model M that M describes the real world. Yet, being nondescriptive, M does not even purport to describe the real world. The lawlike generalization view forces us to characterize nondescriptive economic models in a way that is not appropriate to their nature.

However, the modal view of economic models does not commit us to inappropriate descriptions of nondescriptive models. According to the modal view, the Tiebout model is a theoretical model whose set K contains the axioms of the model which are set out in section 6.2, as well as the deductive consequences of those axioms. The Tiebout model's set L is a set of hypothetical objects including consumer-voters and local communities having different tax systems and mixes of public goods. A term like 'consumer-voter' in the axioms and theorems of the Tiebout model does *not* denote inhabitants of real world local communities, but rather denotes the hypothetical consumer-voters in the model's set L. Thus the Tiebout model is not seen by the modal view as describing what happens in real world local communities. Instead, the axioms and therefore the theorems of the model afford a true description of what happens in the model's domain of hypothetical objects. Obviously, the account the modal view gives of the Tiebout model is entirely faithful to the fact that the model does not purport to describe real world phenomena. Moreover, the role the Tiebout model is designed to play is easily understood in terms of the modal view. Recall that Tiebout developed his model in order to show that it is possible for local governments to provide the quantities of public goods which approximate what consumer-voters want. On the modal view, Tiebout tried to establish such a possibility by developing a set of assumptions which afford a true description of a *hypothetical* domain. He reasoned from his assumptions to the theorem or conclusion that when the Tiebout model is in equilibrium, the consumer-voters in this hypothetical domain come at least fairly close to getting the quantities of public goods they want insofar as local government can supply these. That this theorem, interpreted as being about hypothetical objects, follows from the assumptions of the Tiebout model, establishes that it is possible for local governments to provide approximately the quantities of public goods consumer-voters want. The modal view's description of the Tiebout model makes readily intelligible how the model manages to establish the possibility it is designed to.

On the basis of our discussion of the Tiebout model, we can say that the lawlike generalization view of economic models seems unable to account for the fact that some economic models are nondescriptive. But the modal view is entirely compatible with the fact that economics includes nondescriptive models. According to the modal view, nondescriptive models like the Tiebout model afford true descriptions of hypothetical objects. Consequently nondescriptive models as understood by the modal view do not purport to describe real world phenomena, and of course this is exactly what a nondescriptive model is. The modal view's ability to account for nondescriptive models in economics is a second significant advantage of the modal view over the lawlike generalization view.

I turn now to comparing the merits of the structuralist view of economic models with those of the modal view. An advantage which has been claimed for the structuralist view is that it explains what D. Wade Hands has called 'the empirical immunity' of economic theory. Hands describes this as follows:

> Despite the fact that most economists openly advocate the severe testing of economic theories, they in fact almost never practice what they preach. Negative evidence, if acknowledged at all, is never quite sufficient to dislodge (or cause the rejection of) a professionally popular theory. (Hands, 1985, p. 322)

There is no general agreement on how much evidence there is which disconfirms theories which economists persevere in accepting. Alexander Rosenberg believes that economics has failed to show an increase in improvement over the last century or two. As noted in section 3.3 above, in developing this view Rosenberg makes such claims as that half of the predictions of the theory of perfect competition have turned out to be false. But others dissent from Rosenberg's view. Some grounds for scepticism about Rosenberg's view were developed in section 3.3. And other methodologists, such as Hands in the mid 1980s, have expressed disagreement with Rosenberg. Hands says the following:

> But systematic predictive failure is *not* a standard methodological criticism of

applied economic theory. The reason why such predictive failure is not a standard criticism is quite simple: Rosenberg has exaggerated the extent of this failure. Predictive failure is simply not the ubiquitous fact of modern economic theory which Rosenberg assumes. While nowhere near the standards of the best natural science, applied economic theories (both micro and macro) do generate an ocean of successful predictions, on everything from the impact of trucking deregulation to the demand for consumer credit. (Hands, 1984, p. 497)

So the empirical immunity of economics is controversial. That is, it is controversial as to what extent there exists evidence disconfirming economic theories economists none the less continue to accept. But, for the sake of argument, let us grant that economists do continue to hold on to economic theories in the face of what some take to be adverse evidence.

The structuralist view of economic models is supposed to make sense of the empirical immunity of economics in the following fashion. On the structuralist view, there may be empirical evidence that disconfirms a particular *theoretical hypothesis* such as 'Paul Samuelson is a rational consumer'. But an economic model itself is not disconfirmed by such empirical evidence. Indeed, an economic model is not the sort of thing that could be disconfirmed by any empirical evidence whatsoever, since an economic model is identified with a definition of a predicate like 'is a rational consumer' or 'is a Keynesian economic system'.[14] It is no wonder, then, that economists hold on to their models in the face of what some take to be adverse evidence; it is not really evidence against the models themselves. Now the modal view of models can make sense of the (alleged) empirical immunity of economics as readily as the structuralist view can. On the modal view, empirical evidence can disconfirm an *applied* model corresponding to some theoretical model. But such evidence does not impugn the theoretical model at all. Empirical evidence of whatever sort is powerless to disconfirm a theoretical model. For empirical evidence is formulated by statements characterizing real world economic phenomena, while a theoretical model includes *truths* about hypothetical economic phenomena. Since on the modal view putatively adverse evidence does not tell against theoretical models, it is not surprising that economists persevere in accepting theoretical models in the face of evidence that some have taken to disconfirm economic theories. In sum, the ability to explain the empirical immunity of economics does not distinguish the structuralist view of economic models from the modal view.

Another advantage which has been claimed for the structuralist view is expressed in the following passage from Hausman:

> An absolutely crucial step is constructing new concepts – new ways of classifying and describing phenomena. Much of scientific theorizing develops such new concepts, relates them to other concepts, and explores their implications. This kind of endeavor is particularly prominent in economics, where theorists devote a great deal of effort to exploring the implications of perfect rationality, perfect information, and perfect competition. These explorations, which are separate from questions of application and assessment, are, I believe, what economists (but *not* econometricians) call 'models.' One can thus make good use of the semantic view to help understand theoretical models in economics. (Hausman, 1994a, p. 13)

As the context from which this passage is drawn makes clear, Hausman is using the term 'the semantic view' to refer to the structuralist view of economic models. Given the reference to perfect competition and the like, Hausman seems to claim here that the structuralist view of models has the advantage of enabling us to understand or account for nondescriptive models in economics such as the Tiebout model and the model of perfect competition. This claim implies that nondescriptive models can be viewed along structuralist lines without distorting their nature or role in economic theorizing. This implication seems plausible enough. We might reconstruct the Tiebout model along structuralist lines by recasting the model as a definition of the predicate 'is a Tiebout system of local governments'. The definition would be as follows:

(Df3) X is a Tiebout system of local governments iff X satisfies axioms (A1) to (A7) (see section 6.2 for the statements of these axioms).

A set or system of *hypothetical* consumer-voters and local governments could be specified as a realization for the model. This set of hypothetical objects would be denoted by the predicate 'is a Tiebout system of local governments'. Theorems of the model can be interpreted in terms of the set of hypothetical objects in question, including the theorem that when the Tiebout model is in equilibrium, consumer-voters come at least fairly close to getting the quantities of public goods they want. The fact that this theorem so interpreted can be deduced establishes the possibility that local governments can supply at least close to the quantities of public goods people want. This structuralist presentation of the Tiebout model seems compatible with the fact that it is a nondescriptive model, as well as the fact that its role is to establish the possibility just mentioned.[15] Yet the apparent fact that viewing nondescriptive models along structuralist lines does not distort their nature or role, affords *no* reason for preferring the structuralist view of economic models over the modal view. As indicated above, the modal view is entirely consistent with the presence in economics, and the functioning, of nondescriptive models.

The last two paragraphs may give the impression that the structuralist and modal views of economic models are pretty much tied as far as their worth or merits go. But this is not the case. The modal view enjoys a significant advantage over the structuralist view. The modal view is a much better description than the structuralist view of the way economists *in fact* present their models apart from applications of them to the real world. As a matter of fact, in presenting or developing a non-applied model, economists do *not* usually give a definition of a predicate of the sort the structuralist identifies with an economic model. For example, Charles Tiebout simply did not state a structuralist style definition of a predicate such as 'is a Tiebout system of local governments'. Economists do set out assumptions or axioms when they develop a model. And *sometimes* presenting a model includes giving one or more definitions. But the definitions are *not* invariably like a structuralist definition of a predicate which is identified with a model. For example, the usual development of the model of the behaviour of a firm in perfect competition includes a definition of a perfectly competitive market. The definition specifies conditions individually necessary and jointly sufficient for a market being perfectly competitive, such as the condition that firms on the sellers' side of the market produce a homogeneous good. But the definition does not say that a market is perfectly competitive iff it satisfies the axioms of the model such as 'Firm managers act so as to maximize profits'. So the structuralist view just does not fit the way economists actually present their models apart from applications to the real world. The modal view affords a better fit here. On the modal view a theoretical model may be presented by providing one or more definitions, such as the definition of a perfectly competitive market, and a model's presentation definitely includes a separate list of axioms or assumptions. The modal view does not represent the presentation or development of economic models as invariably including a definition of a predicate along structuralist lines. And, as I just indicated, this is in fact how economists present their non-applied models.

It might be admitted that the structuralist view does not afford as faithful a description of the way non-applied economic models are actually presented as does the modal view. But, it might be said, the structuralist view should not be seen as a description of how economists actually present non-applied models. Instead it should be seen as characterizing a way in which economic models can be reconstructed which is philosophically illuminating.[16] And we should compare the structuralist and modal views as illuminating reconstructions of economic models, rather than descriptions of the actual manner in which models are handled in economics. In response to this, the modal view itself involves a certain amount of reconstruction of economists' models. On the modal view, a theoretical model includes a set of hypothetical objects whose behaviour is described by the axioms and theorems of the model. But in presenting their models, economists usually do not specify a set of objects explicitly identified as hypothetical whose behaviour the model describes.

Furthermore, I am willing to grant that economic models can be reconstructed or restated along structuralist lines. For a given economic model, economic methodologists can invent a predicate and recast the model so that it is a structuralist style definition of that predicate – this was done above for the Tiebout model. But what gain in illumination would flow from restating economic models along structuralist lines which we do not get from the modal view? As we have seen, viewing economic models from the structuralist perspective can make sense of the (alleged) empirical immunity of economic theory. But recall that the modal view can do this just as well. It has been claimed that the structuralist view enables us to understand nondescriptive models in economics. But, as indicated above, the modal view also affords us this understanding. In short, I do not see that anything illuminating results from structuralist reconstructions of economic models which the modal view does not also give us. But since the modal view is a better description of how economists actually present their non-applied models, the modal view is the better of the two accounts of economic models.[17]

The modal view has been compared to the structuralist and lawlike generalization view of economic models. On the basis of our discussion, the modal view can be said to be preferable to either of its two rivals.

7.4   CONCLUDING REMARKS

I want to conclude by relating the modal view to the partial instrumentalism which I embraced in section 6.3. As the modal view is described in section 7.1, it affirms that the non-definitional statements in an *applied* model are true or false statements about the particular real world situation, or class of real world situations, to which the model is being applied. Is the modal view then committed to saying that when an economist formulates and adopts an applied model, he puts forward the axioms and so the theorems of the applied model as *true* of the real world situation or class of situations to which it is being applied? If this question has to be answered affirmatively, then the modal view would be committed to what is called the 'naive view' by Gibbard and Varian. They say:

> An investigator who applied a model to a situation might hypothesize that the assumptions of the model are true of the situation. This suggests a theory of economic models which we shall dismiss as the *naive view*: that when an investigator legitimately applies a model to a situation, he investigates the hypothesis that the assumptions of his applied model are true of the situation. (Gibbard and Varian, 1978, p. 668, italics in original)

Gibbard and Varian reject the naive view because it does not correctly describe economists' practice. Instead they claim that the non-definitional assumptions of an applied model are typically only seen by economists as *approximately true*. I am not prepared to reject this common view, though it does place a certain amount of weight on the somewhat problematic concept of approximate truth.[18]

The modal view of economic models does not have to adopt the naive view. The modal view is consistent with the claim Gibbard and Varian make. The non-definitional (and non-normative) statements in an applied model being seen as only approximately true, is compatible with these statements being true or false descriptions of the real world, as is required by the modal view. A proponent of the modal view like myself can, then, accept the Gibbard and Varian claim that economists put forward their *applied* models as only approximate truths about the real world. By adopting this claim, an advocate of the modal view is just as committed to partial instrumentalism as he would be were he to say that economists put forward their applied models as exactly true. Recall that partial instrumentalism says that (A) some economic models are not put forward as even close to true descriptions of the real world, and (B) a realist view is appropriate for *other* models and individual hypotheses, that is, economists put forward other models and hypotheses as true, or approximately true, descriptions of reality. By adopting the Gibbard and Varian claim, a proponent of the modal view clearly embraces part (B) of partial instrumentalism.

NOTES

1. This account characterizes applied models in terms of a relation to theoretical models. It should not be taken to imply that all applied models actually are obtained from pre-existing theoretical models. Some models seem to start out as applied models without being obtained from a theoretical model that has been antecedently constructed. An

example is Gary Becker's model of the optimal use of resources for crime control discussed above in section 6.2. The general terms and variables in Becker's own development of his model seem best interpreted in terms of the class of real world situations in which criminal acts occur and criminal justice systems attempt to control crime. Becker's model started out as an applied model.

2. Gibbard and Varian (1978, p. 672) usefully distinguish between casual applications of economic models, and applications employing the techniques of econometrics. Here I am only describing casual applications of models.

3. The version of the modal view adumbrated in section 7.1 should be sharply distinguished from the view, discussed by Hausman, that the inexact laws of economics make modal or counterfactual claims. In describing this latter view, Hausman (1992a, p. 129) says '... Mill sometimes explains the inexactness of economic laws by arguing that these "laws" state how things *would be*, were certain conditions met. They do not describe actual regularities. When the hypothetical conditions implicit in the laws are not met, things may not be the way the laws say they would be. This counterfactual view of the inexact "laws" of economics....' The modal view of models in section 7.1 is *not* a view about how to construe alleged inexact laws in economics. The modal view does not even imply that there are any scientific laws, inexact or otherwise, in economics.

4. But Hausman himself does not adopt the lawlike generalization view of models. Instead he accepts the structuralist view to be discussed below.

5. Sometimes a lawlike generalization view is put forward as holding for mini-theories in social science generally, and therefore for economic mini-theories or models in particular. See Brodbeck, 1968, pp. 457–8. Alexander Rosenberg has held that the general statements of neoclassical microeconomics are lawlike generalizations whose subject matter is real world economic phenomena. See Rosenberg, 1976, Chapters 3, 6 and 8. Since neoclassical models typically incorporate the sort of neoclassical general statement Rosenberg examines, presumably he would endorse the lawlike generalization view of neoclassical models. The Rosenberg of 1976 believes that the lawlike generalizations of microeconomics are qualified by explicit or implicit *ceteris paribus* clauses (Rosenberg, 1976, p. 130, 133–8). And the lawlike generalization view of economic models can readily allow that the lawlike generalizations in economics models are qualified by *ceteris paribus* clauses, whether they be precise or vague *ceteris paribus* clauses.

6. Versions of the structuralist (or semantic) view of scientific theories are found in Suppes (1957), Stegmüller (1976), Van Frassen (1980) and Giere (1991).

7. Hausman (1992a, p. 78) says 'It is a category mistake to ask whether they [economic models] are true or to attempt to test them'. Yet Hausman regards models as definitions. And he (1992a, p. 75) says 'Definitions are trivially true....' It may well be that when Hausman says, in the first remark I have just quoted, that models are without truth value, he means that the assumptions or axioms of a model lack a truth value. He could then consistently regard a model itself as trivially true, given that the model is a definition. In any case, a proponent of the structuralist view of economic models holds that the axioms of a model lack a truth value. But he may believe that a model itself is true, though, like any definition, trivially so.

8. Structuralists usually speak of models of a theory (Suppes, 1957, p. 253). I have used the term 'realization' instead of the term 'model' here to avoid confusion between economic models and models as items which satisfy a set of axioms.

9. The structuralist view might *identify* an economic model with an ordered n-tuple containing, among other things, the set of intended applications of the model

(Stegmüller, 1976, p. 118; Hands, 1985, p. 311). As I have presented the structuralist view of economic models, it identifies a model with a definition of a predicate rather than an ordered n-tuple of the sort just mentioned. The structuralist position I present is closer to Hausman's. Hausman is the sole prominent economic methodologist I know of to accept structuralism about economic models.

10. Hausman's version of the structuralist view of models has another element not described so far in my treatment. Hausman (1981, p. 47) says 'One can infer from a theoretical hypothesis what I shall call "closures" of the assumptions of the model'. From the examples Hausman supplies, it seems that a closure of an assumption of a model is a true or false statement resulting from interpreting the schematic letters or free variables in that assumption as denoting a real world object or a class of real world objects. For example, consider clause (B) of the model of a rational consumer which is (Df2) above. In (Df2) clause (B) is without a truth value. But from the singular theoretical hypothesis 'Paul Samuelson is a rational consumer', we can infer 'Paul Samuelson maximizes his utility'. This statement is a closure of assumption (B) of the model of a rational consumer.

11. In Hausman's version of the structuralist view, a set of closures of the axioms of an economic model, together with their deductive consequences, is the closest thing to an applied model of the modal view.

12. It is interesting that Hausman makes such a strenuous effort to show that economics does meet the positivist condition for science, and yet he does not adopt the lawlike generalization view of economic models but instead the rival structuralist view. Some philosophers who accept the general structuralist conception of scientific theories *reject* the positivist view of science as requiring laws, at least if laws are seen as true, universal generalizations. See Giere, 1990, pp. 82–6, 102–4.

13. A theoretical model *M* has an indefinite number of *corresponding* applied models according to the modal view. An applied model corresponding to *M* results by interpreting the general terms and variables in *M* in terms of a particular real world situation or a whole class of real world situations. See section 7.1 on the notion of interpreting general terms and variables in terms of real world situations.

14. As indicated in note 9, the structuralist view of economic models might identify a model with an ordered n-tuple containing the set of intended applications of the model as well as other items. Were the structuralist view to adopt this identification, it would still be true that an economic model is not the sort of thing that could be disconfirmed by empirical evidence. See Hands, 1985, pp. 322–3.

15. Economic methodologists have applied the structuralist view of models to Walrasian general equilibrium models (Händler, 1980; Hands, 1985). Hands (1985, p. 329) says that the set of intended applications of general equilibrium models is *empty*. The same is true of the set of intended applications of the structuralist reconstruction of the Tiebout model. No set of real world local communities or governments is going to satisfy the axioms of the Tiebout model like (A2).

16. Logical empiricist or positivist philosophers of science make a rather similar claim about their view that a scientific theory is associated with a formalized deductive system. For example, Richard Rudner (1966, p. 18) says 'It would be a serious mistake to construe the foregoing account [of theories as formalized deductive systems] as a description of the *actual* process by which theories are, or should be, formulated. It is *not* a description of any *process* of theory construction, actual or proposed; it is, rather, an account of the logical or structural characteristics of theories' (italics in original).

17. Hands makes the sensible suggestion (1985, p. 304) that a *good* philosophical account of economic models either helps us better understand such models, or accurately

describes how economists actually handle their models, or both. My case for the modal view relies on Hands's criterion. The structuralist view does not enable us to explain anything about economic models which the modal view cannot also explain; and the modal view is a more accurate description of how economists present their non-applied models. So, on Hands's criterion for a good philosophical account of models, the modal view is better than the structuralist view.

18. To say a statement in an applied model is approximately true concerning a particular real world situation, is to say that the real world situation in question closely resembles the way the world would be if the statement were true. But this account of approximate truth does not indicate how to *tell* whether a statement in an applied model is approximately true. And efforts by philosophers to supply an adequate analysis of the concept of approximate truth or verisimilitude have not met with success, leaving the concept in a rather unsatisfactory state.

8. Explanation in Economics

8.1   CAUSAL EXPLANATION IN ECONOMICS

As I said at the start of section 6.2, economics is to a significant degree an explanatory enterprise. This view is fairly common among economists themselves. For example, Donald McCloskey says:

> For another, economics *is* a science, a successful sort at that. Economics explains as much about business people and resources as evolution explains about animals and plants, and for identical reasons. No one who knows the subject will deny it; those who do not know it can become persuaded by reading Mancur Olson's *Logic of Collective Action* or Thomas Schelling's *Micromotives and Microbehavior* or another of the accessible jewels of the discipline. (McCloskey, 1985a, p. 56)

This chapter treats two types of explanations of real world phenomena which economics affords. They are explanation-why and explanation-what. It so happens that history provides the same two types of explanation of the phenomena it studies. Indeed, a theme of this chapter is the close similarity between economics and history. This section will treat explanation-why in economics, offering a *causal* theory of explanation-why. Subsequent sections will examine explanation-what. The discussion of this chapter will emphasize the role of models in the two kinds of economic explanations. This will serve to illustrate the claim of this monograph that much economic thinking is the construction of models and their utilization in various cognitive activities.

Even a relatively cursory familiarity with the work of economists reveals that they are interested in explaining *why* some phenomenon occurs or has occurred. Economists seek to explain why the Great Depression took place, why the price of health care has risen so rapidly in the USA since World War II, why the general level of prices rose dramatically in the Confederacy during the American civil war, and so on. In addition to seeking explanations of *individual* phenomena like those just listed, economists also seek explanations of *kinds* of phenomena or recurring patterns of phenomena. Economists seek to explain why involuntary unemployment occurs, why some goods have a low price elasticity, why some firms have more monopoly power (ability to set price above marginal cost) than other firms, and so on. I will use the term 'explanation-why' to refer to an explanation of why some phenomenon, whether individual or kind, occurs or has occurred. Again, it is plain that economists seek explanations-why.

Philosophers have proposed various theories about explanation-why. Perhaps the best-known is the covering law theory. According to this theory, to explain why a phenomenon occurs or has occurred is to subsume the phenomenon under one or more scientific laws.[1] Since subsumption here means deduction, the theory may be said to affirm that to give an explanation-why of a phenomenon is to deduce the occurrence of the phenomena from a set of premises which include one or more scientific laws. The covering law theory allows that explanations-why that people actually give are often not complete. Actual explanations are often elliptical, mere explanation sketches, or the like. But any full or complete explanation-why must include one or more scientific laws. However, the covering law theory is unacceptable. The objections to the theory by philosophers such as Michael Scriven and Richard Miller have, in my opinion, shown that the theory is fundamentally mistaken.[2]

I suggest that instead of the covering law theory, we adopt the causal theory of explanation-why. Richard Miller (1987, p. 60) says 'An explanation is an adequate description of underlying causes helping to bring about the phenomenon to be explained'. This is an expression of the causal theory of explanation-why. Relying on a Humean analysis of causation, a covering law theorist might say that the causal theory of explanation-why is just a special case of the covering law theory of explanation. Carl Hempel, the pre-eminent covering law theorist of the twentieth century, says:

> Causal explanation is a special type of deductive nomological explanation; for a certain event or set of events can be said to have caused a specified 'effect' only if there are general laws connecting the former with the latter in such a way that, given a description of the antecedent events, the occurrence of the effect can be deduced with the help of the laws. (Hempel, 1965, pp. 300–31)

So, given the nature of causation, a causal explanation subsumes the event to be explained under one or more scientific laws. But the causal theory of explanation-why in the form I accept it rejects entirely a Humean analysis of causation. (By a Humean analysis of causation, I mean one that relies upon the idea of a scientific law in analysing the concept of causation.) Indeed, following Miller, I take the concept of causation to be incapable of any analysis, Humean or otherwise, which purports to supply without circularity a list of logically necessary and sufficient conditions for one phenomenon causing another. Miller says:

> Why suppose that there is any definition of 'cause', informative, noncircular and valid a priori? It seems much truer to the facts about causality to take the category as covering a variety of processes, whose title to causal status does not derive from a fit with such a definition. At the core of the family of causes are a variety of processes of making things happen, recognized as such by primordial common sense, processes as diverse as pushing's changing the position of an object, a desire's leading someone to pursue a goal, a blow's causing pain, or pain's making someone cry. (Miller, 1984, p. 285)

So causation is not a concept definable in terms of a set of necessary and sufficient conditions. Rather it is a concept to be understood in terms of paradigm or core cases like the ones Miller cites in the quoted passage, and then extended by various analogical links to other cases. That causation is not susceptible of a non-circular, necessary and sufficient conditions analysis, is the best explanation for the failure of any philosopher to produce such an analysis which has survived criticism. On the view of causation I have endorsed, the concept of a scientific law is not part of the concept of causation. This means that the causal statement 'A caused B' does not entail a scientific law of the form 'Whenever an A-like event occurs, a B-like event follows'. (Here A and B represent descriptions of individual events or phenomena.) And it also means that the fact that A caused B does not entail that there is a scientific law connecting A and B under some description of them, perhaps drawing on a vocabulary quite different than that used in the descriptions A and B.

In light of these remarks about the concept of causation, it is clear that the causal theory of explanation-why does not reduce to the covering law theory. The former theory says that to explain a phenomenon is to cite a cause of it. But given what has been said about causation, explaining a phenomenon B by citing a cause A, is not subsuming B under any scientific law which connects A and B under any descriptions. There need be no such law for A to be a cause of B on the conception of causation that is sketched in the previous paragraph.

My view that not much can be said in a non-circular way about the *analysis* of causation, does not imply that there is little that can be said about the *testing* and *justification* of causal statements. This is a large and complex topic. But it is worth making some remarks about it, and applying them to the case of economics.

Richard Miller says the following about justifying causal statements:

> The comparison of rival hypotheses is an aspect of testing that can also provide empirical warrant for explanations in the absence of covering-laws. Sometimes, an investigator has reason to believe that one or another of a limited group of factors is more likely than not to have caused a phenomenon, if a phenomenon of that kind occurs in the population in question. This list of likely causes may be available even if none of those factors is likely to have that sequel, as an effect.... Sometimes, an investigator can use auxiliary principles to compare these alternatives in light of the data. He or she may be in a position to conclude that one of the factors is the most likely cause of what happened, but not in a position even to sketch a covering-law. (Miller, 1987, pp. 50–51)

Miller is describing a procedure for justifying a causal statement which begins with a short list of factors or conditions C1, C2, ... Cn amongst which the cause of a phenomenon P is likely to be found. Additional evidence is then marshalled that warrants saying that one of the conditions, say, C2, is (probably) the cause of P. Let us call this procedure for justifying causal statements 'the comparison of rival hypotheses method', or for short, 'the CRH method'. The CRH method is essentially a matter of selecting the best of a number of plausible, competing hypotheses.[3] As Miller remarks in the quoted passage, the CRH method may be successfully applied even though the investigator is unable to supply one or more scientific laws under which the occurrence of the phenomenon P is subsumable.

So economists supply explanations-why. And, I submit, their explanations-why are, like explanations-why generally, typically causal explanations; that is, economists' explanations-why typically fit a causal theory of explanation-why. In addition, I have put forward a philosophical thesis about the nature of causation to the effect that it is not definable in terms of necessary and sufficient conditions, but rather is a concept to be understood in terms of paradigm cases and then extended to other cases on the basis of similarities to paradigm cases. The CRH method of justifying causal statements has also been described. The point of the philosophical thesis about causation and the description of the CRH method, is to make clear that scientific laws as defined in section 4.1 are not essential to causal explanation.[4] It is important to make this point for the following reason. As indicated in section 4.5, there is something of a paucity of scientific laws in economics. So, if scientific laws are essential to causal explanation, economics would have a rather limited ability to provide causal explanations of real world phenomena. But, as scientific laws are not in fact essential to causal explanation, the paucity of laws in economics is not a barrier to the discipline providing causal explanations.

I want to illustrate and provide support for my claims about economic explanation-why by considering two explanations-why offered by economists. The examples will also illuminate the crucial role *models* often play in economic explanation-why. The first explanation I want to consider is given by Robert Paul Thomas in an elementary book that applies neoclassical micro theory to real world situations. Thomas (1981, pp. 33–4) notes that there was a bicycle boom in the USA from 1970 to 1973. Over this four year period the number of bicycles went from around 20 million to over 65 million. Thomas sets out to explain why this happened. He says:

> The bicycle boom, then, was generated by a sudden (apparently unforeseen) increase in demand which generated a movement of the demand curve outward along the supply schedule, the increase in output reflecting the increase in consumer demand and the higher prices reflecting the higher unit cost of producing an expanded output. (Thomas, 1981, p. 34)

So Thomas explains *why* the bicycle boom occurred by citing an increase in the demand for bicycles – an outward shift of the bicycle demand curve. And his explanation-why is clearly a *causal* one. The bicycle boom was caused by an increase in demand. Notice also that Thomas is employing the well-known supply/demand model of microeconomics textbooks in constructing his explanation. He applies this model to the market for bicycles in the USA in the early 1970s. This applied model implies that an increase in demand is a possible cause of the bicycle boom, and Thomas identifies an increase in demand as the actual cause of the bicycle boom. (The applied model also implies that an increase in supply – a rightward shift of the supply curve – and the resulting decline in bicycle prices is a possible cause of the increase in the quantity of bicycles demanded; but Thomas implicitly rules out this as the actual cause on the basis that the price of bicycles *rose* during the bicycle boom.) This illustrates the key *heuristic* role models often play in the construction of economic explanations-why. A potential cause within the *model* is picked out or identified as the cause of the real world phenomenon to be explained.

Thomas does not regard his explanation as complete as it stands. He further asks why the demand for bicycles increased in the United States in the early 1970s. He says:

> The increase in demand could have resulted from a number of factors. The

prices of related goods – complements or substitutes – could have changed, causing the demand for bicycles to be affected.... The income of consumers could have increased or consumers could have suddenly altered their expectations for future prices, fearing that prices in future would significantly increase. Or the tastes of consumers could have changed in favor of the bicycle. Any or a combination of these changes could account for an increase in demand. (Thomas, 1981, p. 35)

Thomas is operating with a version of the supply/demand model which includes a demand function that makes the quantity of a good demanded a function of prices of related goods, income of consumers, expectations of consumers, and tastes of consumers. Notice that it is the model, applied to the bicycle market in the USA in the early 1970s, which provides Thomas with a list of plausible factors which might have caused the increase in demand that is directly responsible for the bicycle boom. This again illustrates the *heuristic* role models often play in the construction of economic explanations-why.

It so happens that Thomas explicitly uses the CRH method described above to establish his explanation of the bicycle boom. The demand function of the supply/demand model provides Thomas with the short list of possible causes for the increase in bicycle demand required by the CRH method. And he (1981, p. 35) says 'There are several reasons to believe that it was the last of the four possible factors – a change in tastes – that accounts for most of the increase in demand'. Thomas relies upon various pieces of evidence to eliminate as causes of the increase in demand the operation of the other three independent variables in the demand function. For example, about consumer income he says the following:

While the period from 1970 to 1973 was a recovery period of relatively rapid economic growth in the United States, the median incomes of households increased only from $14,465 to $15,437, an increase of less than 7 percent. Such a small increase hardly seems sufficient to account for a large expansion in the demand for bicycles. (Thomas 1981, p. 35)

Thomas says 'This process of elimination leaves only a dramatic change in the tastes of consumers to explain the bicycle boom'. This is a clear and very explicit example of the use of the CRH method to establish a causal explanation in economics.

The example just considered perhaps suggests the idea that explanation-why in economics is easier and more mechanical than it really is. To become disabused of this notion one need only look at the literature treating the cause of the Great Depression. The Great

Depression in the USA (and elsewhere as well) was not just a garden
variety recession. In the United States the unemployment rate rose to
around 25%, and real GNP fell over the period 1929–33 by about 29%.
Peter Temin on the one hand and Milton Friedman and Anna Schwartz
on the other, are major sources of the two competing explanations of the
Great Depression. These two competing explanations are initially
described by Temin as follows:

> The two classes of explanations for the Depression have different events at
> their cores. What I have called 'the money hypothesis' asserts that the collapse
> of the banking system was the primary cause of the Depression, while 'the
> spending hypothesis' asserts that a fall in autonomous aggregate spending lay
> at the root of the decline. (Temin, 1976, p. 7)

As Temin (1976, p. 63) notes, the issue these two hypotheses address is
not why the economy in the USA turned down in 1929, but why the
1929–33 downturn was so extraordinarily severe. And it is clear from
Temin's language that the explanation-why sought by the proponents of
the two hypotheses is a *causal* explanation.

According to Temin's elaboration of the spending hypothesis, in 1930
there occurred a large decline in autonomous, real (inflation adjusted)
consumption spending and a smaller decline in real exports. This implied
a sizeable decline in total demand for output which, through the
multiplier process familiar from Keynesian macro theory, caused the very
substantial decline in national income characteristic of the Great
Depression. The competing money hypothesis traces the very severe
decline in national income in the Great Depression to a fall in the stock
or quantity of money in the economy in the USA. And the fall in the
stock of money was due, not to a decrease in the demand for money, but
to a decrease in the supply of money. The most important cause of this
decrease in the supply of money was the banking failures which began in
late 1930. Temin's spending hypothesis acknowledges the decline in the
stock of money during the Great Depression. But Temin (1976, p. 9)
describes this as due to a decrease in the demand for money caused by
the severe decline in national income. This in turn occasioned a
movement down along the positively sloped money supply curve (graphed
against the interest rate). So, on the spending hypothesis, the fall in the
money stock was a symptom or effect of the Great Depression rather
than its cause.

Temin argues for the spending hypothesis as the explanation of the
Great Depression. His reasoning is considerably lengthier and more
complex than that used by Thomas to establish the cause of the bicycle

boom in the USA in the early 1970s. But, like Thomas, Temin employs the CRH method in arguing for the spending hypothesis. Temin is faced with two competing explanations for the Great Depression, the different sets of conditions each cites as the cause of the Depression in effect being a short list of potential causes. And he cites various pieces of evidence for thinking the money hypothesis does not correctly identify the actual cause of the Great Depression. For instance, Temin (1976, p. 101) says that a decline in the money supply will likely be followed by a rise in the interest rate. Temin argues that this predicted effect should most reliably show up in short-term interest rates, such as the rates on Treasury bills and commercial paper. After a careful examination of the behaviour of short-term interest rates in 1930 and 1931, Temin concludes the following:

> Yet a glance at Figures 4 and 5 [depicting the behaviour of short-term rates in the American economy from 1919–39] is sufficient to show that no such interruption of [the downward] trend is visible at the end of 1930. There is, in other words, no evidence in the interest rates of the monetary stringency cited in the money hypothesis as the cause of the Great Depression. We must conclude that the money hypothesis has failed its most important test. (Temin, 1976, p. 126)

Temin argues for the spending hypothesis on the basis that the set of conditions it cites is probably the cause of the Great Depression.[5] And the particular form of argument he employs is the CRH method. It is worth noting that there are various ways in which economic *models* play a heuristic and justificatory role in Temin's reasoning. For example, as noted above, in arguing against the money hypothesis by appeal to data about interest rates, he claims that a decline in the money supply will likely be followed by a rise in the interest rate. Temin (1976, pp. 99–100) explicitly justifies this claim by appeal to the IS–LM model familiar from macroeonomics textbooks.

I will conclude this section with a brief and very limited discussion about the relation between causal explanation in economics and econometrics. (Recall that explanation-why in economics is typically causal.) A standard view among econometricians is that econometrics is powerless to supply causal explanations. In an econometrics text Damodar Gujurati says the following:

> Although regression analysis deals with the dependence of one variable on other variables, it does not necessarily imply causation. In the words of Kendal and Stuart: 'A statistical relationship, however strong and however suggestive, can never establish causal connection: our ideas of causation must come from

outside statistics, ultimately from some theory or other.' (Gujurati, 1978, p. 16)

This view has been challenged recently. James Woodward has defended the view that econometric techniques can provide causal explanations of a certain type. Woodward thinks that many regression models, whether of the single equation or the multi-equation variety, represent or purport to express what he calls 'autonomous relationships' as opposed to mere empirical associations or correlations. He (1995, p. 12) says 'In the most general sense the degree of autonomy of a relationship has to do with whether it would remain stable or invariant under various possible changes or "interventions"'. And Woodward provides a counterfactual test of the degree of autonomy of a relationship. He says:

> In asking whether (2.8) [that is, a statement of the form 'All *As* are *Bs*'] is autonomous or possesses a significant degree of autonomy, we ask the following counterfactual question (or really, set of questions). If initial and background conditions were to change in various ways, would (2.8) [All As are Bs] continue to hold? (Woodward, 1995, p. 20)

The importance of autonomous relationships for Woodward is that they are *causal* in nature and can be used to construct explanations.[6]

Woodward (1995, p. 24) acknowledges that his interpretation of many regression models as representing or purporting to capture autonomous relationships creates an *underdetermination* problem. *Such* regression models are underdetermined by the statistical evidence, by the patterns of association observed so far in a given population. And this is so because a regression model that represents autonomous relationships implies – given Woodward's counterfactual test for autonomy – how these relationships *would behave* under various changes that have not in fact occurred. The problem then arises as to how to select as *correct* or *best* a particular regression model, out of the perhaps numerous models consistent with the same observed statistical associations. And Woodward (1995, pp. 54–5) apparently takes the correct regression model to be the model that captures the autonomous relationships that *in fact exist* in the domain under investigation. This seems tantamount to saying that the correct regression model is the one that accurately represents the real world mechanism generating the observed data. (The view that econometrics seeks the correct model in this sense is rejected by some econometricians – see Kennedy, 1992, p. 73, and Hoover, 1994, p. 73.)

Woodward (1995, pp. 24–9) attempts to meet this problem at least in a large measure by appealing to background knowledge of a primarily causal character. In constructing a regression model that is to capture autonomous relationships, the econometrician must rely on assumptions about what are the causally relevant variables to include in the model, before attempting to estimate it using some data set. In addition, the econometrician must rely on assumptions about the direction of causal relations among variables which will be included in the regression model he will estimate. Woodward's appeal to background knowledge of a largely causal character is an explicitly causal interpretation of the familiar point that econometricians regularly rely on economic theory to tell them which variables to include in a regression model, as well as which variables are dependent and which independent. And Woodward views the assumptions about causally relevant variables and causal direction as reducing the plausibility of alternatives to the regression model the econometrician selects. (Woodward adopts the view, reflected in the CRH method described above, that establishing a causal explanation requires ruling out or eliminating competing alternatives.) Yet, Woodward is not at all sanguine about the capacity of these assumptions to rationally select as correct a particular regression model. He (1995, p. 30) says 'At bottom, the problem is that statistical data and background causal information in such contexts [contexts of nonexperimental inquiry such as econometrics] are often simply not powerful enough to permit the convincing ruling out of competing alternatives that is central to successful causal inference'.

None the less Woodward thinks that many estimated regression models purportedly supply causal explanations of a certain type which he describes as follows:

> The alternative conception I favor has three basic features. First, many structural models have what I shall call a contrastive structure and represent attempts to explain the actual variation of some quantity of interest in a particular population. Second, the coefficients in such models are quantitative estimates of the weight or relative importance of different causal factors contributing to this variation. (Woodward, 1995, p. 46)

So, many estimated regression models purport to be explanations of a causal nature as to why a quantity varies within a certain population. Should the model be *correct*, then presumably it is a successful or acceptable causal explanation of the variation in the quantity in question.

To make Woodward's position clearer, let me use an economic example.[7] Let us also restrict the discussion to single equation regression models. Consider a simple version of Irving Fisher's theory of interest rates. This – let us refer to it as 'Fisher's hypothesis' – says that the nominal interest rate r in a country i is determined by the real interest rate r^* and the rate of inflation f in country i. (Assuming free flow of capital between countries, the real interest rate will be the same in all countries.) A regression model specified using Fisher's hypothesis might be as follows:

$$r_i = a + bf_i + U_i \qquad (8.1)$$

with r_i being the nominal interest rate in country i, a being a parameter representing the real interest rate r^*, f_i being the inflation rate in country i, U_i being an error term, and b being another parameter. (According to Fisher's hypothesis, b equals one, though of course an econometric estimate of equation (8.1) is not likely to yield an estimate of b exactly equal to one.) Now suppose we estimate a and b using ordinary least squares and a data set including nominal interest rates and inflation rates in a number of countries in 1989, such as the USA, Japan, France, Italy, and India. Let us suppose that we get the following estimated model:

$$r_i = 5.0246 + 1.6722f_i + U_i \qquad (8.2)$$

In fact, the different countries in the population sampled had different nominal interest rates and different inflation rates in 1989. Woodward (1995, p. 46) apparently would say that equation (8.2) *itself claims* that the *variation* in nominal interest rates in the different countries is partly explained by the differing inflation rates in these countries.[8] (Note the real interest rate estimated in equation (8.2) is *the same* in all the countries.) So, for Woodward, some regression equations themselves *claim* that differing values of the dependent variable in the population under investigation, are partly caused by variations in values of explanatory variables in the regression equation. And should these regression equations be *correct*, they are true (partial) causal explanations of variations in values of the dependent variable within the population in question.

Perhaps reflecting the view about econometrics and causality expressed in the passage from Gujurati quoted above, Kevin Hoover has criticized Woodward's position. Hoover (1995, p. 84) says '... regressions are not explanations, contrastive or otherwise, but data-based calculations, that may help us observe facts for theoretical interpretation'. He (1995, p. 84) adds 'I want to say, absent a theoretical account, that the regression merely describes a correlation, and, at best, suggests factors that may be important in the explanation'. So Hoover denies that a regression equation *is* a causal explanation of any sort, and affirms that regression equations – presumably estimated ones – are merely descriptions or expressions of correlations. These claims are based on Hoover's analysis of the example Woodward uses to illustrate his own view, an example which involves regressing time of fall through the Earth's atmosphere against various explanatory variables such as density of the falling object. It seems to me that Hoover's denial that regression equations are explanations is clearly correct. Consider the estimated regression equation (8.2) above. Surely equation (8.2) itself does *not say* that variations in nominal interest rates in the countries in the population sampled is partly caused by differing inflation rates in those countries. Equation (8.2) just says that the nominal interest rate in the country i equals 5.0246 plus 1.6722 times the inflation rate in country i plus the value of the error term U for country i. The concept of causation is simply not an ingredient in what equation (8.2) expresses. But presumably equation (8.2) is an instance of the type of regression equation Woodward takes to be a causal explanation of variations in values of a dependent variable in a population. For Fisher's hypothesis, which is used to specify the regression model which equation (8.2) estimates, is a causal hypothesis; the concept of 'determined by' used in Fisher's hypothesis expresses the notion of causality. So, it seems wrong to claim, as Woodward does, that regression equations *are themselves* causal explanations, whether correct or incorrect, of variation in values of dependent variables in a population of interest.[9]

It has been argued that estimated regression models are not themselves causal explanations. But this does not mean that econometric techniques have no role whatever to play in the testing and justification of causal hypotheses in economics; it just means that any causal hypotheses or explanations tested are not themselves regression models. Textbook presentations of econometrics often claim that econometric techniques can be used for the testing and confirmation, or disconfirmation, of economic theory (for instance, see Gujurati, 1978, pp. 4–5). This claim would seem to imply that econometric techniques are usable to test causal hypotheses in economics. It is considerably beyond the scope of this discussion to treat this use of econometric techniques. But one might be a bit sceptical about the utility of econometric techniques to test causal hypotheses in economics. At least often establishing a particular causal hypothesis or explanation requires eliminating one or more competing alternatives. Yet the use of econometric techniques does not have a particularly good record by way of successfully eliminating rival hypotheses to establish a given causal explanation. For example, Peter Temin's effort to establish the spending hypothesis as the explanation of the Great Depression includes a careful analysis of the use of econometric techniques by Lawrence Klein and others to establish the spending hypothesis. Temin concludes his analysis with the following remarks:

> Despite these drawbacks, the econometric models of the interwar period embody the most precise descriptions of the various forms of the spending hypothesis, that is, they pinpoint most clearly the falls in autonomous spending that are thought to have caused the Depression. As noted above, none of these models can be considered to have proved its point, in the sense of showing that the view of the Depression embodied in it is *superior to the alternatives*. (Temin, 1976, p. 53, emphasis added)

Temin rightly assumes that justifying the spending hypothesis as the correct explanation of the Great Depression requires ruling out the competing money hypothesis. And he is making the claim, which he persuasively establishes, that the use of econometric techniques has signally failed to do this, and so does not really establish the spending hypothesis.

8.2 EXPLANATION-WHAT

Once again, much economic thinking consists in the construction of models and/or their utilization in various cognitive activities. The previous section treated explanation-why in economics, which is typically causal explanation. And the heuristic and justificatory roles of models in causal explanation in economics was highlighted with the description of a number of actual examples of such explanations. It is fairly widely recognized that economics attempts causal explanations of real world phenomena. But it is much less widely recognized that economics also affords explanations of real world phenomena of a very different kind. These are explanations-what, a type of explanation which William Dray has claimed is prominent in historical studies. This section will treat explanation-what in general terms. The next section will discuss explanation-what in economics, bringing out the key role models play in explanation-what in economics.

To characterize explanation-what we need to borrow some of William Dray's ideas about explanation in history. Dray (1959, p. 403) notes that often historians offer explanations that are not intended to answer the question of *why* some event occurred. Instead the explanations furnish an answer to the question of *what* something really was. About this sort of explanation Dray says this:

Indeed, explaining what a thing is, where this means explaining it as a so-and-so, might be characterized in a preliminary way as explanation by means of a general concept rather than a general law. For the explanation is given by finding a satisfactory *classification* of what seems to require explanation. (Dray, 1959, p. 404, italics in original)

Explanations answering the question of what something is – following Dray, let us call them 'explanations-what' – are subsumptions of the explanandum phenomenon under a concept. Explanations-what explain something *as* an *F*, where *F* represents classificatory terms such as 'renaissance', 'political revolution' and 'social transition'. More needs to be said to make clear what is really involved in explanation-what.

Again, an explanation-what – or, as it is also called, an 'explanation by concept' – explains *X* as an *F*. This implies that an explanation-what subsumes the explanandum under the concept of an F.[10] In history, a series of events or a change is often said to constitute or be an *F*, and this sort of remark is typically the statement of an explanation-what. An example Dray uses in his original treatment of explanation by concept is conveyed in the following passage:

In his *Short History of the British Commonwealth*, after describing some of the changes which took place in late 18th century England – the enclosure of agricultural lands, the beginnings of industrial production, the improvement of communications, etc. – Ramsey Muir observes: 'It was not merely an economic change that was thus beginning; it was a social revolution.' (Dray, 1959, p. 403)

Thus Muir explains the set of changes in late 18th century England cited in this passage as a social revolution. It is important to note that an explanation-what such as Muir's is *not* the application of an arbitrary label or name to a specific series of events taken together. It is not that Muir simply identified some changes in late 18th century England and labelled *these* changes 'social revolution', as one might label a particular dog one encountered 'Fido'. 'Social revolution' is a general classificatory term, and so a series of events *other than* the ones Muir cites do or could constitute social revolutions.

A genuine explanation-what is not merely the subsumption of something under a general classificatory concept. In the following passage from the first edition of his book *Philosophy of History*, Dray cites a key feature of explanation by concept:

A second kind of procedure generally referred to as explanation in history, although sometimes as 'interpretation,' is explanation of what an event 'really

was,' or what it 'amounts to.' Once again, this is to be distinguished from
explaining why the event occurred. The operative notion is less that of
discovering necessary and sufficient conditions than of relating parts, at first
not seen to be such, to a whole of some kind. Thus the historian explains a
host of occurrences in fifteenth century Italy as a 'Renaissance'; he explains
a series of incidents in eighteenth century France as a 'Revolution.' (Dray,
1964, p. 19)

The subsumption under a concept involved in an explanation-what allows
one to see the events or phenomena explained as a unified or connected
whole. Indeed, as I will suggest below, it is precisely this unification
effected by an explanation by concept that gives it its explanatory power.
In giving an explanation-what, a historian or other inquirer is not merely
grouping together some events and applying a general term to the events
taken collectively. In subsuming the events taken together under a
general concept, an explanation-what exhibits the events in question as
forming a unified or connected whole. C.B. McCullagh makes the same
point about colligation in history (recall from note 10 that explanation-
what is colligation using general terms). He (1978, p. 269) says 'Walsh
has consistently, and I think correctly, described colligation in history as
a procedure for making sense of events by showing how, together with
other events, they constituted some sort of connected whole'.

It may be helpful to illustrate the feature of explanation-what just
described with an example. Consider the following passage in an article
describing the break-up of so-called secular, rational humanism in
Western countries such as the USA:

> What Mr. Kristol and others see is a yawning philosophical vacuum in
> American life, with people urgently trying to fill it in myriad ways. 'There's a
> transition going on – but to what, nobody knows,' he says. This great
> transition is the common denominator of a host of social phenomena that
> otherwise seem unrelated. Membership in evangelical religions is growing,
> even as New Age philosophies proliferate. The environmental movement, the
> feminist movement, the rise of alternative medicine, the explosion of street
> gangs – each represents a hunger for something beyond scientific rationalism,
> beyond material progress. 'People want more,' Mr. Kristol says. 'They want
> community and they want transcendence.' (Farney, 1994, A8)

Here a number of events or phenomena – growing membership in
evangelical religions, the feminist movement, and so on – are explained
as constituting a social transition. The transition is from a society
dominated by scientific rationalism and material progress to a different
social state, the character of which is left unspecified. The explanation-

what in this case does not merely consist of applying the concept of a social transition to a number of social phenomena taken collectively. In developing the explanation, the phenomena – the explosion of street gangs, the feminist movement, and so on – are said to be linked or connected by a unifying factor; to wit, each of the phenomena manifests a desire for more than what scientific rationalism and material progress offer, a desire for community and transcendence. Thus the phenomena in question form a connected whole, and each individual phenomenon is part of the whole that *is* the social transition.

To sum up, an explanation-what explains something as an *F*, with *F* representing general classificatory terms. Of course, this implies that an explanation-what classifies something as an *F*. Explanation by concept, however, is not merely classification. The events or phenomena explained must constitute a unified whole, with each individual phenomenon being part of the whole. Explanation-what is classification plus synthesis of phenomena into wholes.

Before proceeding, it is necessary to deal with a sceptical doubt about explanation-what. It might be said that explanations what, explanations by concept, are not really explanatory; they are not genuine explanations at all. Marvin Levich expresses this view in the following passage:

> On the other hand, Dray takes to be an argument against the covering-law model the discrepancies of its logical structure with the procedures of classifying historical material by general concepts and of recounting 'what it *really was* that happened.' These procedures he labels in a revealingly grating phrase 'explaining what' in history. Yet, what generalizations are cited in his essay – for instance, describing changes in late eighteenth-century England as a 'social revolution' – are matters, not of explanation, but of historical interpretation. We *interpret* the nature of changes in eighteenth century England; we explain, given their nature, how they came about. (Levich, 1965, p. 341, italics in original)

Levich denies that the procedure Dray calls explanation-what is explanation; Levich says that instead it should be regarded as interpretation. Note in the last sentence of the quoted passage the tacit stipulation that the concept of explanation is to be restricted to answers to the question of why something happened, or how it came about. This stipulation, which is quite arbitrary, is Levich's basis for refusing to regard so-called explanation by concept as explanation at all.[11] Saying that an arbitrary stipulation is the basis for Levich, and others, excluding explanations-what from the class of real explanations, does not establish that they are truly explanatory. Accordingly, I will consider two ways of making a positive case that explanation by concept is explanatory. It will be argued that only one of the two ways is successful.

Despite the many criticisms of it, the covering law theory of explanation continues to have a strong hold on many. The crux of the theory is that any genuine explanation must involve at least one scientific law. Covering law theorists have been concerned primarily with applying their theory to explanations of *why* something happened. Some prominent covering law theorists have extended their theory to explanation by concept. Specifically, they appeal to scientific laws to distinguish between subsumptions under concepts that are truly explanatory and such subsumptions that are not explanations. For instance, May Brodbeck says this:[12]

> If we explain what something is by subsuming it under a concept, is this type of explanation different in kind from subsumptions under general laws? In his paper Dray argues persuasively that it is. He is making more than the merely verbal point that in common discourse we use 'explain' both for telling what and for telling why. Dray believes, not unjustifiably, that subsumption under a social concept such as *social revolution*, is truly explanatory, in contrast to subsumption a nonsocial concept, such as *dog* or *green*. Although I do not believe that this explanatory power is gained without the use of laws, Dray's discussion usefully illuminates the complexity of our social categories.... But that concept is 'explanatory' only insofar as it is not at all a single concept or conjunction of concepts, but a suitcase term for a whole set of rather crude generalizations. To put things differently, *national character*, like many other everyday social categories, is not a true attribute or variable. That is, it is not a term that can occur in either the antecedent or consequent of a law, for it is itself shorthand for an indefinite set of laws.... Similarly, the concept of social revolution may incorporate not merely specific changes in the institutional structures, but also implicit regularities about the causes and effects of these wide-ranging changes in the relations among men and in the nature of their activities. (Brodbeck, 1968, pp. 339–40)

In his original paper on explaining-what in history, Dray (1959, pp. 404–6) argues that explanation by concept is *distinct from* explanation by subsumption of the explanandum under a scientific law. Subsuming X under a single law is deducing the occurrence of X from a statement affirming the occurrence of antecedent events or conditions C1, C2, ..., Cn, *plus* a law connecting the types of conditions C1, C2, ..., Cn instantiate and events of the type X instantiates. In the passage from Brodbeck just quoted, she admits that Dray's argument on this score is persuasive, as indeed it is.[13] Brodbeck nevertheless thinks that explanation by concept conforms to the covering law theory. This is indicated by her saying, in the passage quoted, that the explanatory power of subsumption under a concept is not 'gained without the use of laws'. But how exactly are scientific laws supposed to be involved in genuine explanations by concept? It is not easy to find an answer to this question in the writings of covering law theorists. As far as I am aware, they offer no general, informative answer. Instead, they just refer to examples of explanations-what and attempt to show that these sample explanations in some way involve laws.

It is fair, if uninformative, to say that for a covering law theorist like Brodbeck, a genuine explanation-what subsumes the explanandum under a concept that *incorporates* one or more laws. Recall that in the passage quoted Brodbeck says that the concept of social revolution incorporates regularities. The problem then becomes one of making useful sense of the notion of a *concept incorporating* scientific laws. In this connection an example from Hempel is suggestive:

> It applies as well, for example, to the explanation of certain complaints 'as symptoms of measles', which *rests on* general hypotheses to the effect that if a person suffers from the measles, then he will exhibit symptoms of such a kind; here, the explanatory concept is referred to in the protasis rather than the apodosis. (Hempel, 1965, p. 456, emphasis added)

In Hempel's example, certain complaints are brought under the general *concept* of symptoms of measles, and Hempel suggests that what makes *this* use of the concept explanatory is that classifying the complaints as symptoms of measles *rests on* or is supported by the generalization that if a person suffers from the measles, then he will exhibit such-and-such symptoms. Generalizing from Hempel's example, I suggest the following:

(Df1) The concept of an *F incorporates* a scientific law *L* iff the (complete) justification for classifying something as an *F* must include *L*.

For covering law theorists such as Brodbeck and Hempel, a subsumption of *X* under the *concept* of an *F* is thus explanatory only if the concept incorporates one or more scientific laws in the sense defined by (Df1). Let us call this view 'the covering law theory of explanation by concept'.[14]

The trouble with the covering law theory of explanation by concept is that there are counter-examples to it. To borrow an example from Dray (1959, p. 407), an intellectual historian may *explain* a range of phenomena in 18th century Europe – the spread of a faith in reason and a highly critical attitude toward traditional institutions such as the Catholic church, among others – by subsuming them under the concept of an age of enlightenment. The historian's notion of an age of enlightenment does not incorporate any scientific laws; a (complete) justification for classifying the European phenomena in question as an age of enlightenment would not include any scientific laws. What laws would they be? Consider Irving Kristol's explanation-what cited above. It can be expressed as follows:

(KE) Growing membership in evangelical religions, the environmental, the rise of alternative medicine, the feminist movement and the explosion of street gangs constitute a social transition in the USA.

Fully justifying applying the concept of a social transition to the phenomena cited in (KE) would require two things: (A) providing some sort of definition of or criterion for a social transition, and (B) showing that the phenomena cited in (KE) taken together fit the definition or criterion. The definition of a social transition is the passage of a society from one state to another state, with a stage of society determined by a dominant set of values, ideas or social practices. This definition certainly is not a scientific law. As indicated toward the end of section 4.1, definitions do not count as laws.[15] As for (B), Kristol, in the passage quoted above, is represented as saying that American society hitherto has been dominated by scientific rationalism and material progress. Kristol further claims that the phenomena cited in (KE) have a unifying theme; to wit, each represents a hunger for something beyond scientific rationalism and material progress. Of course, by implication Kristol is saying that American society is moving from a society dominated by scientific rationalism and material progress to a society that is not dominated by these two values or ideas. In discharging (B) in this way, Kristol does not appeal to any scientific laws. And yet he does *not fail* to provide a justification of his explanation by concept.

In sum, the covering law theory of explanation by concept is not correct. Perhaps some explanations-what do conform to it, but not all do. This makes the situation of the covering law theory of explanation-what the same as its close relative, the covering law theory of explanation-why. It is well known that the latter theory is also subject to a variety of counter-examples.

Recall that the covering law theory of explanation-what was initially invoked to afford a basis for saying that explanations by concept are explanatory. But if their explanatory force is not in general derived from the concepts incorporating scientific laws, what does make explanations by concept explanatory? My suggestion is simply that such explanations *unify* a range of events or phenomena under a *single* concept. It is by providing a unification of otherwise disparate phenomena that an explanation by concept achieves explanatory power. This point connects with an important strand in the philosophy of science that stresses the relationship between scientific explanation and unification. Wesley Salmon nicely describes this strand as follows:

> The strongest intuitive appeal of that view comes much more from explanations of laws than from explanations of particular facts. One great example is the *Newtonian synthesis*. Prior to Newton we had a miscellaneous collection of laws including Kepler's three laws of planetary motion and Galileo's laws of falling objects, inertia, projectile motion, and pendulums. By invoking three simple laws of motion and one law of gravitation, Newton was able to explain these laws – and in some cases correct them.... Quite possibly the most important feature of the Newtonian synthesis was the extent to which it systematized our knowledge of the physical world by subsuming all sorts of regularities under a small number of very simple laws.... The watchword in these beautiful historical examples is *unification*. A large number of specific regularities are unified in one theory with a small number of assumptions or postulates. (Salmon, 1992, p. 33, italics in original)

Of course, an explanation-what does not subsume a collection of scientific laws under a few simple postulates. But recall that explanation by concept is not mere classification, like describing an object as a pen or a rock. It also involves exhibiting the events or phenomena explained as forming a unified whole. The unification of a range of facts or phenomena under a single concept is analogous to the unification involved in the scientific examples Salmon cites. Therefore, if explanatory power is achieved in the examples Salmon cites, it should also be achieved in the case of explanation by concept.

In the next section I will indicate that economics, like history, affords explanations-what. Obviously, explanations-what are *non-causal* explanations. Yet, as section 8.1 indicates, economics also provides causal explanations of real world phenomena of world interest to economists. That economics affords explanations-what, and so non-causal explanations, of phenomena, is entirely consistent with the discipline *also* supplying causal explanations. Causal explanations answer the question of *why* something occurs or occurred, while explanations-what answer the question of *what* something really is. And the same phenomena or group of phenomena is obviously susceptible to *both* sorts of explanations. The case of history, which in fact provides both sorts of explanations, proves the point. So, one should not think that any tension would arise within economics from its provision of both explanations-what as well as causal explanations.

8.3   EXPLANATION-WHAT IN ECONOMICS

Section 8.1 brought out the role of economic models in the provision of causal explanations of real world phenomena. Models play an essential role in the construction of explanations-what in economics. To give a more precise statement of the thesis of this section, we need to recall the distinction between theoretical and applied models made in section 7.1. Often in developing or constructing a model, an economist is doing so in abstraction from any particular real world situation, or kind of real world situation. Such a model is a theoretical model. An applied model is a model that is being applied to a particular real world situation, or a whole class of real world situations. Further details about the character of applied models are supplied in section 7.1. The claim of this section is that *applied* models often furnish explanations-what, explanations by concept, of particular real world situations. Of course, economic models are *not* themselves concepts. But in developing this section's thesis, I will indicate how a model, while not being a concept, can still provide an explanation by concept.

Consider the supply/demand model found in microeconomics textbooks. The presentation of the model typically begins with a definition of a (perfectly) competitive market. Defining features of such a market include the existence of numerous market participants implying that each buyer and each seller is too small to be able to exert any influence over market price; the good exchanged is homogeneous; and there are no barriers to entry into and exit from the market. The model also includes a demand function and a supply function that can be represented respectively as follows:

$$Qd = f(P,T,I,R,N)$$

$$Qs = f(P,M,V)$$

with Qd being the quantity of the good demanded, Qs the quantity of the good supplied, P the price of the good, T the tastes of consumers, I consumers' income, R the prices of related goods, N the number of consumers, M the level of input prices, and V the level of technology. The equilibrium condition included in the model is this:

$$Qd = Qs$$

Supposing that $Qs > Qd$, the price of the good will fall until it reaches the level at which the equilibrium condition is met. If $Qd > Qs$, the price will rise to the level at which $Qd=Qs$. In short, one conclusion or theorem of the model is that the market price will be the price at which $Qd=Qs$.

In deriving the conclusion of the model just cited, it was assumed tacitly that there is no outside interference with the market. Now let us develop a variant of the above model by assuming that the government imposes a price ceiling below the equilibrium price. The effect of this is usefully depicted in Figure 8.1. This diagram conveys the model of a competitive market with a price ceiling. The price ceiling Pc is a price above which the market price is not allowed to rise. The result is that $Qd>Qs$, with Qd minus Qs being the shortage created by the price ceiling. That a price ceiling creates a shortage or excess demand is a major conclusion of the model.

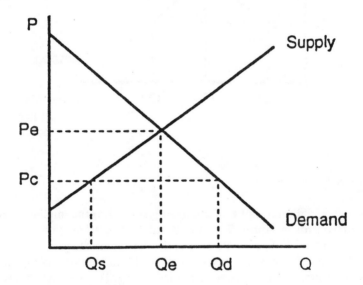

Figure 8.1 A Price Ceiling

So far we have before us two related theoretical models. Let us now set out an economist's application of the model of a competitive market with a price ceiling to a particular real world situation.[16] The situation is the market for rental housing in Santa Monica, California. Rent control was put into effect in Santa Monica by a citizens' initiative in April 1979. The application of the model of a competitive market with a price ceiling to the Santa Monica situation is conveyed in Figure 8.2.

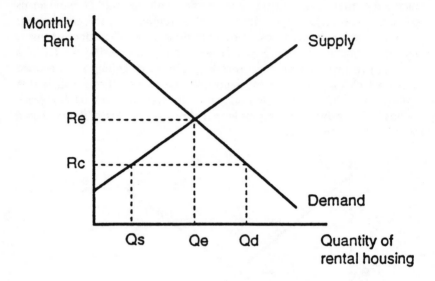

Figure 8.2 Rent Control

Re is the equilibrium rent that obtained just prior to the implementation
of rent control in April 1979. The April 1979 citizens' initiative froze
rents in Santa Monica for three months, and then rolled them back to
their 1978 levels. *Rc* is the maximum allowed rent landlords could charge
after the rollback; therefore *Rc* is a price ceiling. The diagram shows that
the application of the model to Santa Monica predicts a shortage of
rental units. This shortage is represented on the diagram by *Qd* minus
Qe.[17] If a shortage of rental units has already been ascertained, the
application of the model explains why the shortage exists; to wit, a price
ceiling has been placed below the market clearing price, and this causes
the quantity of rental units demanded to exceed the quantity supplied.

Note that the application of the model to the Santa Monica situation
does not even purport to say *why* rent control was imposed in Santa
Monica in the late 1970s. The application does subsume the Santa
Monica rental housing market with rent control under the economist's
concept of a competitive market with a price ceiling. Santa Monica's
rental housing market is explained as a competitive market with a price

ceiling. Generally, to apply the economic model of an F in the manner indicated by our example is to subsume the situation in question under the *concept* of an F. This is how an economic model, despite not being itself a concept, can provide an explanation by concept. In addition, the implementation of rent control in April 1979 and the other elements of Santa Monica's rental housing market – the demand curve of renters, and so on – are *unified* into a connected whole by applying the competitive model with a price ceiling to that housing market. The twin elements of explanation-what – classification plus synthesis into a whole – are found in our application of the model in question to the Santa Monica situation. Thus the application fits the general account of explanation by concept given in section 8.2.[18]

An important point about the application of models to real world situations is suggested by the previous paragraph. An economic model M can be used to give an explanation-what of a situation S even though not all of M's assumptions are exactly true when applied to S *or* a feature used to define a concept in M is not present in S. Obviously rental housing in Santa Monica is not a homogeneous good, though one defining feature of a competitive market is that the good exchanged is homogeneous. Still, the model of a competitive market with a price ceiling can be used to give an explanation-what of the Santa Monica rental housing market after 1979. All that is required for a model M to be usable to give an explanation-what of a situation S is that *enough* of M's assumptions be true, or approximately true, when applied to S, and *enough* of the features of a concept in M be present in S. Thus an economic model might be compared to a general term on the cluster theory of general terms often ascribed to the later Wittgenstein. On the cluster theory, a general term such as 'lemon' or 'game' is associated with a cluster of properties. An object need not have *all* the properties in the cluster for the general term to apply to it. The object just has to have *enough* of the properties in the cluster.[19]

The features of the Santa Monica situation from April 1979 on make it relatively easy to determine which economic model should be used to give an explanation-what of that situation. This is not always the case. Sometimes *different* economic models may seem applicable to a single real world situation, and evidence must then be marshalled that favours applying one of the competing models in order to get a single explanation by concept of the real world situation of interest. For example, neoclassical microeconomics includes a variety of theoretical models of the pricing behaviour of firms in an oligopoly market. One is the model of price leadership, which assumes a single dominant producer that is the price leader and a group of fringe producers taking the price leader's price as a given in their decisions. (For a good presentation of this model, see Nicholson, 1983, pp. 419–20.) Another model of oligopoly is the model of a centralized cartel. This model assumes that producers form an association that makes decisions about the price of the product and other matters, such as the quantity to be offered for sale by each producer. The cartel operates like a multiplant monopolist. (For a presentation of this model, see Leftwich, 1979, pp. 299–302.)

Now consider OPEC. Which of the two models of oligopoly just briefly described should be used to give an explanation-what of OPEC? OPEC is often described as a cartel, and some aspects of its behaviour – the periodic meeting of OPEC oil ministers to agree on a price of crude oil – seem to provide some evidence for subsuming OPEC under the concept of a centralized cartel. Yet some economists would dissent from this classification of OPEC. Walter Nicholson says the following:

> Another view of the world oil market assumes a much greater degree of competitiveness than does the cartel model. In this view, Saudi Arabia is treated as a price leader with the other OPEC nations and, indeed all other oil producers, constituting a competitive fringe.... If this model is correct, the elaborate, regular meetings of the OPEC oil ministers are simply a gaudy ritual with no particular significance for the actual pricing of oil. And Saudi Arabia's much-heralded position as a moderate in oil pricing simply derives from their position as a price leader with low marginal costs of production. On the whole, recent evidence seems to be most consistent with the price leadership model of OPEC behavior. Most OPEC members are producing at what appears to be full capacity and prices seem to be below those a cartelized monopoly would charge. (Nicholson, 1983, pp. 421–2)

Nicholson modestly prefers seeing OPEC as a case of price leadership, with Saudi Arabia as the price leader. He cites some evidence for preferring to subsume OPEC under the model of price leadership instead of under the model of a cartel. The most important piece of evidence for Nicholson seems to be that current (early 1980s) oil prices are inconsistent with those a centralized cartel would charge. In any case, the point here has been established. Sometimes different economic models can yield *prima facie* plausible explanations-what of a given real world situation. Evidence will then have to be appealed to in order to support saying that one of the competing explanations-what is the more acceptable one.

8.4 CONCLUDING REMARKS

Chapter 2 of this book criticizes the rhetorical conception of the metatheory of economics, as well as views about economics itself implied by this conception. Chapter 2 recommends the retention of the traditional conception of economic metatheory which the rhetorical conception was intended to displace. Chapters 3 to 5 treat several varieties of the effort to understand economics which each set a standard for empirical science, and then try to determine whether or not economics meets the standard. The varieties of the 'Is it science?' approach to economics discussed do conform to the traditional conception of economic metatheory. But Chapters 3 to 5 argue that they are all unsuccessful. Chapter 6 suggests that we replace the failed 'Is it science?' approach to economics with the view that much economic thinking consists in the formulation of models and/or their utilization in various cognitive activities. Explanation of real world economic phenomena is one of the most important of such cognitive activities. This chapter has described two kinds of explanations of real world phenomena which economics supplies, to wit, causal explanations and explanations-what. And it has brought out the key role that models play in the construction of both types of explanation.

NOTES

1. The covering law theory can be traced back at least to David Hume. It received clear expression in J.S. Mill's writings. Its pre-eminent advocate in the twentieth century is Carl Hempel. For a brief but lucid presentation of the theory, see Hempel, 1966, Chapter 5.
2. See Scriven, 1959b; Miller, 1987, Chapter One.
3. The CRH method is a special case of inference to the best explanation (IBE). IBE is justifying a hypothesis H on the basis that H is the best of the competing, potential explanations of the data. The CRH method is a *special* case of IBE, since the conclusion of the CRH method is a causal statement whereas IBE can serve also to justify conclusions that are non-causal. In its justifying a causal hypothesis by elimination of rival hypotheses the CRH method is importantly similar to Mill's Methods for establishing causal claims. Mill's Methods – which are competently presented in many elementary logic texts – are *eliminative* in nature. They seek to establish that a condition is the cause of a phenomenon because it is the only one of a list of plausible candidates to meet the requirements for a cause. (A historical and philosophically useful account of Mill's Methods is in Skorupski, 1989, pp. 175–92; and some further discussion of the relation between IBE and Mill's Methods is in Rappaport, 1996.)
4. This claim should not be taken to imply that generalizations never have anything to do with causal explanation. There are various ways in which generalizations may be

relevant to a causal explanation, though the generalizations need *not* be scientific laws. One way is indicated by a distinction which Michael Scriven (1959b, pp. 445–7) makes between an explanation and the justification or grounds for an explanation, a distinction applicable to causal explanations. One type of grounds for an explanation are *role-justifying grounds*. These are grounds for thinking the explanans (the statements formulating the explanatory information) are an adequate *explanation* for the explanandum phenomenon. The role-justifying grounds for a particular causal explanation may include generalizations. But these need not be scientific laws on the standard philosophical conception of laws set out in section 4.1. Scriven (1959b, pp. 456–8) correctly notes that *truisms* are often all we are able to supply by way of role-justifying grounds for a causal explanation of an individual event. (Scriven (1963, pp. 351–4) acknowledges that appealing to truisms does not preclude the need for eliminative reasoning in justifying causal explanations.)Truisms are generalizations. But there would be exceptions to them, and so they would be false, except that they are modified, explicitly or implicitly, by some clause such as '*ceteris paribus*', 'typically', 'under standard conditions', and so on (Scriven, 1959b, pp. 464–6). And we cannot say that truisms are hedged laws of the sort discussed in sections 3.4 and 4.1. For many truisms such as 'Power corrupts' do not meet the reliability condition used in section 4.4.

5. The spending hypothesis, as well as Temin's attempt to justify it, are far from uncontroversial. An interesting evaluation of Temin's critique of the money hypothesis is in Mayer, 1978.

6. Woodward does not think that statements expressing autonomous relationships are necessarily scientific laws. And he wisely rejects the idea that causal explanation in the social sciences must involve scientific laws. He (1995, p. 26) says 'A better way of thinking about these matters, it seems to me, is to sever this supposed connection between cause and explanation on the one hand and laws on the other. My alternative suggestion, which I think fits much better the actual practice in economic [sic] and other social sciences is this: what is crucial in identifying causal relationships and constructing explanations is not the discovery of laws per se but rather the discovery of invariant or autonomous relationships. Laws are just one kind of invariant relationship.'

7. In developing a non-economic example to illustrate his position, Woodward makes a technical error which Kevin Hoover pointed out. Woodward (1995, p. 56 note 25) acknowledges the error, but says his view that regression models can be causal explanations of the type in question is unaffected by the error.

8. Woodward imagines an equation which regresses time of fall through the Earth's atmosphere against various explanatory variables such as density of the falling object. He (1995, 46) says 'The regression equation identifies factors such as surface area that vary for different objects in P_1, and what *it claims* is that these variations partly explain the differences in time of fall for different objects in P_1' (emphasis added).

9. As I have indicated, in the main body of his article Woodward affirms: (W1) many regression equations are themselves causal explanations of differing values of the dependent variable in the population of interest. Following Kevin Hoover, I have suggested that (W1) is false. In responding to Hoover's criticism in a footnote, Woodward (1995, p. 57) claims: (W2) different values of the explanatory variables in many regression equations are used by econometricians to causally explain the differing values of the dependent variable in the population under investigation. Yet (W2) does nothing to support (W1). One could adopt (W2) and consistently reject (W1). (W2) does not imply that any regression equations *themselves* are causal explanations of

differing values of the dependent variable in terms of different values of the explanatory variables. What could make (W2) true is that associated with many regression equations is a causal hypothesis which is distinct from the regression equation itself. This causal hypothesis is the result of applying *economic theory* (economic models in the sense of section 6.1 and individual hypotheses like Fisher's hypothesis) to the population under investigation. It is this causal hypothesis which says that differing values of the dependent variable in the population of interest are due (at least in part) to different values of the explanatory variables in the regression equation. The source of the attempt at causal explanation (W2) alludes to is economic theory, not the regression equations themselves.

10. C.B. McCullagh (1978) follows W.H. Walsh in rightly thinking that one way historians make events intelligible is by colligation, that is, the subsumption of events under colligatory concepts. Subsumption of events or facts under *general* colligatory concepts is explanation-what in Dray's sense. It should be noted that McCullagh (1978, pp. 277–9) argues that some colligations are subsumptions under singular, not general, terms. But Dray (1981, pp. 163–4) shows that even singular colligatory terms involve classification of what is colligated.

11. It is not uncommon to exclude explanation by concept from the class of genuine explanations by arbitrary stipulation. Von Wright (1971, pp. 133–4) does the same thing.

12. Hempel (1965, pp. 454–5) also acknowledges that some so-called explanations by concept really are explanatory. He thinks that what makes them explanatory is that they rely upon lawlike generalizations, which, in the event that they are true, are scientific laws.

13. Dray (1959, p. 405) correctly notes that often accounts of what something really is – a social revolution, a renaissance, and so on – simply do not provide an answer to the question of why it came about. Subsumption of a phenomenon under a scientific law, however, is supposed to do just that, answer the why question. Dray does admit that in *some* cases, subsumption under a concept is in fact subsumption of the explanandum under a law. This does not contradict his claim that explanation by concept is not the same as, or a species of, explanation by subsumption under a scientific law.

14. From the fact that X is subsumable under a *concept* incorporating a law L, it does not follow that X is subsumable under L in the sense of 'subsuming X under a single law' defined above. That is, it does not follow that the answer to the question of *why* X came about involves or appeals to L, even assuming the covering law theory of explanation-why. This in turn means that on the covering law theory of explanation by concept, explanation by concept is distinct from explanation-why as this latter type of explanation is analysed by the covering law theory. Recall that Brodbeck herself acknowledges this distinction in the long passage quoted above.

15. Dray (1959, p. 406) suggests that one sort of generalization is essential to explanation-what. It is generalizations of the form 'x, y and z amount to a Q (e.g., a social revolution)', with x, y and z the particular phenomena that are brought together under the concept of a Q. Advocates of the covering law theory would be mistaken to think that this is an admission by Dray that the concept applied in an explanation-what does after all incorporate a scientific law. For statements of the form 'x, y and z amount to a Q' are not generalizations of the kind that could be scientific laws. They are just statements applying a concept to a fully specified group of individual phenomena taken collectively.

16. The economist on whom I am relying in developing this application is Timothy Tregarthen (1985).

17. The Santa Monica initiative controls landlord uses of rental units they own. Santa Monica landlords were unable, without permission of the rent control board, to do things like convert rental units to owner occupied condominiums. The quantity of rental units *supplied* with rent control would be closer to Qe than to Qs on Figure 8.2. One observable manifestation of the shortage of rental housing created by rent control is the time prospective renters wait for a unit to rent. Some data on this waiting time in Stockholm, Sweden – a city with rent control – is found in Nicholson (1983, pp. 368–9).

18. As indicated, the model of a competitive market with a price ceiling includes as a theorem the lawlike generalization 'Price ceilings cause excess demand'. It should not be inferred that the *concept* of a competitive market with a price ceiling *incorporates* this generalization. Fully justifying an application of the concept of a competitive market with a price ceiling to a particular real world situation does *not* require appealing to 'Price ceilings cause excess demand'. As the following paragraph indicates, an economic model can be used to give an explanation by concept even though *not all* of the model's assumptions, and so not all of its theorems, are true when applied to the situation in question. Moreover, the concept of a competitive market with a price ceiling may *correctly* apply to a particular real world situation even though the price ceiling imposed in the situation in question does *not* create a shortage. The government entity imposing the price ceiling may place it below equilibrium and yet require by law that the sellers of the good supply the quantity that satisfies demand at the ceiling price. Indeed, as note 17 above indicates, this partially happened in the Santa Monica case.

19. A useful account of the cluster theory of general terms and its ascription to Wittgenstein is in Schwartz (1977, pp. 14–20). If an object O has enough of the properties in the cluster associated with the general term 'lemon', then it is *true* that O is a lemon, even if O lacks some of the properties in the cluster. Similarly, if enough of the assumptions of the model of an F (e.g., a competitive market with a price ceiling) are true, or close to true, of a real world situation S (e.g., the Santa Monica rental housing market), and enough of the features used to define concepts deployed in the model are present in S, then it is *true* that S is an F. (The hypothesis that S is an F expresses the economist's explanation-what.) And this is the case even if some assumptions of the model are not even close to true of S, or some features used to define concepts in the model are not present in S.

References

Argyrous, George. (1992), 'Kuhn's paradigms and neoclassical economics', *Economics and Philosophy*, **8**, 231–48.

Aristotle. (1954), *Rhetoric*, trans. W. Rhys Roberts, in *Aristotle: Rhetoric and Poetics*, New York, NY: Random House.

Ayer, A.J. (1946), *Language, Truth and Logic* Second Edition, New York, NY: Dover Publications.

Barro, Robert. (1984), *Macroeconomics*, Homewood, IL: John Wiley & Sons.

Baumol, William. (1977), *Economic Theory and Operations Analysis* Fourth Edition, London, UK: Prentice-Hall International.

Baumol, William and Alan Blinder. (1994), *Microeconomics*, Fort Worth, TX: The Dryden Press.

Becker, Gary. (1976), *The Economic Approach to Human Behavior*, Chicago, IL: University of Chicago Press.

Benham, Lee. (1972), 'The effect of advertising on the price of eyeglasses', *Journal of Law and Economics,* **15**, 337–52.

Bicchieri, Christina. (1988), 'Should a scientist abstain from metaphor?', in Arjo Klamer, Donald McCloskey, and Robert Solow (eds), *The Consequences of Economic Rhetoric*, New York, NY: Cambridge University Press.

Blaug, Mark. (1980), 'Kuhn versus Lakatos, or paradigms versus research programmes in the history of economics', in Gary Gutting (ed.), *Paradigms and Revolutions*, Notre Dame, IN: Notre Dame University Press.

Blaug, Mark. (1985), *Economic Theory in Retrospect* Fourth Edition, Cambridge, UK: Cambridge University Press.

Blaug, Mark. (1992), *The Methodology of Economics or How Economists Explain* Second Edition, Cambridge, UK: Cambridge University Press.

Bonjour, Laurence. (1985), *The Structure of Empirical Knowledge*, Cambridge, MA: Harvard University Press.

Boyd, Richard. (1992), 'Constructivism, realism, and philosophical method', in John Earman (ed.), *Inference, Explanation, and Other Frustrations*, Berkeley, CA: University of California Press.

Brodbeck, May (ed.). (1968), *Readings in the Philosophy of the Social Sciences*, New York, NY: Macmillan Co.

Cairnes, John E. (1965), *The Character and Logical Method of Political Economy*, New York, NY: Augustus M. Kelly.

Cartwright, Nancy. (1983), *How the Laws of Physics Lie*, Oxford, UK: Oxford University Press.

Cassidy, John. (1996), 'The decline of economics', *The New Yorker* December, 50–60.

Chiang, Alpha. (1974), *Fundamental Methods of Mathematical Economics* Second Edition, New York, NY: McGraw-Hill.

Chisholm, Roderick. (1982), 'The Problem of the criterion', in *The Foundations of Knowing*, Minneapolis, MN: University of Minnesota Press.

Colander, David. (1993), *Macroeconomics*, Homewood, IL: Richard D. Irwin, Inc.

Colander, David. (1997), Review of *Beyond Rhetoric and Realism in Economics: Towards a Reformulation of Economic Methodology*, in *Economics and Philosophy*, **13**, 140–42.

Davidson, Donald. (1986), 'Mental events', in *Essays on Action and Events*, Oxford, UK: Clarendon Press.

Devitt, Michael. (1991), *Realism and Truth* Second Edition, Oxford, UK: Basil Blackwell.

Dray, William. (1959), '"Explaining what" in history', in Patrick Gardiner, *Theories of History*, Glencoe, IL: Free Press.

Dray, William. (1964), *Philosophy of History*, Englewood Cliffs, NJ: Prentice-Hall.

Dray, William. (1981), 'Colligation under appropriate conceptions', in W.H. Dray and L. Pompa (eds), *Substance and Form in History*, Edinburgh, UK: Edinburgh University Press.

Dray, William. (1992), *Philosophy of History* Second Edition, Englewood Cliffs, NJ: Prentice-Hall.

Earman, John. (1992), *Bayes or Bust? A Critical Examination of Bayesian Confirmation Theory*, Cambridge, MA: The MIT Press.

Edel, Matthew and Elliot Sclar. (1974), 'Taxes, spending, and property values: supply adjustment in a Tiebout-Oates model', *Journal of Political Economy*, **82**, 941–54.

Ekelund, Robert Jr and Robert Hébert. (1990), *A History of Economic Theory and Methodology*, New York, NY: McGraw-Hill.

Ellis, Brian. (1985), 'What science aims to do', in Paul Churchland and Clifford Hooker (eds), *Images of Science*, Chicago, IL: University of Chicago Press.

Elster, Jon. (1989), *Nuts and Bolts for the Social Sciences*, Cambridge,

UK: Cambridge University Press.

Farney, Dennis. (1994), 'Chaos theory seeps into ecology debate, stirring up a tempest', *The Wall Street Journal*, 11 July.

Fay, Brian. (1984), 'Naturalism as a philosophy of social science', *Philosophy of the Social Sciences*, **14**, 529–42.

Fisher, Franklin. (1989), 'Games economists play: a noncooperative view', *Rand Journal of Economics*, **20**, 113–24.

Fodor, Jerry. (1983), 'Special sciences', in *Representations*, Cambridge, MA: The MIT Press.

Fodor, Jerry. (1990), *A Theory of Content and Other Essays*, Cambridge, MA: The MIT Press.

Friedman, Milton. (1953), 'The methodology of positive economics', in *Essays in Positive Economics*, Chicago, IL: University of Chicago Press.

Friedman, Milton and Anna Schwartz. (1971), *A Monetary History of the United States, 1867–1960*, Princeton, NJ: Princeton University Press.

Gardner, Michael. (1983), 'Realism and instrumentalism in pre-Newtonian astronomy', in John Earman (ed.), *Testing Scientific Theories*, Minneapolis, MN: University of Minnesota Press.

Gibbard, Allan and Hal Varian. (1978), 'Economic models', *Journal of Philosophy*, **75**, 664–77.

Giere, Ronald. (1988), 'Laws, theories, and generalizations', in Wesley Salmon (ed.), *The Limits of Deductivism*, Berkeley, CA: University of California Press.

Giere, Ronald. (1990), *Explaining Science: A Cognitive Approach*, Chicago, IL: The University of Chicago Press.

Giere, Ronald. (1991), *Understanding Scientific Reasoning* Third Edition, Fort Worth, TX: Harcourt Brace Jovanovich.

Glymour, Clark. (1980), *Theory and Evidence*, Princeton, NJ: Princeton University Press.

Gujurati, Damodar. (1978), *Basic Econometrics*, New York, NY: McGraw-Hill.

Halliday, David and Robert Resnick. (1988), *Fundamentals of Physics*, New York, NY: Wiley & Sons.

Händler, Ernst. (1980), 'The logical structure of modern neoclassical static microeconomic general equilibrium theory', *Erkenntnis*, **15**, 33–55.

Hands, D. Wade. (1984), 'What economics is not: an economist's response to Rosenberg', *Philosophy of Science*, **51**, 495–503.

Hands, D. Wade. (1985), 'The structuralist view of economic theories: a review essay', *Economics and Philosophy*, **1**, 303–35.

Hands, D. Wade. (1994), 'The sociology of scientific knowledge', in Roger Backhouse (ed.), *New Directions in Economic Methodology*, New

York, NY: Routledge.

Hausman, Daniel. (1981), *Capital, Profits, and Prices*, New York, NY: Columbia University Press.

Hausman, Daniel. (1992a), *The Inexact and Separate Science of Economics*, New York, NY: Cambridge University Press.

Hausman, Daniel. (1992b), *Essays on Philosophy and Economic Methodology*, Cambridge, UK: Cambridge University Press.

Hausman, Daniel (ed.). (1994a), *The Philosophy of Economics* Second Edition, New York, NY: Cambridge University Press.

Hausman, Daniel. (1994b), 'Kuhn, Lakatos and the character of economics', in Roger Backhouse (ed.), *New Directions in Economic Methodology*, London, UK: Routledge.

Hausman, Daniel and Michael McPherson. (1996), *Economic Analysis and Moral Philosophy*, Cambridge, UK: Cambridge University Press.

Heap, Hargreaves, Martin Hollis, Bruce Lyons, Robert Snugden and Albert Weale. (1992), *The Theory of Choice: A Critical Guide*, Oxford, UK: Basil Blackwell.

Hempel, Carl. (1965), *Aspects of Scientific Explanation*, New York, NY: Free Press.

Hempel, Carl. (1966), *Philosophy of Natural Science*, Englewood Cliffs, NJ: Prentice-Hall.

Henderson, David K. (1991), 'On the testability of psychological generalizations (psychological testability)', *Philosophy of Science*, **58**, 586–607.

Henderson, James and Richard Quandt. (1980), *Microeconomic Theory*, Tokyo, Japan: McGraw-Hill Kogakusha, Ltd.

Hoey, Richard. (1993), 'The inflation question', *Letter from the Lion*, Summer, 3.

Hoover, Kevin. (1994), 'Econometrics as observation: the Lucas critique and the nature of econometric inference', *Journal of Economic Methodology*, **1**, 65–80.

Hoover, Kevin. (1995), 'Comments on Cartwright and Woodward: causation, estimation, and statistics', in Daniel Little (ed.), *On the Reliability of Economic Models*, Boston/Dordrecht/London: Kluwer Academic Publishers.

Horgan, Terence and John Tienson. (1990), 'Soft laws', in Peter French, Theodore Uehling, Jr and Howard Wettstein (eds), *Midwest Studies in Philosophy*, Vol. 15, Notre Dame, IN: University of Notre Dame Press.

Hull, David. (1979), 'Laudan's progress and its problems', *Philosophy of Social Science*, **9**, 457–65.

Husted, Steven and Michael Melvin. (1990), *International Economics*, New York, NY: Harper-Row.

Hutchinson, Terence. (1984), *The Significance and Basic Postulates of Economic Theory* Second Edition, reprinted in part in Bruce Caldwell (ed.), *Appraisal and Criticism in Economics*, Boston, MA: Allen & Unwin.

Kant, Immanuel. (1965), *Critique of Pure Reason*, New York, NY: St. Martin's Press.

Kaufman, Felix. (1958), *Methodology of the Social Sciences*, New Jersey: Humanities Press.

Kennedy, Peter. (1992), *A Guide to Econometrics* Third Edition, Cambridge, MA: The MIT Press.

Keynes, John Maynard. (1937), 'The general theory of employment', *The Quarterly Journal of Economics*, **51**, 209–23.

Keynes, John Maynard. (1948), *A Treatise on Probability*, New York, NY: Macmillan Co.

Keynes, John Maynard. (1964), *The General Theory of Employment, Interest, and Money*, New York, NY: Harcourt Brace Jovanovich.

Kincaid, Harold. (1996), *Philosophical Foundations of the Social Sciences*, Cambridge, UK: Cambridge University Press.

Klein, L.R. (1984), 'The importance of the forecast', *Journal of Forecasting*, **3**, 1–9.

Klein, Philip and Geoffrey Moore. (1983), 'The leading indicator approach to economic forecasting – retrospect and prospect', *Journal of Forecasting*, **2**, 119–135.

Kornblith, Hilary. (1985), 'Introduction: what is naturalistic epistemology?', in H. Kornblith (ed.), *Naturalizing Epistemology*, Cambridge, MA: The MIT Press.

Kuhn, Thomas. (1970), *The Structure of Scientific Revolutions* Second Edition, Chicago, IL: University of Chicago Press.

Kuttner, Robert. (1985), 'The poverty of economics', *The Atlantic* February, 74–84.

Laudan, Larry. (1977), *Progress and Its Problems*, Berkeley, CA: University of California Press.

Laudan, Larry. (1996), *Beyond Postivism and Relativism*, Boulder, CO: Westview Press.

Leftwich, Richard. (1979), *The Price System and Resource Allocation* Seventh Edition, Hinsdale, IL: Dryden Press.

Leontief, Wassily. (1982), 'Academic economics', *Science*, **217**, 104–7.

Leontieff, Wassily. (1985), 'Theoretical assumptions and unobserved facts', in Wassily Leontieff, *Essays in Economics*, New Brunswick, NJ: Transaction Books.

Lester, Richard. (1947), 'Marginalism, minimum wages, and labor markets', *American Economic Review*, **37**, 135–148.

Levich, Marvin. (1965), Review of *Philosophy and History: A Symposium, History and Theory*, **4**, 328–49.

Levine, George. (1994), 'Why science isn't literature: the importance of differences', in Allan Megill (ed.), *Rethinking Objectivity*, Durham, NC: Duke University Press.

Lewis, David. (1973), *Counterfactuals*, Cambridge, MA: Harvard University Press.

Lichtenstein, S. and P. Slovic. (1971), 'Preference reversals between bids and choices in gambling decisions', *Journal of Experimental Psychology*, **89**, 46-55.

Mäki, Uskali. (1994a), 'Reorienting the assumptions issue', in Roger Backhouse (ed.), *New Directions in Economic Methodology*, London, UK: Routledge.

Mäki, Uskali. (1994b), 'Isolation, idealization and truth in economics', *Poznan Studies in the Philosophy of the Sciences and the Humanities*, **38**, 147–68.

Mäki, Uskali. (1995), 'Diagnosing McCloskey', *Journal of Economic Literature*, **33**, 1300-1318.

Mäki, Uskali. (1996), 'Two portraits of economics', *Journal of Economic Methodology*, **3**, 1–38.

Mansfield, Edwin. (1979), *Microeconomics* Third Edition, New York, NY: W.W. Norton & Co.

Maroney, John R. (1967), 'Cobb–Douglas Production Functions and Returns to Scale in U.S. Manufacturing Industry', *Western Economic Journal*, **6**, 39–51.

Mayer, Thomas. (1978), 'Money and the great depression: a critique of Professor Temin's Thesis', *Explorations in Economic History*, **15**, 127–45.

Mayer, Thomas. (1993), *Truth versus Precision in Economics*, Aldershot, UK: Edward Elgar Publishing Ltd.

McCloskey, Donald. (1985a), *The Rhetoric of Economics*, Madison, WI: University of Wisconsin Press.

McCloskey, Donald. (1985b), *The Applied Theory of Price* Second Edition, New York, NY: Macmillan Co.

McCloskey, Donald. (1988), 'Two replies and a dialogue on the rhetoric of economics: Mäki, Rappaport, and Rosenberg', *Economics and Philosophy*, **4**, 150–66.

McCloskey, Donald. (1989), 'The very idea of epistemology', *Economics and Philosophy*, **5**, 1–6.

McCloskey, Donald. (1994), *Knowledge and Persuasion in Economics*, New York, NY: Cambridge University Press.

McCullagh, C.B. (1978), 'Colligation and classification in history', *History and Theory,* **17**, 267–84.

McGuire, J.E. (1992), 'Scientific change: perspectives and proposals', in Wesley Salmon, *et al.*, *Introduction to the Philosophy of Science,* Englewood Cliffs, NJ: Prentice-Hall.

Mill, J.S. (1970), *A System of Logic Rationative and Inductive,* London, UK: Longman Group.

Miller, Richard. (1984), *Analyzing Marx,* Princeton, NJ: Princeton University Press.

Miller, Richard. (1987), *Fact and Method,* Princeton, NJ: Princeton University Press.

Musgrave, Alan. (1981), '"Unreal assumptions" in economic theory: the F-twist untwisted', *Kyklos,* **34**, 377–87.

Nagel, Ernest. (1973), 'Assumptions in economic theory', in Alan Ryan (ed.), *The Philosophy of Social Explanation,* Oxford, UK: Oxford University Press.

Nicholson, Walter. (1978), *Microeconomic Theory* Second Edition, Hinsdale, IL: The Dryden Press.

Nicholson, Walter. (1983), *Intermediate Microeconomics and its Applications* Third Edition, Hinsdale, IL: Dryden Press.

Oates, Wallace. (1969), 'The effects of property taxes and local public spending on property values: an empirical study of tax capitalization and the Tiebout hypothesis', *Journal of Political Economy,* **77**, 957–71.

Pindyck, Robert and Daniel Rubinfeld. (1992), *Microeconomics* Second Edition, New York, NY: Macmillan Co.

Quine, Willard. (1966), *The Ways of Paradox and Other Essays,* New York, NY: Random House.

Quine, Willard and Joseph Ullian. (1978), *The Web of Belief* Second Edition, New York, NY: Harper & Row.

Rappaport, Steven. (1986a), 'What is really wrong with Milton Friedman's methodology of economics?', *Reason Papers,* **11**, 33–61.

Rappaport, Steven. (1986b), 'The modal view and defending microeconomics', in Arthur Fine and Peter Machamer (eds), *PSA 1986* Volume I, East Lansing, MI: Philosophy of Science Association.

Rappaport, Steven. (1988), 'Arguments, truth, and economic methodology: a rejoinder to McCloskey', *Economics and Philosophy,* **4**, 170–72.

Rappaport, Steven. (1989), 'The modal view of economic models', *Philosophica,* **44**, 61–80.

Rappaport, Steven. (1992), 'The as-if view of economic motivational hypotheses', *Review of Social Economy,* **50**, 82–101.

Rappaport, Steven. (1993), 'Must a metaphysical relativist be a truth relativist?', *Philosophia,* **22**, 75–85.

Rappaport, Steven. (1996), 'Inference to the best explanation; is it really different from Mill's Methods?', *Philosophy of Science*, **63**, 65–80.

Rescher, Nicholas. (1978), *Peirce's Philosophy of Science*, Notre Dame, IN: Notre Dame University Press.

Robbins, Lionel. (1994), 'The nature and significance of Economic Science', in Daniel Hausman (ed.), *The Philosophy of Economics* Second Edition, New York, NY: Cambridge University Press.

Roemer, John. (1988), *Free to Lose*, London, UK: Hutchinson & Co.

Rorty, Richard. (1982), *Consequences of Pragmatism*, Minneapolis, MN: University of Minnesota Press.

Rosenberg, Alexander. (1976), *Microeconomic Laws*, Pittsburgh, PA: University of Pittsburgh Press.

Rosenberg, Alexander. (1980), 'Obstacles to nomological connection of reasons and actions', *Philosophy of Social Sciences*, **10**, 79–91.

Rosenberg, Alexander. (1985), 'Davidson's unintended attack on psychology', in Ernest LePore and Brian McLaughlin (eds), *Actions and Events*, Oxford, UK: Basil Blackwell.

Rosenberg, Alexander. (1989), *The Structure of Biological Science*, Cambridge, UK: Cambridge University Press.

Rosenberg, Alexander. (1992), *Economics – Mathematical Politics or Science of Diminishing Returns?*, Chicago, IL: University of Chicago Press.

Rosenberg, Alexander. (1995), *Philosophy of Social Science* Second Edition, Boulder, CO: Westview Press.

Rubin, Ronald and Charles M. Young. (1989), *Formal Logic: A Model of English*, Mountain View, CA: Mayfield Publishing Co.

Rudner, Richard. (1966), *Philosophy of Social Science*, Englewood Cliffs, NJ: Prentice-Hall.

Salinas, Roberto. (1989), 'Realism and conceptual schemes', *The Southern Journal of Philosophy*, **27**, 101–23.

Salmon, Wesley. (1967), *The Foundations of Scientific Inference*, Pittsburgh, PA: Pittsburgh University Press.

Salmon, Wesley. (1992), 'Scientific Explanation', in Wesley Salmon, *et al.* (eds), *Introduction to the Philosophy of Science*, Englewood Cliffs, NJ: Prentice-Hall.

Schlesinger, George. (1991), *The Sweep of Probability*, Notre Dame, IN: University of Notre Dame Press.

Schwartz, Stephen. (1977), *Naming, Necessity, and Natural Kinds*, Ithaca, NY: Cornell University Press.

Scriven, Michael. (1959a), 'Explanation and prediction in evolutionary theory', *Science*, **130**, 477–82.

Scriven, Michael. (1959b), 'Truisms as the grounds for historical explanations', in Patrick Gardiner (ed.), *Theories of History*, Glencoe, IL: Free Press.

Scriven, Michael. (1963), 'New issues in the logic of explanation', in Sidney Hook (ed.), *Philosophy and History*, New York, NY: New York University Press.

Skorupski, John. (1989), *John Stuart Mill*, London, UK: Routledge.

Stegmüller, Wolfgang. (1976), *The Structure and Dynamics of Theories*, New York, NY: Springer-Verlag.

Stigler, George. (1952), 'The kinky oligopoly demand curve and rigid prices', in George Stigler and Kenneth Boulding (eds), *Readings in Price Theory*, Homewood, IL: Richard D. Irwin, Inc.

Suppes, Patrick. (1957), *Introduction to Logic*, Princeton, NJ: D. Van Nostrand Co.

Temin, Peter. (1976), *Did Monetary Forces Cause the Great Depression?*, New York, NY: W.W. Norton & Company.

Thomas, Robert Paul. (1981), *Microeconomic Applications*, Belmont, CA: Wadsworth Publishing Company.

Tiebout, Charles. (1972), 'A pure theory of local expenditure', in Matthew Edel and Jerome Rothenberg (eds), *Readings in Urban Economics*, New York, NY: Macmillan Co.

Tregarthen, Timothy. (1985), 'Rent controls: do ceilings make roofs cheaper?', *The Margin* July, 6–8.

Tversky, Amos. (1969), 'Intransitivity of Preferences', *Psychological Review*, **76**, 31–48.

Van Fraassen, Bas. (1980), *The Scientific Image*, Oxford, UK: Clarendon Press.

Von Wright, Georg. (1971), *Explanation and Understanding*, Ithaca, NY: Cornell University Press.

Wallis, Charles. (1994), 'Representation and the imperfect ideal', *Philosophy of Science*, **61**, 407–28.

Watkins, J.N.W. (1965), *Hobbes's System of Ideas*, London, UK: Hutchinson & Co.

Weintraub, Roy. (1985), *General Equilibrium Analysis*, Cambridge, UK: Cambridge University Press.

Weintraub, Roy. (1988), 'On the brittleness of the orange equilibrium', in Arjo Klamer, Donald McCloskey, and Robert Solow (eds), *The Consequences of Economic Rhetoric*, New York, NY: Cambridge University Press.

Williams, Bernard. (1990), 'Auto-da-fe: consequences of pragmatism', in Alan Malachowski (ed.), *Reading Rorty*, Oxford, UK: Basil Blackwell.

Woodward, James. (1995), 'Causation and explanation in econometrics', in Daniel Little (ed.), *On the Reliability of Economic Models*,

Boston/Dordrecht/London: Kluwer Academic Publishers.

Zedlewski, Edwin. (1995), 'When have we punished enough?', in Thomas Swartz and Frank Bonello (eds), *Taking Sides: Clashing Views on Controversial Economic Issues*, Guilford, CT: Dushkin Publishing Group.

Index